Brief Counseling in Action

ACTION
ACTION
ACTION
ACTION
ACTION
ACTION
ACTION

A Norton Professional Book

Brief
inCounseling

ACTION
ACTION
ACTION
ACTION
ACTION
ACTION
ACTION

John M. Littrell

Professor and Program Coordinator
Counselor Education

Iowa State University

W. W. Norton & Company
New York   London

Desktop composition by Tom Ernst
Manufacturing by Royal Book
Book design by Lane Kimball Trubey

Library of Congress Cataloging-in-Publication Data
Littrell, John M., 1944–
    Brief counseling in action / John M. Littrell.
        p.   cm.
    Includes bibliographical references and index.
    ISBN 0-393-70265-0
    1. Brief psychotherapy. 2. Solution-focused therapy. I. Title.
RC480.55.L58   1998
616.89' 14--dc21   97-39263   CIP

W. W. Norton & Company, Inc., 500 Fifth Avenue, New York, N.Y. 10110
                    http://www.wwnorton.com
W. W. Norton & Company Ltd., 10 Coptic Street, London WC1A 1PU

            1 2 3 4 5 6 7 8 9 0

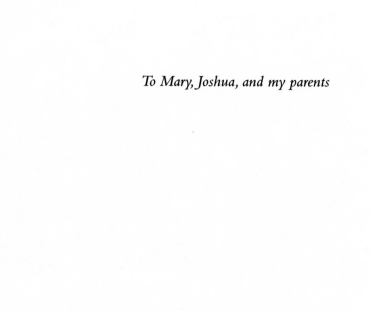

To Mary, Joshua, and my parents

Foreword

Clarity, simplicity, and humor combine with scholarship in this ground-breaking book. Brief therapy is a powerful and vital system leading toward human change, but the actions required to be a brief counselor or therapist have remained somewhat obscure. The great strength of John Littrell's writing is that he brings to us a transparent and lucid interpretation of brief work. In short, this is a book that can make a significant difference in your counseling and clinical practice.

By the end of Chapter 1 you will have a clear definition of brief therapy in concrete terms. And in Chapter 2 you will understand the most vital models of brief work. More than that, you will see brief therapy in action via a clear—and reproducible—case example. As you continue through this action volume, you will continue to expand your knowledge and expertise. John Littrell shows us how to integrate theory and practice. If you take the ideas presented here into your own clinical work immediately, by the end of the book you will likely be anticipating what Littrell has to say. You will be well on your way to utilizing brief principles as part of your clinical portfolio.

I teach the psychoanalytic course at the University of Massachusetts. Object relations, Lacan, and long-term therapy are part of my being. I love to think and I love to think about thinking. Yet, my interest in depth exploration of the human condition is not what many, perhaps most, clients want or need. While I remain convinced that the psychologist, social worker, or psychiatrist who does not understand psychoanalysis is at least slightly handicapped in terms of understanding, I am respectful and appreciative of brief approaches.

Clients come to us seeking change. They want amelioration of the difficult issues they face. I am not one who believes that brief is always better, but I do believe that any counselor or therapist today who is not equipped to provide brief therapy for clients is ill-equipped. Although I sometimes like to come from an analytic frame, I value the skills and flexibility that brief work provides. Brief work can be completed as an end in itself or it can be readily combined with other approaches to therapy, ranging from psychodynamic to cognitive-behavioral to existential/humanistic.

One wonder of brief therapy, particularly as presented by John Littrell, is the respect with which the client is held. Brief therapy as he presents it moves toward an egalitarian approach and makes the client a co-investigator with the therapist. Perhaps even better, brief therapy recognizes that the client is the expert rather than the professional helper. Throughout this enlightening book, Littrell shows real regard for clients and their past and present capacities.

You will find that the book ends with an in-depth analysis of a brief session, including some comments from the client on the usefulness of the experience. One thing that stands out to me as I read this chapter is John Littrell's interest in client positives and strengths. He is consistently able to enable clients to use these strengths to their own advantage.

You will also find Littrell useful to you in assessing and utilizing your own personal strengths as a professional counselor and therapist. Theory sometimes makes us feel a bit inadequate, as it is so difficult to measure up to the model of the expert. Littrell is perhaps the ultimate expert. He shows us and clients how we can build on what we have for a more impactful and important future.

Enjoy this book. It will make a difference in your career.

Allen E. Ivey, Ed.D., A.B.P.P.
Distinguished University Professor
University of Massachusetts—Amherst

Contents

Acknowledgments

In the 1930s, Agatha Christie, Dorothy Sayers, and other writers of members of the Detection Club collaborated in writing *The Admiral Floats*, a murder mystery. The stories told in this book are not unlike the collaborative efforts of the Detection Club. Significant ideas for both thinking about and practicing brief counseling have been provided by many different writers and practitioners, whose contributions are gratefully acknowledged.

I wish to acknowledge the following people who have assisted in writing this book. First, to my wife Mary who believes in me—sometimes more than I believe in myself. I specifically thank her for issuing this challenge: "If you get this book written within one year, it will be the biggest organizational job you've ever pulled off." The challenge was a superb example of brief counseling—and it worked (at least as a motivational tool to write the book, but not in meeting the one-year time line). Life's journey is a living miracle because of her. Our son Joshua proved an excellent testing ground for trying out innovative brief counseling ideas. As a "volunteer" participant, his reactions were a first-rate reality check about what worked and what did not. My parents continue to be my inspiring teachers.

Second, I owe so much to the many participants in my brief counseling workshops in the U.S. and abroad, many of which were sponsored by the American Counseling Association and planned by Pat Christoff and Mark Hamilton. The participants in my workshops made sure I knew about the "realities" of the counseling world outside the confines of a university. This book addresses these "realities" by providing ideas that are marketplace tested.

I thank the counseling students and professionals who have worked with me in exploring brief counseling through research projects, papers and presentations, especially Jeff Angera, Mei-Wei Chen, Paul Crandell, Jeannette Cruz, Sue Johnson, Matt Kunz, Julia Malia, Diana Nesselhuf, Roger Nichols, Jan Olson, Kara Sanford, Bob Thompson, Claudia Vangstad, Jane Yeh, Charles Yorke, Lorrie Young, and Kirk Zinck. You made the hard work fun.

I appreciate the contributions of the following counselors who contributed case examples—Cheryl Chopard, Kim Combes, Melissa DeRadcliffe, Pam Lehman, Cindy Moore, Rick Raulston, Scott Rix, Tamsel Tack, Rosie Walter, Lorrie Young, and Kirk Zinck.

Thanks to readers who contributed time, patience, enthusiasm, and wonderful suggestions for improving the manuscript: Jeff Angera, Debbie Durham, Gale Livingston, Jean Peterson, Allison Walsh, and Kirk Zinck. Marla Smith saved me countless hours of editing because of her meticulous attention to detail. Mary Littrell's insistence on structure and organization proved invaluable for a process-oriented person like myself.

Special thanks to Susan Munro, my editor at W. W. Norton. Susan could see this book's big picture as well as its details. Her observations about ways to strengthen the book were presented in the most gentle and affirming manner. She is a master of solution-focused editing. Thanks also to Aaron Katler for the marketing efforts.

Based on the premise that counselors often possess tacit knowledge of how to proceed, the book represents a mosaic of field-tested ideas gathered from counselors, books, articles, workshop participants, and my own professional counseling and teaching experiences, as well as my own personal life. The following is a list of people whose writings I have scrutinized, demonstrations I have observed, or workshops I have attended. These people in particular have influenced my thinking about and my practice of brief counseling: Ellen Amatea, Connirae Andreas, Steve Andreas, Richard Bandler, Insoo Berg, Steve de Shazer, Robert Dilts, Milton H. Erickson, John Grinder, Richard Fisch, Scott Miller, William (Bill) O'Hanlon, Jane Peller, Lynn Segal, Matthew Selekman, Moshe Talmon, John Walter, Paul Watzlawick, John Weakland, and Michele Weiner-Davis. I especially wish to thank Allen Ivey for being my role model of an outstanding counselor educator and for his special contributions to this book.

Finally, I wish to thank my clients and the clients of the counselors who have contributed to this book—they are the true testers of the helpfulness of brief counseling and any other type of counseling. Ultimately, this book is for them.

Introduction

Counseling invites involvement. We extend to our clients invitations to participate in examining choices and making changes. We cheer them on. This book evokes a similar process. I invite you to become involved as you read each chapter. I will ask you to examine what you do when you are counseling. What are the assumptions you make about change, about clients, and about the nature of counseling?

I will encourage you to go beyond just reading this book. My straightforward goal is that you will incorporate many new patterns into your counseling as you learn intriguing ideas. In my brief counseling workshops people report that it is one thing to watch demonstrations but quite another to actually practice the new skills. Therefore, I will cheer you on as you put your new learning into practice.

Cases

Since stories invite our involvement, I have included 55 brief counseling cases. Some cases are serious; others humorous. Several cases recount people's struggles with problems, but most are focused on how to reconceptualize problems and implement solutions. Because I have taught evening classes during most of my academic career and been greeted at 5:30 in the late afternoon by people who have worked all day, I have learned that cases must be engaging and entertaining if people are to stay awake and learn. I have endeavored to make this book and the specific cases within it both engaging and entertaining so that you will stay actively involved in learning. Cases from a wide variety of settings form the basis for the varied solutions offered in this book. These cases are important because they encourage us to discover and invent who we are and how we interact with others.

Theoretical Frameworks

Counseling theoretical frameworks also invite our involvement—some are complex and labyrinth-like, while others are simple and straightforward. The field of counseling is enriched by extraordinary theoretical frameworks about making choices, taking risks, and engendering change. As counselors, we often acknowledge that we have a favorite framework by a favorite theorist, yet most of us would say we enjoy many different frameworks written by diverse theorists. Just as a steady diet of only John Grisham adventures or Agatha Christie mysteries can be tedious and boring in the long run, so can a steady diet of only behavioral or Transactional Analysis or gestalt frameworks. While old familiar frameworks offer the comfort and reassurance of tradition, new theoretical frameworks awaken our potential to respond in new ways to the constantly changing challenges our clients present. *Brief Counseling in Action* invites counselors and counseling students to listen to and learn from new frameworks that can make a difference in their professional practice.

Counseling Strategies and Techniques

Counseling strategies and techniques can be understood as tools that assist clients in achieving desired states. The frameworks in this book will add to counselors' repertoires of strategies and techniques and thus increase their effectiveness as counselors. The strategies and techniques of brief counseling (alternatively called brief therapy, short-term therapy, and solution-focused therapy in the literature) offer practical and exciting ideas to help you assist people who are struggling to make changes in their lives as quickly as possible.

Intended Audience

Brief Counseling in Action was written for the overworked practitioner who desires shorter-term models of counseling and for counseling students who want to learn a model that is brief and effective. I assume this may apply to you, the reader, since it describes most counselors and counseling students I know. This book will help you accomplish one or more of the following:

1. explore revolutionary ideas in the field of counseling about how to help people make changes in their lives,
2. acquire new ideas and methods for helping clients reach their goals more effectively, thus speeding up the process of change,
3. learn about multiple ways of looking at the process of change,
4. confirm that the things learned on the job have legitimacy and backing (i.e., "I can trust my helping instincts"),
5. become more solution-focused rather than problem-focused,
6. experience counseling as an occupation that can be fun, interesting and exciting—elements often overlooked or missing in other counseling books and sometimes forgotten in the press of day-to-day helping,
7. possess a handy reference book of ideas suggesting possibilities for increased flexibility when dealing with clients who are stuck, and
8. bring about desired changes in your own life.

Prominent Features

To translate brief counseling ideas into a practical format, I have designed each chapter to function as a handy desk reference for professional helpers. Inviting your involvement in brief counseling are the following seven prominent features.

Client-focused. All 18 chapters are client-focused. Each begins with a client's complaint or concern about the counseling process. These concerns are not unique to brief counseling since they occur across many types of counseling. One contribution of this book is to address how these clients' complaints would be handled from a brief counseling perspective.

Skill-enhancing. Individual chapters are skill-enhancing in that brief counseling ideas (e.g., strategies, techniques, ideas, frameworks, suggested phrases) for dealing with the concerns are provided. Counselors may borrow and use these ideas as presented or modify them for a better client fit.

Entertaining Chapters. We have all read our share of counseling books that plod along from chapter to chapter. I have actively tried to avoid such boredom by designing each chapter around a metaphor, simile, image, case, or explicit activity. This design serves several purposes. First, metaphors, similes, images, cases, and activities are concrete and specific ways of remembering more abstract and complex material. Second, they are more fun to read than traditional formats. One of my not-so-hidden agendas is to make learning about counseling an entertaining and enjoyable experience. Because I try to practice what I teach, I applied a "pleasure principle" to the writing of this book. I set a goal that I would enjoy writing each chapter. The thematic motifs for each chapter helped ensure that the actual writing was fun, interesting, and exciting. Finally, the motifs evoke stories, and stories are much of what clients share with us.

User-friendly and Engaging. A typical textbook format has been eschewed. Chapters are written in a user-friendly style that is designed to engage and involve you. Tasks of this nature follow from the metaphor, simile, or image and serve to reinforce the ideas in the chapter. Even cartoons have been added for good measure and "instructive" chuckles. Occasionally, chapters illustrate brief counseling in action by including dialogues from actual cases. Finally, esoteric psychological jargon has been studiously avoided so the book is 99.44% jargon free (with no additives or preservatives).

Faster Change. Helping clients reach their goals quickly is a major goal. Specific ideas about speeding up the process of client change are offered in every chapter. I was once asked by a participant at a day-long brief counseling workshop, "If you were practicing what you preach, how much shorter could this workshop be?" The sentiment behind this participant's question has been taken into consideration—each chapter is relatively brief.

New Ideas, Options, and Concepts. The premise underlying all chapters is simple: If something is not working for the client, the counselor needs to help the client do something different. Based on the assumption that counselors often possess tacit knowledge of how to proceed, the book presents a mosaic of field-tested ideas gathered from counselors, workshop participants, my own professional counseling and teaching experiences, as well as my own personal life. Ideas, options, and concepts from a wide variety of sources have been gathered and applied to client concerns and serve to augment the theoretical and operating assumptions of brief counseling.

Do Something Different. Each chapter ends with counselor and client applications of the ideas presented in the chapter. This section is called *Do Something Different*. You can take steps on the journey toward becoming a master at brief counseling by completing these activities. I believe that we increase our empathy for clients' experiences when we apply to our own professional and personal lives what we are learning; thus, I encourage self-application of new strategies and techniques in addition to the assumed client applications.

As you read these chapters and experiment with new ways of helping people make changes in their lives, you will not always feel comfortable and you may experience a lack of support. It takes time for a new counseling approach to become part of who we are. Therefore, as you add to your counseling repertoire, find that optimal state where the doing is challenging and fascinating but not overwhelming and scary.

Who Changes?

Authors have expectations when they write books. My hope is that this book will contribute to and sustain readers' evolution as counselors. I also hope that for some readers the brief counseling ideas will create a revolution in how they view clients, counseling, change, and themselves.

The process of becoming a brief counselor is exceptionally demanding, evolutionary, and continuous. As counselors, we learn to become more aware of who we are and how we appear to others. We explore and study the complex world around us to better understand individuals and the systems of which they are a part. We continually acquire new skills to assist people in making changes in their lives. Becoming a brief counselor is not a brief process—it takes time to acquire the necessary awareness, knowledge, and skills. The process of becoming a brief counselor is also evolutionary, in that new awareness, knowledge, and skills are continually being added to existing ones. Even revolutionary ideas must find a relationship with existing ideas. Finally, becoming a brief counselor is a continuous process because we constantly encounter new opportunities and challenges.

I repeat my invitation for your involvement as you read this book. The constantly challenging stories that our clients tell us and that we tell about them are filled with despair, discouragement, pain, and suffering. At the same time these stories teem with strengths and resources. The stories of how change occurs are stories that reflect the struggles we all share as human beings. The promise of brief counseling is that it offers a powerful means for conceptualizing clients' and counselors' stories and for drafting new ones filled with increased resources, greater flexibility, and new hope. In summary, this book is about increasing clients' choices, helping them make changes as quickly as possible, and cheering our clients on with an unshakable belief in their capacity to reach their goals and to reach them rapidly.

Part I

•
•
•
•
•

Establishing
a
Brief Counseling
Mindset

CHAPTER 1

Defining Characteristics of Brief Counseling

CLIENT: *In non-jargon terms, what exactly is brief counseling?*

Brief counselors are committed to helping people alleviate their discomfort and reach their desired states as quickly as possible. Briefness is not endorsed for its own sake; rather, briefness is valued because it encourages clients to get on with their lives without counselors' assistance. Stated from the perspective of brief counselors, the goal is to make ourselves quickly dispensable in our clients' lives.

Eight characteristics define brief counseling as a unique approach and serve to highlight issues that are clarified and illustrated more fully in the remaining chapters. Brief counseling is: (1) time-limited, (2) solution-focused, (3) action-based, (4) socially interactive, (5) detail-oriented, (6) humor-eliciting, (7) developmentally attentive, and (8) relationship-based. When counselors holistically integrate these eight characteristics, they can swiftly help clients alleviate their discomfort and reach their desired states.

1. Brief Counseling Is Time-limited

Attempts to expand the length of professional helping began with the psychoanalysts. Freud once wrote about a case involving a single session, but as psychoanalytic theory developed, short-term assistance no longer seemed sufficient. More sessions were deemed necessary to understand clients' psychological lives and help them make deep and permanent changes. In the course of several decades, long-term therapy became the accepted norm; short-term counseling was viewed as inferior and consequently neglected.

Attempts to limit the length of counseling began with clients. History has not recorded the name of the first client who invented single-session counseling, but at some point a client terminated after one session and never returned. Because the client did not mention if sufficient help had been provided, and because the client had not behaved according to theoretical expectations, the counselor made the assumption, as have generations of subsequent counselors, that the client's termination was premature. The field of counseling had begun a long tradition of avoiding time limits on the change process. If counseling was short, it was not because it was planned that way; it was assumed that these clients were not good candidates for psychoanalysis.

In the 1960s, Bob Dylan's song *The Times They Are A-Changin'* reflected the era's turbulence. The song's title also mirrored new changes in how some counselors were beginning to view time. A group at the Mental Research Institute (MRI) in Palo Alto, California, deliberately imposed a limit on the number of sessions that counselors met with clients. These proponents of time-limited counseling restricted the number of sessions to ten. They also set forth a four-step model to assist clients in changing and developed strategies to make sure the job was done within the allotted limits.

Once it was demonstrated that setting time limits did not adversely affect clients' ability to change, other counselors joined in the effort. A Milwaukee group led by Steve de Shazer declared that counselors were focused on the wrong end of the counseling process. Counseling would go faster if counselors emphasized clients' solutions and not their problems. To help clients focus on solutions, the Milwaukee group asked "miracle" questions and employed innovative scaling techniques (see Chapters 5 and 9).

The ultimate in brief counseling was reached when some, including the author, sought to determine how much could be accomplished if there were but a single session. Once again, the negative prognosis offered by proponents of longer-term counseling was upended. Since the 1960s when the MRI group successfully challenged the assumption that longer is better, counselors have been freed to manage time more creatively. The major difference from the past is that brief counseling has become a viable option, not just for clients, as it has always been, but now also for counselors.

2. Brief Counseling Is Solution-focused

Brief counselors believe that solutions are more likely to be found and created when the focus is on what works in clients' lives, rather than on what does not work. In brief counseling we assist clients by focusing on three areas: (1) exceptions to the problem, (2) untapped resources, and (3) goals (Littrell & Angera, in press; Zinck & Littrell, 1998). A major way of heading toward solutions is to focus on what clients do that works. Here we focus on when clients are *not* stuck. Stated another way, we help clients discover how every so often they engage in patterns that are exceptions to their problem states. Effective interventions accent and encourage successful exceptions so that clients do more of what works.

Exceptions to problems are a potent source of information. We repeatedly ask questions such as, "When is this *not* a problem for you?" and "How did you *do* that?" Often clients are amazed at the times problems were nonexistent or diminished; they have focused exclusively on the problem parts of their lives and failed to notice when problems had not occurred.

Brief counselors also head clients toward their futures. Counselors and clients co-create goals as a way of clarifying clients' desired states. The co-creating process means that the future is fluid and that many futures are possible. Clients begin to experience freedom from being stuck as new choices become possible. For some clients, setting goals is a liberating experience and they know what they need to do to reach them. For other clients, goal-setting is scary because they cannot see how to achieve their goals; these clients can benefit from tapping unused and often unrealized resources.

Resource identification assists clients in believing they can achieve their goals. Clients are often unaware of the multitude of internal and external resources they possess and that can be used to move from their present states to future states. Brief counselors are experts in helping clients tap their resources.

3. Brief Counseling Is Action-based

Brief counselors plunge their clients into new experiences as quickly as possible. These new experiences let clients know that new patterns of behavior are possible; hope emerges. A highly effective way to ensure that clients have new experiences is through action-based activities of giving directives and assigning tasks.

Giving directives influences clients during the counseling session. When clients are fixated on problems, they adopt physiological postures of defeat. Their heads hang and their shoulders slump; they lack vitality. Rather than waiting for clients to spontaneously change, brief counselors direct clients to change their physiology. For example, a counselor might direct a client by saying, "Show me what you would look like when you've made the changes you'd like to have happen." Remarkable and empowering psychological transformations follow shifts in physiology. Brief counselors orchestrate physiological changes to speed up the counseling process.

Assigning tasks influences clients beyond the counseling session by moving them into new experiences and toward their goals. Tasks head clients into action, rather than just further talk. For example, the following generic task aims clients toward their target goals, "During this next week, do something different as a way of moving in the direction of your goal." Giving directives and assigning tasks are two methods to prompt client action. The ultimate aim of action is to move clients closer to their desired states.

4. Brief Counseling Is Socially Interactive

Brief counselors recognize that while they spend considerable time on their clients' actions, thoughts, and feelings, their clients live in socially interactive worlds of families, friends, colleagues, and peers. Clients and those around them powerfully influence one another in reciprocal ways. As brief counselors we utilize these reciprocal interactions by tapping into need-satisfying qualities of socially supportive relationships.

We attempt in four ways to help clients be more aware of the social supports found in their worlds and more skilled in accessing them. First, we determine the "cast of characters" germane to our clients' worlds so we and our clients are aware of the potential social supports. Second, we explore with our clients how to ask for and receive help from other people. Third, we examine clients' goals to determine how ecologically sound they are (i.e., how will reaching goals affect other people who will, in turn, affect our clients' worlds?). Finally, we assign tasks that include other people in supportive ways because clients will achieve their goals more often if they receive social support than if they do not. The socially interactive nature of brief counseling is a recognition that, while many clients are moving toward more independence, the larger social framework of interdependence also allows clients to experience the joys of win-win social support.

5. Brief Counseling Is Detail-oriented

Brief counselors concentrate clients' attention on concreteness, specificity, and details because this attention helps clients move from vague abstractions in their minds into "real world" possibilities. The details we collect are not about what fails to work in clients' lives—they are more than willing to share that information. Brief counselors go into detail about what works.

We explore the details of clients' desired states. We ask, "What will you look like, be saying, and be doing when you reach your goal?" We might ask clients to imagine that they are watching made-for-television movies of their lives to see and hear the changes they are wanting.

We also catalog clients' resources. What works in clients' lives? What are the resources, strengths, abilities, and talents they can draw on to affect the changes they want? Brief counselors are persistent and tenacious in accessing what has worked and is working. We want clients to fully experience their power so that they can use that power to change.

6. Brief Counseling Is Humor-eliciting

The seriousness of counseling is vastly overrated by both counselors and clients. In part, this seriousness is predicated on the belief that, because pain is a common response to problems, pain must continue during the process of moving toward solutions. In brief counseling we challenge this belief. We find humor to be a miracle salve with analgesic qualities. It helps in healing wounds and allows for the present and future to be explored with considerably more hope.

Many clients discover that when patterns are not working in their lives they react with the emotions of fear (flight) and/or anger (fight). On the other hand, when we tap clients' capacities for humor, we elicit variations of life-embracing emotions such as liking, loving, and exuberance. Once when working with a client named Grace, I was wowed by her strengths even in the face of overwhelming difficulties. I endeavored to see the world from her point of view and even shared my belief in her strengths by singing a verse of "Amazing Grace." My client beamed as I, functioning as her personal cheerleader, acknowledged her strengths and affirmed what worked in her life. The song also proved memorable in another way. Grace owned a cassette tape containing the song, and she agreed to play it on occasions when she needed a reminder of her strengths. With a twinkle in her eye and an impish grin, Grace let me know that the voice on her tape was a bit better than mine. Together we enjoyed her humor.

7. Brief Counseling Is Developmentally Attentive

Brief counselors are attentive to clients' developmental stages and needs because understanding them provides a broader perspective from which to view problems and solutions. When clients struggle with a problem, they get bogged down in exhausting and discouraging repetition. Their more-of-the-same solutions fail to work; new solutions are elusive. As brief counselors we believe that human beings develop and are inherently free to move on to new things.

The hypnotherapist Milton Erickson was mindful of his clients' developmental stages and knowledgeable about how clients often became stuck at times of key transitions from one life stage to another. Erickson employed his understanding of developmental frameworks when he designed interventions to make developmental transitions as smooth and natural as possible. In brief counseling we draw on our knowledge of human development to ensure we are helping clients not only with the immediate task at hand but also with mastering the broader developmental challenges they face.

In addition to paying attention to developmental stages, brief counselors are attuned to four psychological human needs postulated by William Glasser (1986): love/belonging, power, freedom, and fun. We help our clients meet their needs for love/belonging by emphasizing the socially interactive nature of counseling (Littrell, Zinck, Nesselhuf, & Yorke, 1997). Clients' needs for power are met by highlighting their internal and external resources. Freedom is stressed by having clients continually make their own choices rather than living by the dictates of their internalized "shoulds" and/or responding non-assertively to others' unreasonable demands. Finally, as mentioned before, fun is elicited in the solving of problems and the finding of solutions through eliciting humor. Brief counselors recognize that clients' solutions work best when developmental perspectives are acknowledged and embraced.

8. Brief Counseling Is Relationship-based

A considerable portion of this book focuses on strategies and techniques designed to assist people in changing. However, the relationship-based characteristic of brief counseling reminds us that strategies and techniques are ineffectual if the facilitative conditions of warmth, genuineness, and empathy do not permeate the counseling process. Warmth, genuineness, and empathy are not extras to be added if the counseling relationship calls for greater rapport or more credibility; they are necessary conditions for successful counseling. Clients must believe we care about them as people. Clients must know we are being genuine—that we can be trusted when they share their life stories with us. Finally, clients must truly experience being heard, as if we understand from their points of view.

While the facilitative conditions are necessary, they are not sufficient. As brief counselors we must have in our repertoires a wide range of helping skills, including myriad strategies and techniques. It is only when the emphasis on establishing and maintaining a facilitative relationship with our clients combines with the other seven characteristics of brief counseling that a powerful way of helping synergistically evolves—the strategies and techniques of brief counseling unite with our humanness. We use ourselves along with our complete package of brief counseling tools to help clients alleviate their discomfort and reach their desired states as quickly as possible.

Do Something Different

1. Think about your own evolution as you continue to learn more about how to be an effective counselor. What are the events—teachers, clients, personal events, books, workshops, etc.—that marked new directions in your evolution as a counselor? How did your counseling change at each important stage? What patterns do you see? If you knew what your next marker would be, what would you say it would be?

2. Take a minute and free associate to the word "change." Were the associations words like *quick, easy,* and *fun,* or words like *slow, difficult,* and *painful*? If the latter, to what extent are you willing to give the former serious consideration?

3. What is an example from your own life when you experienced making a significant and painless change in a very short period of time? How did you do it? What resources did you use?

CHAPTER 2

Theorizing about the Journey of Change

CLIENT: *I assume you know where you're going because I sure don't.*

To live means to experience—through doing, feeling, thinking. Experience takes place in time, so time is the ultimate scarce resource we have.
—Mihalyi Csikszentmihalyi, 1997, p. 8.

Change is a journey through our most scarce resource—time. Some journeys consume inordinate amounts of time, while others, barely any. Modifying patterns of smoking, drug abuse, gambling, and excessive drinking may take a person years from the beginning of the journey when the behavior is recognized as problematic to the final destination when the person finally declares, "This is no longer a problem for me." Other problems are associated with brief journeys. For example, the four-year-old who wets and soils his pants will eventually become a five-year-old with dry and clean pants.

John Weakland (Thomas, Jr., 1995) once observed that "When you have a problem, life is the same damn thing over and over. When you no longer have a problem, life is one damn thing after another." His observation reminds us that life continues to present unsettling difficulties. Most of the time people tackle these difficulties on their own. However, some people are unable to break patterns; instead, they persistently recycle their failed solutions. Professional counselors, therapists, ministers, and social workers assist people struggling to free themselves from cycles of failed solutions. Professional helpers are experienced guides who know the territories of change. They provide their expertise in helping people with the same-damn-thing-over-and-over-again problems reach their desired destinations.

In this chapter, we will explore four theory-derived approaches used by experienced counselors when they provide assistance to those needing help on the journey of change. The four approaches are: (1) utilize maps, (2) work cooperatively, (3) agree on destinations and paths, and (4) inventory and requisition needed gear. In the presentation of each approach, brief counseling's theoretical frameworks will be highlighted and their originators recognized.

Approach #1: Utilize Maps

Counselors are guides on the journey of change. They know the territory to transverse and the processes to be employed. They possess the skills to assist people over difficult terrain. Effective guides have one or more master maps that describe the overall journey as well as numerous detailed maps to expedite getting from one specific point to another. Maps are valuable because they help counselors and clients appreciate where they have been, ascertain where they currently are, and anticipate the challenges ahead.

Three master maps have proven useful in implementing brief counseling. The first map, while not intended as a brief counseling map, offers a way of understanding how counselors and clients may work together in a short-term framework even when the total journey is lengthy. The second master map plots the change process across four stages from problems to solutions. The third master map places the emphasis on the search for solutions rather than the examination of problems. Just as a road map and a contour map can display common territory while accenting different features, so also do the three master maps. None of the three is better than the other two—each simply highlights unique features of the journey of change. Astute brief counselors have a choice of master maps and select those most appropriate for each of their clients.

Master Map #1. A valuable master map of change has been fashioned by Prochaska, Norcross, and DiClemente (1994). This global map was drawn by teasing out the stages of change across many types of problems. Prochaska's model delineates six stages or territories (see Table 1). Following the name of each stage in the table is a statement of how I imagine a client might summarize his or her stage of the journey.

Table 1. Stages in the Journey of Change

1. *Precontemplation*—"I am *not* thinking about a change journey."
2. *Contemplation*—"I have begun my change journey. I am intending to take action in the next six months."
3. *Preparation*—"I am moving along on my change journey. I am intending to take action within the next month."
4. *Action*—"I have really been traveling on my change journey. I have taken action on my problem within the last six months."
5. *Maintenance*—"I've traveled far on my change journey. I solved my problem more than six months ago."
6. *Termination*—"I don't think much about my prior change journey. My previous behavior is no longer problematic."

Modified from Prochaska, Norcross, and
DiClemente, *Changing for Good,* 1994, p. 68.

Prochaska's model was developed based on the natural processes people used when attempting to change across a wide variety of problem behaviors, e.g., smoking, troubled drinking, depression, high fat diets, and sedentary life. Prochaska and his colleagues found that people first began by moving from the precontemplation stage to the contemplation stage. For example, clients referred for problem drinking often are in the precontemplation stage. They do not understand that they have a problem. For them, the biggest problem is that others won't leave them alone. Moving into the contemplation stage implies that they are at least willing to examine the possibility that their drinking is adversely affecting themselves and others. They have weighed the pros and cons of continuing their present behavior.

Some problem drinkers move from the contemplation stage into the preparation stage, during which they lay the foundation for changing their behavior. From the preparation stage people might move to the action stage. This is where the ritual of drinking is modified, new friends are cultivated, new behaviors are learned. Eventually some problem drinkers arrive at the maintenance stage, which involves "sustained, long-term effort" and a "revised lifestyle" (Prochaska et al., 1994, p. 204). While we might debate whether problem drinkers ever reach the termination stage, some seem to do so. Four criteria for terminators are a new self-image, no temptation in any situation, solid self-efficacy, and a healthier lifestyle. For most people attempting change, the journey is not a linear progression from the precontemplation stage to the maintenance or termination stages, but a recycling process in which stages are frequently revisited.

For brief counselors the usefulness of Prochaska's master model is twofold. First, the model points out that three stages precede the action stage. Many of the interventions in counseling are aimed at the action stage, where people are *doing* new things. The three steps prior to the action stage suggest that we proceed with caution. In our haste to help in a brief manner, we must not forget the necessary work people have to do prior to successful action.

Second, the client's statements in Table 1 remind us that the overall process of change requires time. Brief counselors believe in going only as far on the client's journey of change as is needed. Because as counselors we find pleasure in helping people with their journeys, we sometimes overestimate how much assistance we need to provide. Brief counselors have an implicit goal, which can also be made explicit to clients. When discussing my role with new clients, I have used the following statement about my goal:

> My goal is to make myself dispensable as quickly as possible in your life because I want you to get on with your life without me. You should be dealing with life with your family, friends, colleagues, associates, peers, etc. Professional helpers like me are just temporary guides through a rough time in your life. I think you'll like it much more—and it will be considerably cheaper in terms of time, energy, and money—to deal with problems using your own resources.

Returning to Prochaska's model, all clients do not need to go through all the stages of change with us. Many clients find one counseling session is all that is needed in moving from one stage of change to another (Talmon, 1990). They are not asking us to go the whole journey. They just need help in moving from one state to the next. Brief counselors respect their clients enough to stop when clients have the skills to find their own way.

Master Map #2. The second global map for the change journey is responsible for revolutionizing the counseling profession. Prior to the introduction of this model, placing limits on the number of counseling sessions was considered unconscionable. However, the ten-session limit placed on this model's implementation speeded up the process of change. Clients acknowledged the ten-session limit by making needed changes within the shorter time frame.

This second model was developed by the staff of the Mental Research Institute (MRI; Fisch, Weakland, & Segal, 1982; Watzlawick, Weakland, & Fisch, 1974). As shown in Figure 1, the MRI model has four recognizable

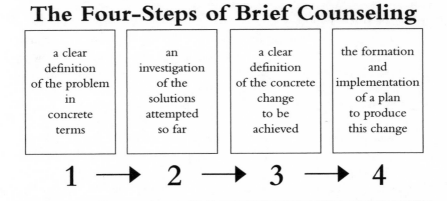

Figure 1: Steps of Brief Counseling
Modified from Watzlawick, Weakland, and Fisch, *Change*, 1974, p. 110

territories: (1) a clear definition of the problem in concrete terms, (2) an investigation of the solutions attempted so far, (3) a clear definition of the concrete change to be achieved, and (4) the formation and implementation of a plan to produce this change (Watzlawick et al., 1974, p. 110). Part of the beauty of the MRI model is how parsimoniously it breaks the global change process into just four major territories.

In a condensed form, the theory underlying the MRI four-step model is simple. A person attempts to effectively deal with one of life's problems. Occasionally, the person's attempted solution not only fails to achieve the desired outcome but in fact even exacerbates it. When the problem is not solved by the attempted solution, the person takes a more-of-the-same approach. To extricate the person from the more-of-the-same trap, the counselor assists the person in clarifying goals and doing activities that are not in the more-of-the-same category. This master map is deceptively simple in that, while it seems easy, the skills needed to guide clients through the territories are complex.

Master Map #3. Yet another highly useful global map is a solution-focused one (de Shazer, 1985, 1988). Rather than begin with problems, the solution-focused model emphasizes exceptions to clients' problem situations and builds on those exceptions. When no exceptions can be found, the emphasis is placed on the hypothetical—what clients believe they will be doing when their problems are solved. In *Becoming Solution-focused in*

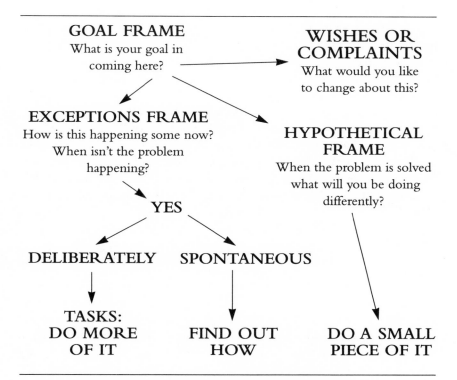

Figure 2: Pathways of Constructing Solutions
Walter and Peller, *Becoming Solution-focused in Brief Therapy*, 1992, p. 64.
Reprinted with permission.

Brief Therapy, Walter and Peller (1992) effectively summarize in a flowchart the contributions of de Shazer and his associates (see Figure 2).

As shown at the top of the figure, initially some clients are able to specify goals while others express wishes or complaints. Eventually a goal is clarified. Exceptions to the problem are delineated and two tasks follow based on whether the exceptions are deliberate or spontaneous. If the exceptions are deliberate, the client is directed and assisted to "Do more of it." If the exceptions are spontaneous, the client is helped to "Find out how." Sometimes no exceptions can be found, in which case the counselor and client move to a hypothetical frame to determine what the client will be doing when the problem is solved. The counselor assigns the task of doing "a small piece of it."

Whether using the large-scale map of Prochaska et al. or the slightly more specific maps drawn by the MRI group and de Shazer, the counselor assists clients in finding their way through the complex tasks of change.

Models provide information about what is most likely to be encountered and the most common routes through the territory. However, as much as brief counselors value quality models, they know that these maps are not the territory (Korzybski, 1933). The maps make it seem as though clients bring with them *well-structured problems*, i.e., "problems with clear paths to solution" versus *ill-structured problems*, i.e., "problems without clear solution paths" (Sternberg, 1996, p. 171). As Sternberg says, "There just aren't solutions to major life problems that are as clear as the formula for finding the area of a parallelogram or the identity of the person who discovered X-rays" (p. 172). At best, models are a compendium of collective wisdom; they should serve to guide, not to dictate. Thus, brief counselors employ models as but one of many valuable tools in their repertoire to effectively help clients.

Approach #2: Work Cooperatively

The best counselors work cooperatively with clients to achieve their desired states. They use three basic strategies to increase cooperation. First, counselors match their responses to their clients' current stage of change. Second, they discuss topics clients believe are their problems, rather than what others, even counselors, think are their problems. Finally, counselors talk a language that clients will understand, which is, not surprisingly, the language clients use naturally. The bottom line is that cooperative people are easier to work with than those who are not pulling together toward a common end. Brief counselors actively seek cooperative encounters.

Prochaska et al. (1994) found that one of the most serious mistakes counselors make is to mismatch clients' current stages. Mismatching frequently occurs when counselors apply action processes when clients are not yet ready for action. For example, according to Prochaska, approximately 40% of clients seeing a therapist for the first time are in the precontemplation stage, 40% in the contemplation stage, and only 20% in the preparation stage. The mistake is to suppose that most clients are in the preparation stage and ready to move to the action stage when only about 20% of clients are ready to take this step.

A simple and effective tool for assessing the client's stage of change is found in Table 2 (Prochaska et al., 1994). Use of this assessment tool helps counselors match the client's stage and select appropriate change processes. Because motivation to change is enhanced when counselors match their clients' stages, clients are less likely to terminate counseling prematurely (Prochaska et al., 1994). Fisch et al. (1982) recognize stage-matching in *The Tactics of Change*. They delineated three types of clients: window shoppers,

Table 2. Assessment of Stage of Change

Directions: Choose some aspect of your life that you are thinking about changing, are in the process of changing, or have changed. As you think about that aspect of your life, answer **YES** or **NO** to each of the following four statements.

YES	NO	
YES	**NO**	1. I solved my problem more than six months ago.
YES	**NO**	2. I have taken action on my problem within the past six months.
YES	**NO**	3. I am intending to take action in the next month.
YES	**NO**	4. I am intending to take action in the next six months.

Key: Assess the stage of change using the following criteria:
Precontemplation stage—no to all
Contemplation state—yes to #4 and no to all others
Preparation stage—yes to #3 & #4, but no to the others
Action stage—yes to #2, and no to #1
Maintenance stage—truthfully answer yes to #1

Modified from Prochaska, Norcross, and
DiClemente, *Changing for Good*, 1994, p. 68.

complainants, and customers. These three types correspond to clients in Prochaska's first three stages: precontemplation, contemplation, and preparation, respectively. Prochaska's choice of the term "contemplation" avoids the pejorative connotations associated with "complainant."

Brief counselors who use Prochaska et al.'s (1994) master map (see Table 2) know that one way to work cooperatively is to set goals that are only one stage beyond the client's present stage. If a client is in the contemplation stage, the immediate goal is to move to the preparation stage. While the client's big goal may be to terminate the problematic behavior, the most effective interventions to elicit cooperation come when manageable goals are set for achieving the next stage. If needed, new goals can then be set.

Clients' cooperation is enhanced by talking about their problems and avoiding counselors' agendas (Berg & Miller, 1992; de Shazer, 1985, 1988). In their ground-breaking work, de Shazer and his colleagues have delineated

specific ways to enhance cooperation with clients. They have avoided thinking in terms of resistance. When cooperation is lacking, they understand that
to mean that the counselor is not knowledgeable enough about the clients'
worlds to be aware of where they are willing to cooperate. For example, in
Working with the Problem Drinker Berg and Miller (1992) acknowledge the
obvious—clients referred for drinking problems are often not very interested
in discussing what others describe as *the* problem. (Using Prochaska's model,
these clients would be in the precontemplation stage; on Fisch et al's model,
clients like this might be considered *pre*-window shoppers.) Rather than press
clients to talk about problem drinking, Berg and Miller explore what these
clients perceive as problems in their lives. Often they are relationship problems. When clients begin working on their own identified problem they
often reach a point where they mention cutting down on drinking as a way
to solve their relationship problem. Consequently, clients view cutting down
on excessive drinking as one means to a desired end, rather than feeling
forced to change their drinking patterns, behavior they view as their own
business. The message: start where clients are so as to work cooperatively.

A third way of increasing cooperation is to use clients' language rather
than psychological jargon. Brief counselors avoid becoming language
teachers. They take their cue from Milton Erickson, who employed his
clients' language to effect therapeutic change. In the short case that follows,
Erickson talked to a policeman in the language of self-discipline.

Walk to the Grocery Store

A policeman was forced to retire for medical reasons. He had emphyse-
ma and high blood pressure and was obese. He came to Milton H. Erickson
to get help with cutting down on his eating, drinking, and smoking.
Erickson told the man that when he wanted a meal he should walk to a
grocery store a mile and a half away to buy food for one meal. When he
wanted a drink he should walk to a bar a mile away and if he wanted
another drink he should walk another mile. When he wanted a pack of cig-
arettes he should walk across town to get them. The man left Erickson's
office angry and swearing at him. A month later a new patient came in saying that the policeman had referred him to Erickson as "the one psychiatrist who knows what he is doing." (O'Hanlon & Hexum, 1990, p. 19)

While the policeman's initial reaction was one of defiance, the outcome
confirmed that Erickson had talked a language that made intuitive sense to his
client. Erickson surmised that, while the policeman might not like orders, he

had been trained to carry them out. Therefore, Erickson issued a directive that the policeman could not disobey or ignore. Brief counselors reject thinking in terms of client reluctance, resistance, and denial. Instead, in a manner similar to Erickson's, they skillfully employ language to elicit their clients' cooperation.

Approach #3: Agree on Destinations and Paths

Some clients begin their journeys knowing where they want to go. They imagine their destinations; their visions beckon them to future desired states. On the other end of the spectrum, many clients begin their journeys with no idea of their desired state; they know only that they want to leave their present pain behind. Finding their current bind unendurable they are profoundly aware that something needs to change.

In *Stop Setting Goals If You Would Rather Solve Problems*, Biehl (1995) postulates that people approach problems in two major ways. As a means of assessing people's preferences for goal-setting or problem-solving, he asks people to reflect on the following two statements and decide which most nearly matches their thoughts, feelings, or preferences.

1. "I love setting goals, and it is emotionally very satisfying every time I reach a goal I have set."
2. "I love solving problems, and it is very emotionally satisfying every time I solve a problem no one else could solve." (p. 14)

Biehl found that goal-setters couldn't understand the problem-solvers' way of approaching issues any more than the problem-solvers could make sense of the goal-setters' approach. Biehl's dichotomy of goal-setters and problem-solvers finds expression in two major approaches to brief counseling. In a hedging of their bets on either the problem-solvers or the goal-setters, both the brief counseling approaches of the MRI and de Shazer involve elements of problem-solving and elements of goal-setting.

Destinations. The MRI model begins with two problem-solving elements, in which clients' known conditions are made quite salient by: (a) defining the problem—step 1, and (b) determining what attempted solutions have been tried—step 2. On the other hand, de Shazer's (1985) brief counseling approach accents problem-solving in three ways. First, de Shazer does a twist on the problem-solving approach by focusing on exceptions to the problem. He directs his clients' attention to what works (the proverbial half-filled glass of water) rather than what doesn't work (the half-empty water glass). Second, as a general type of task, clients are encouraged to

Table 3. Stages of Change in Which Particular Change Processes Are Most Useful

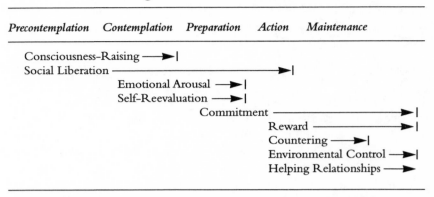

Precontemplation	Contemplation	Preparation	Action	Maintenance

Consciousness-Raising ──▶|
Social Liberation ──────────────────────▶|
　　　　　Emotional Arousal ──▶|
　　　　　Self-Reevaluation ──▶|
　　　　　　　　Commitment ──────────────────▶|
　　　　　　　　　　Reward ───────────────▶|
　　　　　　　　　　Countering ──▶|
　　　　　　　　　　Environmental Control ──▶|
　　　　　　　　　　Helping Relationships ──▶

Prochaska, Norcross, and DiClemente, *Changing for Good*, 1994, p. 54.
Reprinted with permission.

actively do more of what works as a way of solving their problems. Finally, clients are assisted in shrinking problems to manageable size.

Both the MRI and de Shazer approaches incorporate goal-setting strategies as a way of appealing to clients who approach the world by explicitly setting specific and concrete goals. MRI therapists teach their clients goal-setting through the very direct process of defining a goal—step 3. De Shazer's approach is more imaginative but no less precise. In his approach, the goal-setting side of the equation is facilitated by asking miracle questions that serve to open up new horizons (see Chapter 6).

In determining where clients want to go, brief counselors acknowledge clients' preferences in approaching their problems. Some prefer to use a problem-solving method while others want goals to shoot for. This book includes both problem-solving and goal-setting ways of helping clients. The MRI and de Shazer approaches are helpful at times in tailoring the counseling to clients, as opposed to coercing clients to fit one of the approaches.

Paths. In brief counseling, counselors and clients agree not only on destinations but also on paths to help the problem-solvers move from where they are or, conversely, help goal-setters move toward where they want to be. Agreement on the paths to be traveled is essential. Making change involves a maze of choices; wrong turns may delay reaching a desired state. Prochaska's expanded model of the stages of change indicates that at each stage there are change processes which are most useful (see Table 3). Prochaska et al. (1994, p. 54) suggest that moving from the precontemplation stage to the contemplation stage involves *consciousness-raising* (increasing information about self and problem) and also *social liberation* (increasing social alternatives for behaviors that are not problematic). Moving from a contemplation stage into a preparation stage may involve the processes of *emotional arousal* (experiencing and expressing feelings about one's problems and solutions) and *self-reevaluation* (increasing social alternatives for behaviors that are not problematic). *Commitment* (choosing and committing to act, or belief in the ability to change) assists in moving from preparation stage to the action stage. Finally, moving from action to maintenance may involve varying degrees of *reward* (rewarding self, or being rewarded by others for making change), *countering* (substituting alternatives for problem behaviors), *environmental control* (avoiding stimuli that elicit problem behaviors), and *helping relationships* (enlisting the help of someone who cares). For clients to discover by themselves the change processes needed to move from one stage to another (as well as their corresponding techniques) is a Herculean task, often most efficiently accomplished with a guide, rather than learned through trial and error. Counseling may be brief because clients need guidance through only one stage, not all of them.

Approach #4: Inventory and Requisition Needed Gear

Journeys involve preparation. Too often the inventory counselors take of clients' readiness for the journey of change is not of what works but of what doesn't work. Traditionally, counselors highlighted deficits considerably more than assets; there was a preponderance of problem talk. Before beginning a journey of change, it is essential to conduct an inventory of what works in clients' lives—their knowledge and skills.

Two major ways of conducting inventories have gained acceptance by brief counselors. The first way comes from the MRI school. Proponents of the MRI school listen carefully to clients as they describe their prior attempted solutions (step 2 in their model). Attempted solutions are a rich source of information about how clients have been stuck. This information also informs clients and counselors about what not to try. The attempted solution is also viewed as problematic because it is the attempted solution that maintains the problem by continuing to be a solution that doesn't work.

A second way to inventory the available gear is to focus on exceptions to the problem behavior (de Shazer, 1985, 1988). Discovering when a problem is not a problem or is less of a problem provides a foundation of success or partial success on which to build. Accenting prior solutions, whether partially or fully successful, provides clients with new hope that change is possible.

Brief counselors also inventory their clients' strengths, competencies, and abilities. When we know how clients' lives have worked in the past and in the present, we make salient for them an inventory of functional knowledge and skills they can tap for the current journey of change. A colleague, Jim Bergin, describes a simple but effective technique his mother used when he was a child to help him quickly access the resourceful state of being more self-confident. Before Jim would leave home for an important event, his mother would stand in front of him for a final inspection. She would say to him, "Remember the string on the crown of your head." When Jim pulled the invisible string he would instantly stand up straighter, just like a marionette whose taunt strings make for an erect physique. Jim's mother would then add, "All humans have strings on the crowns of their heads."

Brief counselors acknowledge the wisdom of Jim's mother. Brief counselors understand that part of the wizardry of their profession is helping clients locate their strings and then having them pulling them so as to access internal resourceful states. Helping clients locate their own internal resources and employ them challenges counselors to inventory resources, not catalog deficits. When needed resources are not in the repertoire of their clients, counselors assist in requisitioning what is needed.

The Four Approaches in Action

The following single-session case with its subsequent follow-up letters illustrates all four approaches in action. Christine Simpson (the client's real name), had issued "A Call for Help" about her procrastinating behavior.

A Call for Help

I briefly explained to Christine a four-step model for making changes (Fisch et al., 1982; Watzlawick et al., 1974). First, we talked about Christine's problem situation. She had written *Jenny's Locket* (Simpson, 1994), a short book about her daughter's coming to terms with her uncle's death by AIDS. Those who had read *Jenny's Locket* lauded its sensitive handling of how a young girl feared social ostracism in her small community and how she faced her fears. People told Christine how personally moved they had been by her book.

When Christine and I met she was in the process of contacting all 50 state departments of education so as to make the book available for children. Christine had successfully completed 44 of the 50 phone calls she wanted to make, but now she was stuck. She labeled herself a procrastinator. She asked herself why she couldn't complete the calls, since, after all, she had done most of them. Our mutually agreed upon goal was for her to complete the remaining six phone calls.

As we examined paths to her goal, my initial response was to have her make the calls in a fun, interesting, and exciting way, because this particular technique seems to free people from viewing their problem as drudgery. Christine would have none of that. She just couldn't think of a way to make the remaining calls fun. In brief counseling, when something isn't working, the counselor needs to do something different. Finally, I looked at Christine and said,

> Christine, you have convinced me that there is no fun, interesting, or exciting way to make those phone calls. Maybe you're one of those persons who just has to grind it out. In fact, I suspect that for you to make those remaining phone calls is the equivalent of trudging through shit.

The change on Christine's face was amazing. She laughed and said, "You couldn't be more right!" Sensing we were now on the right track and that she had a sense of humor, I added,

> I have this picture in my mind of you standing near your desk making those last six call wearing galoshes to protect your feet from all that shit you're standing in. Are you willing to get some galoshes and make those last six phone calls?

Christine agreed to get a pair of galoshes from her husband and make the calls. Several days following our single session, I sent Christine a short encouraging note with an attached picture of galoshes cut from a Lands' End catalog. Several weeks later I received a letter from Christine. She wrote:

> I received your clipping of my galoshes and chuckled for the next day or so—and every time I look at them. At this point I have finally tacked the photo up at my desk. Well, I sat down to make those last six phone calls. I got all decked out to be the epitome of the absurd with my hubby's grassy, muddy boots on my feet and to my knees, emerald earrings, the whole nine yards. It was all I could do not to laugh when on the phone to Nevada, Ohio, Tennessee, New Hampshire, New York, and Kansas, but I did it.

> Today I got a call back from my contact in Tennessee. You may

think I am making this up, but *I am not*. She loved *Jenny's Locket* and is sending me the necessary paperwork so she can order 1,600 books. One for each school in her entire state! In the past year I sold/gave away 1,000 books. Today I matched that—and all because I got a kick in the rear at the right time.

I did not get a photograph of myself as you requested because no one else happened to be around. But that doesn't matter because I know in my heart and head what happened—and most importantly, someone believes in *Jenny's Locket* and will help me get it into the hands of children. Thank you so much for the "boot" in the rear! Galoshes are very special to me now.

Christine actually wore the galoshes and discovered that they transformed the phone calls from something she had to do into something she wanted to do. She appeared to use the helping relationship of counseling to engage in new actions. At the same time, the galoshes helped her control her environment by transforming the stimuli that elicited problem behavior (sitting at her desk in her office) into a room with shit on the floor for which galoshes were an appropriate and entertaining solution. Ironically, wearing galoshes to deal with a shit-covered floor proved to be highly amusing to Christine and thus belied her earlier belief that the phone calls couldn't be fun, interesting, or exciting.

As counselors we are at best temporary guides who are retained for the explicit purpose of assisting clients through difficult times. Almost never is our contract with clients to go the whole journey. The four approaches to brief counseling suggest the following:

1. *Utilize maps*. Right from the beginning I used one of the brief counseling maps so that Christine and I would be aware of the outlines of the territory we were to transverse.
2. *Work cooperatively*. I worked with Christine in a cooperative framework because I knew she had enough to struggle with without also having to struggle with me. When my proposed framework of "fun, interesting, and exciting" was not working for her, I shifted to her framework of trudging and grinding it out. Ironically, using her framework resulted in her completing the task in a fun, interesting, and exciting manner.
3. *Agree on destinations and paths*. Christine and I agreed on her destination, i.e., where she wanted to go, and we selected a promising path to reach it.

4. *Inventory and requisition needed gear.* Despite her considerable accomplishments in completing 44 of the 50 phone calls, Christine was discouraged. I suspect the needed gear for Christine was to remember her former sense of hope and persistence and her strong desire to really help children. I believe that one of the most therapeutic parts of our short time together was listening to how important it was to have others read her inspiring book. The galoshes were but a small lever for moving her beyond immobilizing discouragement into hopeful action. Christine located the resources she needed to complete her journey.

Brief counselors believe that helping is a temporary condition and that the sooner clients can do what they need to do without our help the better it is for all concerned. Many times we prolong counseling to satisfy our needs for helping. In working with Christine, I derived satisfaction in knowing that she had reached her destination as soon as possible. I also felt satisfaction from knowing that I played a small role in helping another person discover her own resources and strengths so that she could continue her life in more hopeful and fulfilling ways.

Do Something Different

1. The map metaphor in this chapter will appeal to some readers and not others. If maps are not your forte, what is another way of presenting approaches that blends with your way of understanding the process of change?
2. Some clients enter counseling because they are seeking the experiences collected on a journey, rather than seeking to arrive. They might argue that life is in the living experience and that terminating the journey is irrelevant. Assume that you are a brief counselor who finds that the approaches in this chapter make a lot of sense. What are three different ways you might approach a client espousing this philosophical stance?
3. Which guiding approaches are the most intuitive to your way of thinking? Which, if any, are the least? What is your alternative for those that don't fit?

CHAPTER 3

Overcoming the "Quick Fix" Phobia

CLIENT: *My counselor told me, "We'll be done when we're done. Have patience—these things take time. Don't be fooled into believing that counseling offers a quick fix."*

In brief counseling we question traditional assumptions about how long it takes to help people. Basic to brief counseling is the belief that people are very resourceful and that our responsibility as helpers is to be dispensable—as quickly as possible. In brief counseling we simply assume that our help can often be provided in significantly less time than we have been taught to believe. Unfortunately, several factors contribute to the belief that going faster is ultimately injurious to clients. When speedier ways of making change are proposed, a frequent rejoinder is that doing counseling faster is just a "quick fix." The counseling profession holds a collective disdain for the phrase "quick fix"—it has strong negative connotations.

When the phrase "quick fix" is associated with counseling, counselors have tended to make several assumptions. First, if something is a quick fix, then issues will be missed or overlooked. Second, quick fix means superficial treatment, not quality care. Third, quick fix implies dealing with surface issues, not deeper and more real issues, such as the meaning of events in people's lives. Fourth, some counselors contend that a quick fix has no place in counseling since there are no quick answers to the complexity of the human condition. Finally, a quick fix implies that what is done will not last; it is temporary at best.

While quick fix brings to mind negative images and meaning, the dictionary is more complimentary for each word taken separately. The word *fix* used as a verb has the following meanings:

Fix: To alter so as to make efficient or more efficient; to put into good shape or working order again; to find an answer or solution for (a problem or difficulty).

The word "quick" has these meanings as an adjective:

Quick: Moving, proceeding, or acting with great celerity (i.e., rate of movement, performance, or occurrence); able to respond without delay or hesitation or indicative of such ability; shrewdly aware and subtly resourceful; in a rapid manner.

These definitions suggest that counselors who think in terms of quick fixes are justified in responding efficiently, without hesitation, and in a rapid manner to help clients find answers or solutions for problems and difficulties. Those who engage in brief counseling do not have a quick-fix phobia. They assume that helping people make life changes in the fastest ways possible is a perfectly legitimate activity. Helping people as quickly as possible is also viewed as an ethical stance. In other words, in brief counseling the counselor believes that quick fix is one legitimate way, but not the only way, of assisting people. Perceiving quickness as a positive outcome, counselors using brief approaches look for opportunities to speed up the process of change, to hasten progress toward reaching goals, and to say good-bye to clients as soon as possible.

New Assumptions about
How Long Counseling Takes

A faster approach to counseling is possible because brief counselors challenge five established assumptions of traditional counseling. These older assumptions are replaced with a new set of assumptions that seriously question certain causal connections. Brief counselors no longer make causal connections between the length of time needed for effective helping and five variables: (1) the nature of problems, (2) the number of problems, (3) the duration of problems, (4) the severity of problems, and (5) the complexity of problems. In breaking these causal connections, counselors are free to explore with clients changes that may take less time.

In the following five sections, case examples are provided that illustrate how these newer assumptions play out in actual counseling sessions. Each of the clients had expressed discomfort over what was happening and each wanted to be able to manage his or her situation more effectively. The clients were able to reach their goals in from one to six sessions, with three needing but a single session.

1. Nature of Problems. The nature of problems has often been cited as a factor in how long counseling will take. It was assumed that certain types of problems would, by their very nature, take longer. For example, career counseling has often been viewed as rather short-term—one or two sessions. In contrast, drug and alcohol counseling, and recently codependency, have been perceived as long-term—extending a lifetime for some types of treatments. Recent work in solution-focused therapy has challenged the view that helping clients who have substance abuse problems must of necessity be long-term (Berg & Miller, 1992).

Steve de Shazer (1988) provided a brief counseling example of a cocaine addict who sought assistance with her drug problem. She had not taken cocaine for three days and as she sat in the office she appeared quite tense. The counselor emphasized what was working in his client's life by focusing on exceptions to the problem through questions such as, "When have you already successfully overcome the urge or the temptation to take cocaine?" (Exceptions will be presented more fully in Chapter 6.) Extensive exploration was conducted of those times when she had been successful in refusing cocaine. The counselor sought details of how she made sure she said "no" to taking cocaine. The client described how she locked her door and would not let in anyone who wanted to sell or give her cocaine. She told of avoiding people she knew were not good for her. At the end of the session she was given the task of continuing to do those things that were successful in resisting doing cocaine. The woman was seen a total of six times over a six-month period of time. She reported that during that time she had not taken cocaine, had changed her set of friends, and had begun looking for a new job. A half-year later she reported that she had tried cocaine once but that it had not given her the same kick. At a year she had a new job and new friends and was pleased with her drug-free existence.

This example is not given to demonstrate that all or even some drug addiction can be overcome in only several sessions. Obviously, there are clients who struggle with addictions all their lives. The significance of the example is that it points to the possibility that the nature of the problem may be independent of how many sessions counseling will take. In many theoretical approaches, various problems are assumed to have fixed natures that require a minimum length of time. Brief counselors divorce the nature of the problem from assumptions about how long counseling will take. New solutions often emerge when we remove the restriction of always coloring within the lines.

2. Number of Problems. Brief counselors do not assume that the greater the number of problems reported by clients, the longer counseling will last. The number of problems clients report does not tell counselors and clients how many solutions will be necessary. Sometimes only one or several solutions may suffice for a handful of problems.

A master key to an office building is designed to unlock many doors, thus avoiding the time-consuming activity of finding the right key. In a similar way, a master-key solution may serve to unlock multiple problems in considerably less time than if a separate key were applied to each problem. In a case to be fully presented in Chapter 6, "You Can Tie Your Own Shoes," the client Meg had numerous problems. She chose to apply her resources to one problem in particular. When I saw Meg again in two weeks she reported substantial progress in solving the problem. Meg also reported meaningful progress on several other concerns that we had not discussed. When I asked what had occurred, she said she had used her newly discovered resources on other issues as well. Based on what I learned from Meg, I now intentionally ask clients the following question, "Given the resources and strengths that you are going to be using on the issue we discussed, what are other areas of your life where you might also use these same resources?" The question presupposes that there may be other problematic areas not yet discussed that may benefit from change. The question also presupposes that clients may begin to generalize solutions to other problem areas. I have been impressed with people's abilities to take solutions for one problem area and apply them, without much direction on my part, to other areas of their lives.

In the following case, David presented a long list of stressors in his life, any one of which could have been treated as a separate problem or cluster of problems. A modification of a strategy used by Milton Erickson was chosen to help the client regain "control" over his life (Haley, 1984; O'Hanlon & Hexum, 1990).

Give Me the Toothbrush Task

Several years ago David, a student in my counseling class, appeared at my office door. He stood there and said, "I'm depressed. I can't sleep. Give me the toothbrush task." I knew exactly what David meant. Several weeks before in class I had discussed a case by Milton Erickson whose client was experiencing severe insomnia. Erickson arranged for his client to wax a wooden floor for eight hours each night for four nights. The man learned after several nights that falling asleep when he went to bed was vastly preferable to waxing floors.

In telling Erickson's case to my class I had suggested that scrubbing the floor with a bucket of soapy water and a toothbrush might be the preferred way of cleaning modern vinyl floors. David was telling me that he needed this task to help him fall asleep. Prior to assigning "the toothbrush task," I asked David to sit down and explain a bit about what was happening. He gave me the following laundry list of events that had occurred in the last six months:

1. His grandfather had recently died.
2. He and his wife had moved from a house in the country to one in the city.
3. He had been forced to purchase a new car because his other one had caught fire.
4. He had quit a teaching job.
5. He had started graduate school full-time.
6. His graduate assistantship was supposed to be 20 hours per week, but was in reality taking 40 hours.
7. Finals week was approaching.
8. He had a long paper for a class due.
9. He had not been sleeping well during the past week.

On Holmes' scale for measuring stress, David was pushing a very high score. Had he considered suicide? David emphatically stated he had not. We soon established that his "depression" correlated 100% with his lack of sleep. David believed that if he could get several good nights of sleep he could handle all the other "stressors" occurring in his life. I gently quizzed him about this certainty, but he remained convinced that sleep was the key.

After our short assessment and in response to his initial request, I gave David the following short directive, "Do the toothbrush task!" We then worked on the details. David was to lie awake in bed for no more than 15 minutes. If he were still awake at the end of that time he was to get a bucket of soapy water and scrub the kitchen floor with a toothbrush until he became sleepy. When sleepiness began to happen he could go back to bed; however, if after 15 minutes he were awake it was back to the kitchen floor. David agreed to follow through on the task and to report to me the next day.

David appeared at my office the next afternoon looking considerably refreshed. He said he had slept eight hours last night. Because I am insatiably curious about the ways clients individualize the tasks they have been assigned, I asked him to tell me specifically how the task had worked for him. He blushed a bit and told me that he had gone to bed as usual. He lay in bed realizing that he needed to go to sleep within 15 minutes. David said he looked over at his wife lying beside him in the bed and said to himself, "If I go downstairs and scrub that damn floor with a damn toothbrush at this hour my wife is going to think I'm crazy." Then David added, "I knew having her think that about me would be worse than the toothbrush thing, so I just rolled over and went to sleep."

David's laundry list contained real problems. While each problem by itself was not overwhelming, the cumulative effect was. The simple existence of many problems does not mean that the length of counseling must necessarily be extended. The focus on solving the sleep problem was instrumental in providing a master-key solution to the other problems. Brief counselors are not daunted because clients' lists of problems are long. Brief counselors use the long lists as an opportunity to look for master-key solutions that unlock other problems.

3. Duration of Problems. Because clients have struggled with problems for prolonged periods of time does not necessarily mean that counseling must be longer than if the struggles had been of shorter duration. When a person takes a long time to find a workable solution to a concern, we often find that the attempted solution is being recycled *ad infinitum* (Amatea, 1989; Watzlawick et al., 1974). For example, clients often try to force themselves to go to sleep, thus ensuring that sleep will be postponed. Replacing old solutions that perpetuate more-of-the-same approaches with new solutions that introduce differences that make a difference is one way out of the continuous loop.

Often clients have convinced themselves that because they have struggled for a long time with a concern, creation of the solution will take just as long. Unfortunately, counselors are inclined to accept this assumption. Brief counselors challenge the assumed positive correlation between duration of problems and length of counseling in order to find workable solutions. One way to unlink these two variables is to make statements and ask questions such as the following:

- "I have worked with clients who thought that just because they had struggled with a concern for a long time, they would have to spend a long time resolving the concern. Are you willing to entertain the idea that we might find some ways of resolving your concern in a short period of time?" (The first sentence paces the client's belief that change takes a long time. The second sentence gently challenges the client's belief by making the belief less than absolute.)

- "To what extent are you willing to be pleasantly surprised that counseling doesn't take a long time to help you deal with this problem that has lasted so long?" ("Pleasantly surprised" adds an element of fun to what is often perceived as an ordeal.)

- "I have had clients be very skeptical of making changes too fast because they think the changes will not last. Yet they have been wonderfully surprised when the new solutions work. How skeptical are you right now? What would have to happen to overcome your skepticism?" (Again, the first sentence is a pacing of the client's belief. The question about skepticism has the client go on record as to how skeptical he or she is. The last question provides the counselor information about the criteria the client is using to remain skeptical.)

Unlinking the duration of the concern from how long it will take to deal effectively with the concern provides one way of shortening counseling. Clients' beliefs about length of counseling should be heard, considered, and acknowledged, but they do not have to receive our professional endorsement. Mild challenges are often effective in breaking the link between problem duration and length of counseling. In the next case, I tackled a chronic problem with which the client had struggled for years.

Chance, Choice, and Change

Thelma had struggled with her excess weight for many years. Her current description of herself was that she felt "as big as a house." She had tried diet after diet, and she had stuck with each one for about two or three days. I acknowledged and validated her discouragement and sadness over not losing weight.

When I inquired about what she had tried over the years, I was surprised to learn that she had maintained a well-designed exercise regime. On the other hand, her eating patterns were abysmal. Despite seeing a nutritionist for some time she had not eaten vegetables in the last year. Then she dropped the bombshell—she survived on sweets. When I asked what that meant, she said, "I probably eat three to four pounds of sweets a day." I work hard to be empathic with clients but at that point I said, "Pounds?" She looked me in the eye and repeated, "Pounds!" Because of severe medical problems possibly associated with consuming huge quantities of sweets, I established a contract with Thelma to have her receive a complete medical exam as quickly as possible. As it turned out, she had one scheduled for the next day.

Thelma's initial goal was to lose 20 pounds in three weeks. This was unacceptable to me, and we negotiated a three to four pounds loss. A more direct goal involved her maintaining her exercise program and establishing healthy eating patterns. Based on my belief that Thelma was taking chances with her health and needed to be making better choices, I designed a task involving the rolling of a die each morning to see which combination of exercise and eating patterns she would do that day. Each morning she took her chances by rolling a die to determine what her choice was. The die spots and tasks were:

1 = One pound of sweets (or less or none) + regular exercise
2 = Two pound of sweets (or less or none) + regular exercise
3 = Three pounds of sweets (or less or none) + regular exercise
4 = No sweets + day off from exercise
5 = No sweets + half of regular exercise
6 = No sweets + regular exercise

Thelma responded by saying that she planned not to eat sweets even if she rolled a one, two, or three. I provided her with a small die to roll and a large fuzzy die (the kind found hanging from the rear view mirrors of cars) to place near where she ate sweets. The fuzzy die served to remind her of the choices she was making.

We were not able to schedule an appointment until two weeks later. Thelma appeared carrying a plastic bag filled with vegetables. She reported that her medical exam had indicated pre-diabetic signs and that her successful reduction in sweets was all for the best. In the time since we had first met, Thelma had rolled the die daily for one week. Each time she had chosen not to eat sweets on that day. At the end of the first week, she said she looked at the die and said to herself, "Why am I letting this stupid die control my life? I can decide on my own without it." Subsequent follow-ups indicated that Thelma was continuing to exercise, had eliminated sweets from her diet, and was slowly losing weight. She reported being much more in control of her life; she liked the changes that were occurring.

Thelma's case provides an example of how long-standing problems do not necessarily take more time to solve than problems of recent origin. Longer duration may be understood as simply an indication that clients have not yet discovered solutions that work. For Thelma, the die served as a way of making more salient her ability to choose healthy options. Interestingly, while the die functioned as an external means of helping, Thelma eventually internalized the choice process. Brief counselors look for solutions with their clients and spend little time being concerned about how long problems have persisted.

4. Severity of Problems. How much does something hurt? One measure of severity is the amount of discomfort and distress that clients are experiencing. Often a positive correlation is made between the amount of client discomfort and the number of sessions needed to alleviate it. In brief counseling the focus is on helping clients reach their goals as quickly as possible. Reduction in the amount of clients' discomfort may serve as an indicator of how effective counseling is. To the extent that solutions work, clients will experience less discomfort. Discomfort is not seen as a symptom or as a necessary step in clients' recovery. When discomfort is viewed as a symptom of deeper, underlying issues rather than as a problem in and of itself, then counseling will probably take longer. Brief counselors tend to approach clients' concerns about discomfort in a rather direct fashion.

Brief counselors do not assume that discomfort is a necessary condition for people to experience during the time they are in counseling. In fact, discomfort acts as a stressor so that decision-making is more, rather than less, difficult. Brief counselors want their clients functioning at the highest possible levels of effective decision-making. Reducing discomfort is viewed as a highly desirable first step, in that it frees clients to use their cognitive capacities more effectively. Optimal levels of stress may also serve as a motivation to find new solutions. When counselors help clients to use their minds to think about solutions and plan effective strategies of change, they reduce the time clients need counseling.

The following case is an autobiographic one in which I experienced severe distress and the prospects of its continuing unabated for nine weeks. I applied the Neuro-Linguistic Programming (NLP) technique of "anchoring" (i.e., classical conditioning) to a fear I was experiencing (NLP Comprehensive Training Team, 1994). The internal resource tapped was most unusual and the change almost instantaneous. As will be discovered, the change was also quite gratifying.

Fear of Flying (with apologies to Erica Jong)

I had worked with numerous people in helping them overcome their fears using the NLP technique of anchoring, but I had not had the opportunity to try it myself prior to December 1980. As part of my course load at Iowa State University (ISU), I began teaching an extension course in Cedar Rapids in early December. To travel to the class 100 miles from Ames I flew in a small ISU airplane that held five passengers and a pilot. Returning to Ames the night after teaching the first class, we encountered a blizzard. As the plane approached Ames, I watched as the runway and runway lights bounced all over my field of vision. Strong winds and snow buffeted our plane.

I was terrified. My hands were shaking and my palms glistened with sweat. Racing through my mind were ideas about my will and funeral, my grieving wife and son, and my abbreviated life. I experienced tremendous relief when the pilot landed successfully.

Over the next several days I thought about my options. I realized that I was going to need considerable help before I climbed into that small plane for next week's flight to Cedar Rapids and for the eight additional weeks after that. Suddenly the question occurred to me: What did NLP trainers say was necessary to overcome a fear? Instantly I remembered their answer—a resource that is more powerful than the fear. Systematic desensitization advocates would have suggested relaxation. In view of the terror I had experienced, that just didn't seem powerful enough.

The only resource that I could think of that was more powerful than my fear of flying was the joy of making love with my wife. I decided to use the technique of "anchoring" a powerful resource to diminish the fear. That evening I anchored in the wonderful and powerful sensation of love-making. The next week when I got on the plane I used the anchored resource. The experience of flying was transformed by the "magic" of love or, stated another way, my fear of flying was transformed by the joy of sex. I quickly concluded that change can be quick, fun, and long-lasting in spite of the problem's initial severity.

Some people believe change that occurs quickly is not long-lasting. However, since 1980 I have logged several hundred thousand miles. The special anchor that took just minutes to install has allowed me to enjoy flying in all types of weather. Distress and discomfort are indicators that something is amiss, or they may be the problem as in the above case. Solutions that work for clients relieve distress and discomfort. Brief counselors search for ways to help clients find comfort, even as they work on problems that are severe.

5. Complexity of Problems. Finally, problems are often viewed by counselors and clients as complicated knots that can only be untangled slowly. As clients present their knots for our inspection and assistance, we are often impressed by their complexity and hence clients' difficulty in untying them. One frame for viewing clients' knots is to consider them Gordian knots. In antiquity the Gordian knot was so complex that it defied many attempts to untie it. The eventual solution to the Gordian knot was not to untie it. Alexander the Great achieved the solution; he cut the knot. Brief counselors see complexity and respond by cutting the Gordian knot, thus solving the problem boldly and quickly, rather than timidly and slowly.

If as counselors we assume that the whole problem must be untied before anything is going to happen, then it will take longer than if the knot is bypassed with bold interventions. One bold intervention is to begin counseling by asking clients the following question: "If we were to be completely successful in helping you, what would your life be like?" This question bypasses the "problem" and provides clients and counselors with information about what clients want, not information about what is troubling them.

During a counseling internship at Indiana University more than twenty years ago, I caught my first glimpse of how brief counseling could work effectively with complex problems. It was a pivotal moment in my thinking about how short effective counseling might be. Unfortunately, while the experience was memorable, I did not know enough about what had happened to reproduce it in any sort of systematic fashion. My first briefest of brief counseling sessions (one session) occurred in the following fashion.

Client as Saint

I met with Claire, a young woman in her junior year of college. She was upset about her art major, her life in general, but most of all about an affair she was having with a married man. As Claire talked about her experiences, I remembered a photograph and description of Bernini's sculpture "Ecstasy of Saint Teresa" in Kenneth Clark's *Civilisation* (1969). Because the themes of pain and sweetness Claire expressed seemed to be conveyed in the sculpture, I shared with her my remembrance of a description of the sculpture. She became alive with excitement as she vividly recalled the sculpture from an art class and how it was one of her favorite pieces of art. We went on to talk about how Bernini's "Ecstasy of Saint Teresa" conveyed a state of religious ecstasy with simultaneously felt pain and sweetness; Claire described how the emotions exactly described her own situation.

As we continued talking, Claire experienced a dramatic sense of relief. She said that the "Ecstasy of Saint Teresa" captured the conflicting feelings in her life. Her own simultaneously felt pain and sweetness had suddenly acquired new meaning; she could reconcile her seeming conflicting emotions. Claire chose not to elaborate but indicated that she now knew what she had to do in her life. She said we didn't need to meet again. Our first session was our last.

As a beginning counselor steeped in the client-centered approach of Carl Rogers, I was amazed at Claire's rapid change because it certainly did not fit into any of the models of counseling I was studying. Moreover, I was profoundly impressed that a simple solution—talking about a classic sculpture and relating it to one's life—could rapidly provide the help a client needed. I remember wondering how I could help clients reach their desired outcomes as quickly as this client, especially when the situation the client had described was rather complex. My counseling with Claire spurred my search for counseling models that conceptualized change occurring faster than the models I had learned.

Life seldom makes things simple. Complexity evolves quickly even from seemingly simple actions. Rather than attempt to deal with multiple issues, brief counselors aim for simple interventions that will provide the greatest leverage for clients to regain more control of their lives. In brief counseling we sow the seeds of change by beginning with simple changes, ever mindful of the complexity of our clients' lives.

Working Quickly

People approaching counseling have varying expectations. A 45-year-old man seeking to leisurely explore the meaning of his life may find that counseling labeled "brief" is not a good fit. An abused wife with three children probably needs more than several counseling sessions, since many aspects of her life are out of her control. In both of these cases, traditional counseling might take a year or so, while "brief" counseling might effect the needed changes in six months. Brief counseling is "brief" only when compared to what we consider typical treatment length.

Talmon (1990) proposed several types of situations in which clients will benefit from single-session counseling. I believe they also apply to the brief counseling discussed in this book. Talmon suggested that clients who come with "a specific problem," who are "checking if they are normal," and who have "natural supports" are well suited for very short counseling. Talmon also proposed that clients who "can identify, often with counselor's assistance, helpful solutions, past successes, and exceptions to the problem," as well as those who are "stuck on some feeling toward past events," are good candidates for short approaches. Two other situations are clients who "need referral to some other source" and clients who "face unsolvable problems" and therefore need to acknowledge "the impossibility of change" (p. 31). Talmon's list is compatible with the unlinking of problems from the time required to work on them, as proposed in this chapter. Talmon provides ways of understanding when short-term approaches may be appropriate.

This chapter has provided counselors with a heuristic to use in determining if brief counseling is appropriate. The heuristic is: A brief counseling approach asks that we not approach clients with preconceived ideas about how long counseling should take. Sometimes brief counseling is appropriate even when our clients' problems seem long-term by their very nature, fairly numerous, long in duration, quite severe, and/or extremely complex. In breaking the supposed causal connections between these five factors and the assumed length of counseling, we free ourselves to explore with clients solutions that may be quicker, rather than slower. Once we are freed from assuming that counseling necessarily has to stretch out over an indefinite period of time, we are in a position to help our clients change more quickly.

Do Something Different

1. Think about your last five clients. When you began working with them, what was your best guess about how long counseling might take? To what extent did the nature of problems, the number of problems, the duration, the severity, and/or the complexity of problems influence how long you thought counseling would take? Actively challenge your own beliefs about the connection between each of these variables and the length of counseling time.

2. Milton H. Erickson used a phrase when clients held a belief that was not particularly conducive to being helped: "Don't be so sure." Then he would abruptly change the topic before the client had a chance to disagree. Use this seeding technique when clients are convinced that counseling must, of necessity, take a long time.

3. Ask your clients how long they think the counseling will take. If they say longer than you think, then mildly challenge them by letting them know that in your experience the solutions they are exploring will take less time. If your clients say shorter than you think, then tell them, "Let's work to meet your expectation."

4. Challenge your beliefs. How much faster do you believe you could possibly work with clients and still be as helpful as you currently are?

   10%   25%   50%   100%   200%   500%   1000%

   How willing are you to try these different speeds? If you can do in one session that which formerly took ten sessions, then you are helping 1000% faster.

CHAPTER 4

Trusting Clients' Expertise

CLIENT: *My counselor conveyed that she knew me better than I knew myself—she was the expert on my life.*

The Wizard of Oz was a knowledgeable and powerful figure, as attested to by Dorothy, the Tin Woodsman, the Scarecrow, the Lion, and other inhabitants of the Land of Oz. It was well known throughout the Land of Oz that the Wizard possessed amazing powers. The Wizard of Oz was an expert at helping people (and Munchkins). As is typical of people who possess power, the Wizard did nothing to dispute the conventional wisdom of his expertise. In fact, he traded on his reputation as a means of helping people reach their goals.

Our clients, like people seeking the Wizard's help, look to us for assistance with their problems. Often, they confer upon us a mantle of expertise. After a while, it becomes relatively easy to slip into the role of a wizard.[1] We begin to believe and subsequently convey to our clients that we are experts on their lives. The danger of mistaking ourselves for wizards is that in focusing on our own expertise we overlook or diminish our clients' expertise. What is needed is a better balance between counselor and client expertise. I believe four factors contribute to this

[1] I could find no consensus on whether the word *wizard* is sexist. Changing to wizardess is one option but few liked it.

emphasis on counselor expertise at the expense of client expertise.

First, the education of counselors is infused with an emphasis on counselors' knowledge and skills. One of the first courses offered in counseling programs teaches students attending and influencing skills (Egan, 1990; Ivey, Ivey, & Simek-Morgan, 1993). Despite professors' attempts to diminish students' apprehensiveness, beginning students' nonverbal behavior during tape critiquing resembles actors' performances in Mel Brooks' *High Anxiety*. Cognitive dissonance theory would suggest that those of us who have successfully completed this training endeavor would find it hard not to see ourselves as experts. Learning advanced skills in counseling classes reinforces our perceptions of ourselves as experts.

A second reason for the lack of balance between counselors' and clients' expertise has been the choice of counseling theories. In contrast to brief counseling theories, many counseling theories stress the expertise of counselors and their ability to know what is wrong with clients and what needs to be right, what clients' goals *should be*, and how they *should* achieve those goals. Brief counselors operate from the assumption that their clients know much more about their own lives than they are ever going to know. Therefore, brief counselors are wary that their assessment skills can pinpoint *the* problem, such that clients should be more assertive, should deal with their dependency needs, or should be more integrated. In other words, brief counselors do not act as experts in knowing what is best for clients.

The following case illustrates how a therapist saw his role as being the expert in identifying the client's problem while ignoring the client's judgment in the matter.

The Problem Expert

Several years ago I witnessed, over a period of six weeks, a psychotherapist demonstrate short-term therapy using a psychodynamic framework. He began the first session by asking his client, Tina, a college student, what she would like to talk about. Tina mentioned that she would like to lose about ten pounds, as she felt uncomfortable at her current weight. The therapist responded that first he would like to know more about who Tina was. She cooperated with his request. The remainder of the session and continuing throughout the next five sessions, the therapist and Tina explored her relationships with her boyfriend and her parents, as well as her career objectives.

After six sessions the time-limited, psychodynamically-oriented therapy was completed. The therapist asked Tina a series of questions about her experience with brief psychotherapy, which included the following, "Tina, how did this type of short-term therapy work for you?"

Tina replied, "It was very interesting, but I was disappointed about one thing. Initially, I mentioned that I wanted to work on my weight and we never got around to dealing with that."

During his subsequent remarks to the professional audience after Tina had left, the therapist elaborated on his belief that Tina's request for help in losing weight was merely a symptom of her inner conflicts. He implied that as a trained professional he knew better than she what the important issues were and that he was the person who should determine the focus by emphasizing certain topics and ignoring others. Those of us in the audience were assured that Tina's choice of focusing on the weight issue should not distract us from recognizing the client's need to work on her inner psyche and strengthen her ego.

When the sixth session and the analysis were completed, I left thinking that the therapist had expert skills. There was no sin of commission—the therapist had provided opportunities for Tina to explore a number of topics, and he had listened carefully and reflected back the essence of her thoughts and feelings. The problem was a sin of omission—the therapist ignored Tina's knowledge of what was important to her.

A third reason for the lack of balance between counselors' and clients' expertise has been the choice of social influence models for understanding the process aspects of counseling. The prominence of the social influence model has encouraged counselors to focus on their own expertness, as well as their own trustworthiness and interpersonal attractiveness (Corrigan, Dell, Lewis, & Schmidt, 1980; Strong & Claiborn, 1982). The considerable amount of research to date suggests that counselors should establish and maintain high levels of expertness and trustworthiness because these two attributes lead clients to perceive counselors as possessing credibility. Counselors may then use this perceived credibility to leverage client change. Notably lacking in the counselor literature has been how counselors might work to increase clients' credibility—clients' expertise and trustworthiness.

A final reason that clients have not been viewed as experts has been that prominent diagnostic and assessment instruments have focused attention on what does not work in clients' lives. The most widely employed classification scheme for understanding clients is the *Diagnostic and Statistical Manual of Mental Disorders, 4th Edition* (American Psychiatric Association, 1994). The focus of the *DSM-IV* is on categories of disorder, not order. The best known assessment instrument used for diagnosing clients' problems is the *Minnesota Multiphasic Personality Inventory* (MMPI), whose scales reflect serious disorders. Even instruments to measure normal personality characteristics, such as the *Edwards Personal Preference Schedule* (EPPS) and the *California Psychological Inventory* (CPI), are often used to determine and subsequently highlight where persons are maladjusted, rather than where they are experts in their own lives. All too often the emphasis of assessment has dictated the implied rule of thumb—focus on what does not work.

There are significant exceptions to the mainstream emphasis on what does not work in clients' lives. Behaviorists have employed applied behavioral analysis to focus on a blend of what is working and what is not working. Perhaps the most conspicuous example of focusing on what people can do has been in the area of career/vocational counseling. For example, on John Holland's (1985) career assessment instrument, *The Self-Directed Search*, clients' skills, abilities, and capabilities are highlighted. It is an ironic commentary on the counseling profession that counselors who have traditionally focused most on clients' strengths, such as career counselors, are often perceived to have less status than those who do personal/social counseling and have accented clients' weaknesses.

The emphasis on knowledge and skills in counseling programs, the preponderance of counseling theories that focus on deficits, the valuing of counselors' expertise in social influence models, and the predominance of assessment focused on clients' weaknesses and failings—all contribute to a failure to trust clients as experts in their own lives.

Highlighting Clients' Expertise

Expertness is highly desired in brief counseling but there is a twist. Expertness is precisely the characteristic that brief counselors actively seek and successfully find in their clients. For brief counselors, two scenarios are common. In both, counselors adopt the following belief: Clients are experts in their own lives—they know much more about their lives than counselors can ever know (or should want to know). Brief counselors begin counseling believing that because their clients are such experts in their lives it is absolutely necessary to tap clients' expertise if counseling is to be successful.

In the first scenario, counselors perceive their clients as being the experts in their lives but find that clients do not share this perception. Many times clients begin counseling, especially when it is "voluntary," perceiving counselors as the experts. Brief counselors work hard to help clients realize and use their own expertise as quickly as possible.

In the second scenario, counselors perceive their clients as being the experts in their lives and their clients agree. Clients in brief counseling who believe in their own expertise are appreciated and encouraged to maintain that belief. Brief counselors know that these clients are not going to just rely on them, be "dependent," and engage in "yes, but" behavior; these are clients who want to work.

Trusting Clients

For counselors to see clients as experts in their own lives evokes the issue of trust. Brief counselors believe their clients are doing their best at any given time to share their world view. If what is shared is minimal, then it is because their clients' abilities to share their worlds at that point are minimal, not that their clients are trying to hide things from their counselors.

When clients seem to be sharing little, brief counselors understand that they have perfectly legitimate reasons for not disclosing. One reason is the fear that revealing information will be painful to themselves and/or others. A second reason is the fear that information shared with the counselor will be used against them. In brief approaches, counselors trust their clients to know what is hurting. They trust clients to choose (with assistance from counselors, friends, spouse, etc.) important goals to work on. They trust clients to know (with assistance) how to reach their goals. Finally, counselors trust clients to know when they no longer need counseling.

Conveying trust in clients is facilitated by counselors' adopting a stance of not knowing what is best for clients. When I work with clients I am aware that in the short time we meet I have very few clues as to how my clients live their lives. I have even fewer clues about what they want different in their lives. Confronted with my own massive ignorance about who my clients are and what they want, I adopt a posture that says "trust the people you work with to be the experts in their lives."

In the following case, I trusted that my client, Martha, was much more knowledgeable about her world than I would ever be. I supported Martha as she used her own expertise about her own life and that of her daughter to dream up an imaginative approach to communicate more effectively with her daughter. As is typical of people I work with, Martha amazed me with her expertise in inventing a fascinating way to reach her goal.

Give Me a Break

Martha was thoroughly disgusted with her 15-year-old daughter, Gina. Martha was a single parent who worked hard herself but demanded little of Gina except doing the dishes. Day after day Martha returned home from work to find the dirty dishes still in the sink. The usual methods had been tried and all had produced identical results—minimal compliance with maximum complaining for a brief period of time prior to a return to doing nothing.

We negotiated the following goal: "I will communicate with my daughter Gina in such a way that, despite how she responds, I will retain my sense of humor." As we moved to help Martha reach her goal, she was given the task of doing something really different, something that was utterly fun for Martha but would move her out of her endless nagging role. We were looking for something that would interrupt the old pattern and set in motion a new one (O'Hanlon & Weiner-Davis, 1989).

On her own Martha thought up something really new and out of the ordinary that she was delighted to try. The following quote is Martha's description of what she did:

> I was really put out that Gina just sat there on her ass in the other room when I did the dishes. I thought I'd get her attention to the problem in another way without having to nag her, which I hate. We had some old crappy china in the basement and one evening I went down and got some.
>
> The next day I got home and the dishes were still in the sink. Gina was in the other room watching TV. I was pissed but I was also smiling because I had my plan ready. I went to the sink and started washing dishes. After a few minutes I held up one of the china dishes and let it fall on the linoleum floor. It broke and Gina came running in to see what the noise was. I didn't even look up at her and I said in a weary voice, "Oh, I'm just tired and it slipped. Don't think about it. I'll pick it up and finish the dishes myself." Inside I'm just laughing my head off but I didn't let her know that.
>
> Gina went back to watching TV and in a few minutes I let go with another plate. When she came in I just said, "My reflexes must be going in my old age. Never mind. I'll finish up." Gina looked at me in a funny way. I just told her to go back to what she was doing.
>
> The next day when I got home the dishes were washed, dried, and put away. I went into the TV room and thanked Gina for doing the dishes. It was a genuine thank you because I was really thankful. I even added, "Is there anything I can do to help you?" She really looked surprised.
>
> It's amazing! All this last week Gina has done the dishes without me saying a word about them. We're getting along much better now and not

just when it comes to doing the dishes. I guess I really do know how to communicate with my daughter.

Martha demonstrated her inventiveness in designing a way to communicate with her daughter. Whereas one "obvious" solution to the client's problem from the role of an "expert" counselor would have been to teach the mother and daughter better communication skills, the mother found a highly effective technique of getting her message across in record time. She also reported that her relationship with her daughter improved in other areas of their lives.

Similarly, in the next case the client's understanding of her life allowed her to tailor a solution that fit perfectly. We met for only one session.

Choreographing a Life

Andrea and I worked together to help her reach her goal, which she stated as: "Getting the book that is within me written." She had received encouragement from others that her knowledge on the topic was abundant and that she really owed it to others to share it in print. To date she was using a grind-it-out pattern and the book had not written itself. Andrea was becoming an outstanding avoider of that which she professed to want.

I was tempted to play the expert. After all, I was writing a book about brief counseling and I was moving ahead at a steady pace. Surely my knowledge of how to get a book written would be invaluable. I had even found a pithy formula, PAS, that reminded me to keep writing. The PAS formula (Phillips, 1993, p. 1) is:

Persistence (fanny on chair) + Activity (actually writing) = Success (producing something useful)

Luckily, I suppressed my own ideas about what would work best in Andrea's world and stayed with the belief that she was the expert on her own life. Andrea was a dance therapist and so I asked her, "How could you take what you know about dance and apply it to your book writing?" Suddenly we were talking about how she taught her students to dance. Andrea began to conceptualize her book writing as her solo dance. She chose a specific costume to wear when she wrote and a specific time for her fingers "to dance" over the computer's keyboard. As she drew parallels with dance she became more animated; it looked as if she might leap up and dance around the room.

I spoke to Andrea on the phone in a follow-up five weeks after our only session. While Andrea had not yet begun writing, she stated that this was "not negative." She said she did not view the lack of writing as procrastination as she previously had. Andrea added, "I'm getting ready for the writing because there are all kinds of things to prepare. I'm organizing my environment." She laughed and quipped, "I'm nesting." In addition, Andrea said, "I'm not depressed about the writing like I was." Future follow-up interviews are planned.

In both of these cases, "Give Me a Break" and "Choreographing a Life," the women were able to use personal knowledge about their own lives to shape solutions that worked for them. As the counselor working with these two women, I reaffirmed that clients often possess considerable knowledge that can be tapped. My role was not to be a content expert but, rather, an expert at the process of finding solutions. While I facilitated my clients' search for solutions that worked, each client assumed responsibility for generating and implementing the new patterns that finally served as solutions.

Counselors Are Still Experts

The discussion to this point has underscored how counselors have been led to perceive that they are the experts in the counseling relationship and how clients' expertise has been minimized. The thesis has been that we should tap clients' expertise much more than we currently do. However, expertise is not an either/or choice. I believe there are certain domains where counselors certainly possess expertise that may prove beneficial to clients.

Counselors need to be experts in terms of their self-awareness. A potential danger that I have observed in supervising practitioners new to brief counseling is their tendency to forget empathy and caring as they push toward solutions. They have become consumed with finding solutions at the expense of accurately hearing their clients. I have found in my own supervision that I must continually be on guard that my own impatience and desire to "be helpful" do not result in my placing my own agenda first, thus blinding me to my clients' expertise.

The helping professions require that counselors be experts in the issues that clients face—AIDS, child and spouse abuse and laws pertaining to these, poverty, job opportunities, scholarships, peer pressure, and sexual identity, to name a few. The list is lengthy and continues to grow.

Counselors are expected to be skilled experts who know how to assist in helping people change. We want counselors who can validate clients' concerns, set mutually agreed upon goals, and know many methods to help clients reach their goals. Counselors do not need to deny their expertise. Steve de Shazer (1993), who has contributed significantly to the theory and practice of solution-focused therapy, has said, "I certainly want to retain the idea that I am some sort of expert." He continued by listing how he sees himself as an expert.

> I have a lot of knowledge about (a) talk about problems and how they happen, (b) talk about solutions and how they develop, and (c) how language works. . . . I know a lot about (d) what does not work. I also know a lot about (e) where the materials for constructing a solution come from—they come from clients. In fact, I think of clients as experts—they know a lot that I do not know. (p. 88)

Balanced Expertise

Seeking, finding, and trusting clients' expertise reverses the imbalance that has been the prevalent stance in traditional counseling. An expert is one who has acquired special skills in or knowledge and mastery of something. In brief counseling the client is seen as an expert—an expert in the content and context of his or her own life. As such, this way of looking at clients differs radically from traditional approaches to counseling. At the same time, counselors possess expertise that should not be minimized. Correcting the imbalance would do much to release the wealth of knowledge clients have about their own lives and how they can use their expertise to reach their goals.

When we trust our clients as the experts about their lives, we are no longer in the position of having to guess what is not working and what will work. Acknowledging clients as experts takes the pressure off us. We are free to spend our time assisting our clients in demonstrating to themselves how much they already know. When we are tempted to set ourselves up as the great and powerful Wizard of Oz with our clients, we might remind ourselves of the scene in the movie when Toto pulled the curtain aside to reveal the person working the controls of the Wizard's image. We can even say to our clients,

> Remember that scene in *The Wizard of Oz* when the wizard is revealed not to be a real wizard but just a human being? I'm not all-powerful. I'm like the person behind the curtain. But remember that the person behind the curtain had skills at helping Dorothy and her friends find many of the solutions they needed within themselves. That's what I do. I help people recognize that they are experts

already—they just didn't know it. I'll work with you to help you tap your own expertise.

Do Something Different

1. Be direct with your clients and tell them the following:

   > You know, I see you as the expert in your own life. You really do have lots of knowledge and wisdom about who you are and the world you live in. My expertise is in helping you use your own expertise.

2. Remind clients about who the experts were in *The Wizard of Oz*. Point out how Dorothy, the Tin Woodsman, the Lion, and the Scarecrow discovered the expertise they already possessed about their own lives. Tell them you want to be like the person behind the curtain who helps people use their own expertise.

Part II

Mastering
the
Key Steps

CHAPTER 5

Demystifying Counseling

CLIENT: *I had no clue where we were headed. Each session was a guessing game; I was totally mystified.*

Remember back to a time when you watched a skilled magician. How did your body change? What emotional states did you experience? Some common reactions when watching a magician perform are amazement, wonder, irritation, smiles, pleasure, and laughter. Most of us experience puzzlement at what we have just seen—a head-scratching that announces, How did the magician do that? If the magician is first rate, we are totally mystified, unable to explain what we have just witnessed.

Brief counselors and magicians orchestrate their performances, engage in extensive practice of their routine, and perfect their patter so as to perform as flawlessly as possible; however, brief counselors and magicians part company when it comes to mystifying people. Brief counselors seek to demystify what they do by clearly informing clients. Those working in a brief counseling framework fully support the American Counseling Association Code of Ethics and Standards of Practice (1996), which calls for informing, not mystifying, clients. The code of ethics of the counseling profession states that:

> . . . counselors inform clients of the purposes, goals, techniques, procedures, limitations, potential risks and benefits of services to be per-

formed, and other pertinent information. (American Counseling Association, 1996)

Brief counselors believe that demystifying counseling speeds up the process of change in several ways. First, demystifying forestalls clients from assuming a passive role and thereby encourages them to become active participants in the work of counseling. When clients are provided with the purpose of counseling, it often changes their preconceived idea of what will happen. When counseling is explained as a process of decision-making, setting priorities, and devising methods to arrive at goals, then clients normalize the process.

Second, brief counselors want the focus to be on their clients, not on themselves or on taking extensive amounts of time to clarify what counseling is about. Demystifying turns clients' attention to issues and solutions. Demystifying provides more accurate information for people who have formed opinions about counseling and counselors based on popular media images. More accurate information replaces the portrayals on television, in movies and books of counseling and therapy as:

- dens of seduction (the movie *Basic Instinct*),
- asylums for "crazy" people (the book and movie *One Flew Over the Cuckoo's Nest*),
- havens for people who aren't strong (a recent client told me, "I always thought counseling was for people who were weak"), and
- sanctuaries for a lifetime (old Bob Newhart shows where Bob played Dr. Robert Hartley, the psychologist; Woody Allen's movies and his real life).

When counseling is demystified, then clients do not have to spend time worrying about who the counselor is and what the counselor is going to do. Clients focus on working on the issues at hand. The counseling literature supports the idea that people progress faster in the desired direction when they are provided explanations of what is expected and how they are to proceed (Cormier & Cormier, 1991).

A third benefit of demystification is that it speeds up counseling by emphasizing the cooperative alliance and working together of counselors and clients (Molnar & Lindquist, 1989). Words often used to describe the counseling relationship are *mutual, shared, cooperative,* and *collaborative.* Words describing counselors are *straightforward, transparent, open, genuine,* and *self-disclosing*—no deception, no fooling, no magic, no mystifying. Counselors using brief counseling models want to achieve a cooperative relationship, not an adversarial one. Clients' reluctance to participate is lowered when they know what to expect; cooperation is increased. Counseling becomes something that clients do with counselors, rather than something done by the counselors to them or for them.

A final benefit of demystification is that clients learn the process of counseling so that they know how to duplicate the process later with other issues in their lives. By sharing how counseling occurs, counselors teach clients how to help themselves in the future. Brief counselors work to become dispensable, as quickly as possible. Demystifying counseling contributes to that goal.

Ways to Convey Accurate Information

In brief counseling, we ensure that clients are accurately and fully informed. Clients without such information are sometimes blamed for being lost and given labels such as "reluctant," "resistant," and "not motivated." In brief counseling it is not assumed that clients are consciously or unconsciously working against the counselor. Our basic assumption is that clients have few clues about what is expected.

When we do not provide clients with sufficient information, we are asking them to trust us. In workshops where people are learning about the difficulties that people with handicaps encounter, participants are often given an exercise called a Trust Walk. One person is blindfolded and another leads the blindfolded person around for a period of time. When clients are not told what to expect during counseling, we are asking them to execute a Trust Walk. While clients are learning who we are, it may not be easy to trust this stranger called a counselor. Providing information helps reduce the distrust and fosters more willingness to participate.

Used in the broad sense, maps assist in demystifying counseling because they are an effective means of conveying information about counseling. Wurman (1989) described the value of maps in this way: "You cannot perceive anything without a map. A map provides people with the means to share in the perceptions of others. It is a pattern made understandable; it is a rigorous form that follows implicit principles, rules, and measures" (p. 260). Four conceptual maps that demystify counseling are: (1) explaining brief counseling, (2) disclosing counseling information, (3) being straightforward, and (4) engaging in self-disclosure.

Explaining Brief Counseling. A useful map of brief counseling that I often share with clients is from the classic, *Change: Principles of Problem Formation and Problem Resolution* (Watzlawick et al., 1974, p. 110). Their explanation is a four-step model that identifies four recognizable landmarks (see Figure 1, p. 14). When I present this four-step model to my clients, I put it in my own words. I also adjust my vocabulary to fit the particular client. As we begin our first session, I say:

> When I work with people, I have found that using a four-step approach is helpful. First, I like to get a clear idea of how you see your problem in quite specific terms. I really want to understand your situation as much as I possibly can. Second, we'll look at what you've tried so far. What has worked in the past? What have been exceptions to the problem occurring? Third, we'll work together to obtain a clear description of how you want your life to be different. In other words, what will you be doing differently or how will you be different from how you are now? Fourth and finally, we'll make a plan and help you use it to reach your goal. Most of the time I have found we can accomplish all four steps in a relatively brief period of time. We can use future sessions, if needed, to help you make the changes you desire.

Recent developments in brief counseling have modified the basic four-step model by emphasizing miracle questions and exceptions to the problem (de Shazer, 1985, 1988), as well as starting with goals (Littrell, Malia, & Vanderwood, 1995). These solution-focused forms of brief counseling will be illustrated in the next chapter.

Most of the time counselors provide clients information orally, not visually. Some clients do not have good "listening" skills. An alternative is to provide visual maps in the form of handouts or posters. These might include charts, drawings, diagrams, and/or graphics. The advent of computers with easy-to-learn and quick-to-do graphic capabilities allows counselors to design visual aids to match their own counseling preferences. Handouts illustrating the various steps in methods to achieve change may also be produced. For example, just as counselors often appreciate handouts at counseling workshops, so clients are appreciative when, instead of having to remember our orally provided guidelines for methods such as practicing relaxation, they can read our handouts.

Disclosing Counseling Information. Brief counseling can be demystified in a second way. Provide clients with readable information about counseling forms. Ken Mills (1992) assessed the reading level of informed consent forms at a substance abuse recovery center. His findings amusingly suggested that having earned a Ph.D. was a useful prerequisite for comprehending the forms—the sentences were very lengthy and complex. Business writing guidelines suggest sentences be no more than 15 words in length, a length often observed in newspapers. More readable forms increase the chances that clients, often highly stressed, will comprehend their rights and responsibilities, as well as the purposes, goals, and techniques, rules of procedure, and limitations that may affect the counseling relationship (American Counseling Association, 1996). The information form in Table 4 is written in an easy-to-understand style. Any part of this form may be used without obtaining permission; modify it to meet the requirements of your particular setting.

Table 4. Information Form

The Five Cs of Counseling

Counseling—a way of helping people make decisions, face new challenges, set goals, and be supported.

My responsibilities include:
- listening and understanding you and your concerns,
- helping you set goals, and
- assisting you to reach those goals by using your strengths and resources.

Your responsibilities include:
- being as open and honest as possible,
- setting realistic goals, and
- working to achieve those goals.

Confidentiality—not telling others about what you tell me. However, I cannot keep our conversations just between us if you are a danger to yourself or others. In addition, the law requires me to report suspected child abuse.

Caring—I will do my best to provide you the best possible counseling. I will do my best to ensure that you are fully informed about the methods we use to help you reach your goals.

Cost—I charge $ ____ per session. If insurance is being used to pay, then I will help you with the forms. If you are paying out of your own pocket, I will accept either a personal check or cash on the appointment day. If my fee is too much, please let me know and we will try to work something out.

Concerns—Counseling works best when we both believe that we can really work together. If you have questions or concerns about me or about what we are doing, please tell me. While I want to help, in some cases I may not be the best counselor for you. If that is the case, I will help you find another professional helper.

Being Straightforward. Unlike magicians, brief counselors are willing to let their clients see that there is nothing up their sleeves; there are no hidden agendas that will appear later. Being straightforward can be highly effective in demystifying counseling. Unfortunately, while we as counselors want to be straightforward, sometimes we inadvertently mystify clients with our agency's hidden agenda and/or our theoretical goal agenda. All institutions such as schools and social service agencies have agendas in the form of rules, regulations, and norms. When clients are informed of these, then they have choices.

Hidden agendas appear when theoretical goals are not explicitly shared with clients. Many theoretical goals are considerably more global and abstract than the goals clients and counselors explicitly negotiate. For example, the following theories have these goals for clients (Corey, 1991):

Reality Therapy	"To help people become more effective in meeting their needs. To challenge them to evaluate what they are doing to assess how well this behavior is working for them" (p. 450)
Psychoanalytic Therapy	"To make the unconscious conscious. To reconstruct the basic personality. To assist clients in reliving earlier experiences and working through repressed conflicts. Intellectual awareness" (p. 449)

One difficulty with theoretical goals is that they operate outside of awareness so that counselors are placed in the position of unconsciously expecting more from clients than is acknowledged. For instance, the therapist in the case entitled "The Problem Expert" (see Chapter 4) had a goal agenda that he did not explicitly reveal to Tina, his client. Brief counselors attempt to demystify counseling by working with clients on mutually agreed upon goals. For example, brief counselors would avoid concealing a goal like "the client will have higher self-esteem" within, or in addition to, the explicitly stated client goal of "I will spend an hour a day volunteering in my community." Goals that are openly shared are faster to achieve than hidden goals clients must discover over time. Shared goals elicit cooperation; hidden goals promote guessing and wandering. Brief counselors prefer working in a straightforward manner.

In the following case, the counselor Lorrie Young found that being upfront about her agency's agenda and the way she counseled allowed her to work considerably faster because her clients were considerably more cooperative. Lorrie did not have her clients engage in guessing games.

Gentle Lies or Honesty—Take Your Pick

Lorrie carried a caseload of 50 low-income families. When she first began working with them, many were suspicious of her intentions. Her clients believed they had not been told the truth by the small army of professional helpers (e.g., counselors, social workers, school psychologists, counseling psychologists, clinical psychologists, and psychiatrists) who had been empowered to help them. Aware that she was perceived as just another helper marching into and disrupting her clients' lives, Lorrie decided that she needed to demystify what she did.

Upon first meeting with a family, Lorrie informed them of who she was and how she worked. She talked to them about how she wanted to be dispensable in their lives so that they didn't have to have her visit unless they really wanted her there. Then Lorrie performed some magic but in an open and straightforward manner. She told each family the following:

> I suspect that you have had enough counselors and social workers and psychologists parading through your lives to last a lifetime. (Lorrie reports that this statement alone elicited enough head nodding and minimal encouragement to have led client-centered counselors to believe they were in Carl Rogers' heaven.) I also suspect that sometimes you believe that they are not really open and honest with you about what they are thinking. (This statement elicited more head nods and some sighs.)
>
> If that is what you've experienced, I'd like to be different from that. When I work with people, I think they need to know where I stand. However, I've found that when I honestly share with people, sometimes what I say is painful for them to hear, even though they often know that what I am saying really fits.
>
> I want to check something out. Would you rather that I was gentle and easy and sometimes withheld what I was thinking about you and your situation, or would you rather that I was open and honest with you but at the risk of having you possibly experience some pain?

Lorrie reported that when she finished saying the above, some clients even thanked her. By demystifying and sharing with her clients in a forthright manner, Lorrie obtained her clients' consent to tell them things that might prove helpful. Lorrie did not have to subtly persuade her clients in unobtrusive ways; she could just let them know what she thought in a straightforward manner. Like Lorrie, brief counselors avoid hidden agendas, of which clients have every right to be suspicious. We demystify counseling when we are straightforward with clients; our openness about agendas is also a way of conveying that we care.

Engaging in Self-Disclosure. Still another approach to demystifying counseling is through counselor self-disclosure. Research supports the sharing of two to three self-disclosures in an opening session as optimal (Cormier & Cormier, 1991). This amount of self-disclosure lets clients know something about the counselor. Clients find this reassuring, in that they are not working with an unknown entity; there is a real person helping them. On the other hand, too much self-disclosure places the focus on the counselor and not on the client. The following case illustrates how self-disclosure may facilitate client exploration of new solutions.

I Have No Clue

Tim was drowning me in details that were buttressing his own conclusion that he could not change. Unfortunately, I was beginning to believe he was right that change was not possible. After a short while, I stopped Tim's monologue and said,

> Tim, you are a very persuasive person. You have the ability to talk to me, a very optimistic person, and begin to convince me that your situation is unchangeable. In fact, I'm beginning to believe that I am performing a disservice to you in taking your money for this session.

I had hardly finished speaking when Tim began to say things like, "Actually, I think I can change. I have made some changes already." He went on to begin convincing me that indeed changes were possible and that he could make them.

Sometime later, a colleague pointed out that my pessimistic self-disclosing "reeked" of paradoxical intervention and that the "one-down position" I had assumed (Fisch et al., 1982) had elicited a polarity response from my client. While I would have liked to have taken credit for the skillful tactical ploy that my colleague suggested I had used, the fact is that I was genuinely without clues about how to help.

Sharing my pessimism provided an opportunity for Tim and me to examine a process that was not working. We were able to move beyond being stuck. Self-disclosure works best in small doses because it lets clients know us as persons. In larger doses it puts the focus on the counselor to the client's detriment.

Inadvertent Mystifying

There are times when, despite our best efforts to demystify counseling, something malfunctions. I have included the following humorous case because it illustrates how clients may misunderstand what is expected. As the counselor, I believed I had fully informed my client about brief counseling—the mistake was mine.

A Sad Case

A residential substance abuse center invited me to do a brief counseling workshop. I had recently studied Berg and Miller's book *Working with the Problem Drinker* (1992) on applying solution-focused approaches to people with drinking problems. Because I believe that workshop participants should be able to see brief counseling in action, I arranged to conduct a 30-minute interview with one of the new clients. I planned to focus on the many strengths and resources that the client possessed.

When Joe came in, I introduced myself and told him we would be doing a brief counseling interview that focused on his strengths and resources. I asked Joe how he would describe himself. He said, "I'm just an average Joe." I was so intent on my task that I missed his opening humor about his name. The interview progressed and we explored his strengths and resources. When we finished I thanked Joe for his willingness to share with me and the staff. Joe indicated to us that the interview had gone well.

Several days later I received a thank you note from the substance abuse center. The writer commented that the staff had found the workshop very helpful but that Joe later had expressed puzzlement about the interview. He had told a staff member that the doctor (me) hadn't spent any time talking about his sadness. The staff member was confused until Joe added, "I thought he said we were supposed to be doing *grief* counseling." As I put down the letter I was the one who felt sad. In retrospect, I believe I failed to explain brief counseling in sufficient detail so as to preclude Joe's misunderstanding. Perhaps if I had simply used the phrase "short-term counseling," Joe and I would have made more progress.

Occasionally, good magicians and good brief counselors fail, but when they do it is in opposite ways. For magicians, the magic may fail to work and the illusion is lost—audiences understand how the process works. For brief counselors, attempts at demystification may fail and clarity is lost—clients do not understand what is expected. Magicians and counselors owe it to their audiences to do the best possible jobs. Magicians should mystify;

counselors should demystify. When counselors explain brief counseling, provide necessary information about counseling, are honest, and engage in self-disclosure, they contribute to demystifying counseling. If you enjoy mystifying people, take up magic as an avocation, but in your counseling vocation, practice the art of demystifying.

Do Something Different

1. Are you mystifying your clients? Review the information you provide clients. Evaluate your brochures, information forms, evaluation forms, posters, etc. Are they clear? Concise? Inviting? Visually appealing? Informing? To the point? Accurate? If you were a potential new client, would you want to read them? Put your ego on the line and have a friend known for being honest give you feedback about the information you provide. Take the friend's advice.

2. Read one of the following books that your clients might be reading. They are consumer guides to counseling. Evaluate your own counseling in light of the criteria that the lay public is reading about our profession. What are specific changes you would make based on your reading?

   • Prochaska, J. O., Norcross, J. C., & DiClemente, C. C. (1994). *Changing for Good: The Revolutionary Program That Explains the Six Stages of Change and Teaches You How to Free Yourself from Bad Habits.* New York: William Morrow.
   • Seligman, M. E. P. (1994). *What You Can Change and What You Can't: The Complete Guide to Successful Self-improvement.* New York: Knopf.
   • Talmon, M. (1993). *Single-Session Solutions: A Guide to Practical, Effective, and Affordable Therapy.* Reading, MA: Addison-Wesley.

3. For a week solicit feedback from your clients about what they would change about the information you provide. Avoid "yes, butting" as you listen. Get new ideas.

4. Adapt the Five Cs of Counseling for the clients in your work setting. Provide copies to new clients. Surprise current clients by giving them copies.

5. Give pop quizzes about the information you have newly designed. Are clients absorbing the information? What makes sense? What doesn't?

CHAPTER 6

Accentuating Resources

CLIENT: *My counselor continually focused on what wasn't working in my life. We rehashed my problems again and again. I gained some important understanding about my problems but I still stayed stuck and discouraged.*

Recently we entertained some visitors from Finland in our home. At one point the conversation turned to gardening. I casually remarked that, except for growing indoor cacti, I did not have a green thumb. Our guest, Dr. Juha Pietikainen, remarked about my use of the words "green thumb." He said there is a closely related Finnish proverb, "If the thumb is in the middle of the hand, then you can't do anything."

The proverb applies to our clients. So often they tell us stories about how they believe their thumbs are in the middle of their hands. We listen and empathize as they complain about how they cannot do anything right. To the extent clients believe they are helpless, they act on that belief, thus setting in motion a cycle of learned helplessness (Seligman, 1975). The work and play of life are severely hampered when people believe their thumbs are in the middle of their hands, especially if that is what they continually focus on. When our clients see their thumbs in the middle of their hands, they try to succeed while focused on their deficits; eventually they conclude that their situations are hopeless.

Historically, in the field of counseling and psychotherapy the search for patterns has been dominated by a concentration on patterns that currently are not working or did not work in the past. Clients have been asked to tell in exhaustive detail how things are not working in their lives. Sometimes the search for causes has led to equally exhaustive exploration of prior unproductive patterns. When counselors have dwelt on what is not working or what has not worked, clients often experience increased pain. The phenomenon of clients who leave a counseling session feeling worse than before they entered is not atypical. This state of affairs for clients has been dismissed as a reasonable price to pay for making changes; pain and suffering are assumed to be "natural" by-products of counseling. Corey (1991) summed up this point of view with a client's quote, "My God, I was better off before I started therapy. Now I feel more vulnerable than before. Maybe I was better off when I was ignorant" (p. 34). Counselors do not like to see people suffering, so after focusing on problems for an entire session, they normalize their clients' suffering by telling them, "It's not unusual for people to feel worse off temporarily when they enter counseling."

From a brief counseling perspective there is something wrong when people feel worse after talking to a counselor and then are told it is normal. From a brief counseling perspective it makes sense that, if the focus is placed on what does not work and on defenses, then clients can "naturally" be expected to be temporarily demoralized. When counselors put the focus on problems, problems, problems, it is not unusual for a person to be discouraged, demoralized, and depressed.

Unfortunately, many counseling and therapy approaches are problem-focused. As counselors we have usually begun our counseling sessions by asking clients to tell us what is happening in their lives. Indirectly, we are asking about patterns that do not work. They tell us of a preoccupation with problems, they describe their own pain and the pain of others, and they provide detailed descriptions of their struggles.

Once clients begin problem-oriented talk, we have typically used our verbal attending and influencing skills to reinforce problem orientations. In a popular taxonomy of counselor skills, these skills include minimal encouragers, restatements, paraphrases, reflections of feelings, summarizations, self-disclosure, and interpretations (Ivey et al., 1993). We have also used nonverbal attending behaviors, such as head nods, leaning forward, and eye contact, so as to encourage clients to continue their problem-oriented talk. Our training in verbal and nonverbal methods of encouraging responses pays off; we hear of clients' problems interminably. We listen to more than we need to know; clients share more than they want or need to tell.

Our rationale for concentrating on problem-oriented talk has been an assumption that counselors must understand clients' situations in considerable detail before proceeding toward goals. Therefore, we have listened to a recitation of all the problem's pieces. When clients have not been openly forthcoming or have provided incomplete data in the assessment categories we believe are important, we have probed and questioned until we, the counselors, have been satisfied. We have said "um-huh" countless times while nodding our heads to encourage the output of more details of what does not work. Finally, after we and our clients are satiated with problem talk, we have asked our clients what their goals are. In a state conditioned by the confusing focus on what did not work, clients have told us what they did not want. They have made statements such as, "I don't want all this stress in my life." Sometimes they have sighed and stated utopian goals such as, "I just want to be happy."

Patterns of Hope

Jerome Frank (1973) reminded us that clients seek counseling because they are demoralized. They lack hope that they can be instrumental in making changes. One of our tasks as counselors is to assist in the process of restoring patterns of hope. When our clients begin to access previously successful patterns and/or create new patterns, they experience hope and are energized. Patterns of hope sometimes have the following labels:

- inner resources
- external resources
- solutions
- things I like about myself
- inner strengths
- gifts
- attributes
- features
- expertise

- assets
- capabilities
- skills
- possibilities
- reserves
- potential
- qualities
- traits
- answers
- accomplishments

- abilities
- talents
- proficiencies
- repertoire
- flairs
- aptitude
- characteristics
- virtues
- knacks

The words on the above list (e.g., resources, abilities) are patterns composed of thoughts, feelings, actions, and meaning (Ivey et al., 1993). They are not "things" that can be used. Rather, they are merely words that sum up patterns that may be useful in opening up options. As counselors we help clients find and/or create patterns composed of thoughts, feelings, actions, and meaning. We code these patterns with names like "resources" or "abilities" or "inner strengths." Some patterns we rediscover from clients' pasts; some are currently being used but clients have not recognized them as such. We can also co-create new patterns that do not yet exist in clients' repertoire or we can modify current ones.

Brief counselors place a major emphasis on resources that inspire hope (Furman & Ahola, 1992; McGinnis, 1990). This chapter provides nine methods for discovering or creating hope-inducing resources during the counseling process.

1. Start "Counseling" Before Counseling

In the last decade conceptualizations of the helping process have been advanced that seriously question the assumption that even brief counseling should begin with the problem orientation (de Shazer, 1985, 1988; Littrell, Malia, Nichols, Olson, Nesselhuf, & Crandell, 1992; Littrell et al., 1995; O'Hanlon & Wilk, 1987). The most parsimonious place to begin seeking clients' resources is before they begin an outpouring of problems. In other words, do not start with problems. After you have explained about counseling (see Chapter 5—*Demystifying Counseling*), use one of the following opening lines:

- Before we begin, would you share with me what it would be like for you if we were completely successful in getting to where you would like to be?
- Before we begin, how would you like things to be in your life?
- Before we begin, how would your life be different from how it is now if you didn't have this problem?

The phrase "before we begin" creates for clients a nontherapeutic atmosphere that skirts potentially unpleasant emotions and thoughts associated with counseling/therapy. Since you and your client have not begun, the client may feel more at ease. Clients also relax as they realize that they are not talking about problems. When we start counseling before "counseling," problems that have dominated our clients' world view are circumvented.

2. Start Counseling with Goals

The basic four-step brief counseling approach presented in the last chapter begins with a problem focus. Unfortunately, starting this way results in problem talk rather than solution talk. In a recent research project conducted in a high school, my colleagues and I modified the basic four-step model by lopping off its first two steps of defining the problem and discussing attempted solutions (Littrell et al., 1995). The counselors using this new solution-focused model began by helping clients define their goals and moved on to help them reach them.

The solution-focused, two-step approach generated several appealing findings. First, the counselors who had been trained in traditional problem-oriented approaches found it almost painful to give up the focus on problems. They felt a loss—something familiar was missing; it was as though they were attached with super glue to their problem approaches. They were comfortable when listening to clients' recitation of problems because they were on familiar ground. As the counselors gained familiarity with the solution-focused approach, they gained confidence and exhibited enthusiasm. They discovered that approximately one-half the clients with whom they began with the solution-focused approach never turned back from their future-focused efforts to tell them about problems. The counselors found the counseling sessions more gliding than adhering; they enjoyed the change. The counselors also discovered that they could more easily direct into solution-talk those clients who wanted to dwell on problems.

The counselors also discovered that their clients moved more quickly when exposed to solution-focused counseling. Clients did not tend to linger or dwell on what did not work; goals were generated. Clients then came up with many different methods to reach their goals. Sometimes the methods were logical, straightforward, obvious, and very traditional. At other times the methods were imaginative, flamboyant, off-the-wall, and highly creative.

Starting counseling with a solution-focused approach does not mean that problems should not or are not discussed. It does mean that we do not assume that the answers to clients' problems lie in their problems. The last place answers may lie are in problems, a territory where problems are all stuck together. There is a poster that states,

> WHEN YOU'RE UP TO YOUR ASS IN ALLIGATORS,
> IT'S HARD TO REMEMBER THAT YOUR ORIGINAL OBJECTIVE
> WAS TO DRAIN THE SWAMP

Problems and their connections to other problems easily become our focus in counseling. Confronted with problems, it is often difficult to remember our basic objective. A variation on the alligator/swamp poster that is appropriate for counselors is the following:

> WHEN YOU'RE UP TO YOUR
> EARS IN LISTENING
> TO CLIENTS' PROBLEMS,

IT'S HARD TO REMEMBER THAT
YOUR ORIGINAL OBJECTIVE
WAS TO HELP THEM FIND SOLUTIONS

Rather than dwell on what is not working, brief counselors can deliberately focus on what clients want and how to help them get there. Brief counselors move as quickly toward a solution or series of solutions as is practical and possible for clients. Working toward solutions is more satisfying than wallowing in problems for both counselors and clients. Brief counselors invert the sequence of typical counseling that begins and continues with problems; they begin with what has worked and is working. They begin with accessing clients' strengths and resources. When the focus is on what has worked, is working, and can work, clients begin to experience hope.

3. Change the Problem/Resource Talk Ratio

While it may be highly desirable to focus on what has worked in clients' lives, that is not always possible. Some clients have important reasons for starting with problems. Some believe it is essential that we understand their problems before we can possibly help them with solutions. Others are hurting too much to think about solutions before we acknowledge their pain. Still others are simply following our lead of beginning with problems.

In contrast to the focus on patterns that do not or have not worked in clients' lives, brief counselors concentrate their attention on finding useful patterns. The amount of time that we focus on patterns that are not currently working or have not worked in the past, compared to the time we spend focusing on patterns that have worked, currently work, or could work, provides an important ratio. Typically, the problem/resource ratio has been high. Brief counselors invert the ratio so that resource talk is greater than problem talk.

The easiest way to find clients' potentially useful past patterns is to ask for them in a direct fashion, as in the following case. As George Kelly (1955) said, "If you don't know what's wrong with a client, ask . . . ; he [or she] may tell you" (p. 201). A brief counseling adaptation of Kelly's dictum applied to accessing clients' resources might be: If you don't know what your client's resources and strengths are, ask; he or she may tell you.

The following case illustrates how hope can be quickly generated when the problem/resource ratio is high in favor of resources and when resource talk precedes problem talk.

You Can Tie Your Own Shoes

I saw Meg while working at a university counseling center. Meg requested that she be allowed to switch to me as her counselor because she had heard I was an "action-oriented" counselor. With the other counselor's permission we made the switch.

Before seeing Meg I reviewed the previous counselor's case notes. Meg had seen the previous counselor weekly for six months. As I read the case notes I became mildly depressed. My immediate question was, If I were becoming mildly depressed just reading her case notes, what must it be like to be living her life? I began our first session by reviewing the numerous issues I had read about in the case notes. As Meg sat rather listlessly in front of me, she confirmed that these were the issues she was struggling with in her life.

I said, "Meg, you asked for me because you had heard I was 'action-oriented.' I don't know exactly what that means for you, but let's not do what you have been doing in counseling for the last six months. Let's do something different. The first thing I want you to do is make a list of ten things that you like about yourself—your resources and strengths, the things you do well."

Meg sat very still and looked at me. Her posture was hunched over and she appeared to be mildly depressed. She paused for some time before answering, "I can't think of any."

Only because of our slight acquaintance prior to counseling and because I felt that Meg and I had good rapport in the session was I willing to take the following risk to begin generating new possibilities. In a warm and friendly manner and with an obvious twinkle in my eyes as I looked down at her tie shoes, I said "You could put as number one on your list that you can tie your own shoes."

Meg rolled her eyes and then looked at me with an expression that said, Give me a break, John. Yet she also smiled slightly. Meg quickly decided that she could generate more meaningful strengths and resources than I could offer and together we worked to brainstorm them. After a while Meg was generating her own ideas without my assistance. Her list included: going to graduate school, raising two children, being smart, and having a sense of humor.

The second thing I had Meg do was read me her list of resources and strengths and to tell me about them. As she did her posture became more upright. Her voice sounded more confident. By the time she finished she looked and sounded like a person experiencing newfound strengths and resources.

The third and final activity I had Meg do that day was to select one of the issues that she had been working on during the last six months and bring all of her strengths and resources to bear on that one issue. I asked her if she knew how to do that and she said yes. We agreed to meet in two weeks.

When we met two weeks later, Meg reported that she had followed the instructions and that her strengths and resources had really made a difference in dealing with the problem area she had selected. She also spontaneously reported that she had applied the resources to other problematic areas in her life and was seeing changes there as well.

In my experience Meg's transformation is not so unusual. Clients are experts at dealing with their problems. They attend to their problems; they fail to attend to their resources. The tradition of problem talk places a disproportionate emphasis on the nonworking part of clients' worlds. Alter the customary ratio of problem talk to resource talk and observe how clients change more rapidly.

4. Explore Exceptions

Despite their difficulties, clients experience times when things work. Brief counselors help their clients find those times when their problems failed to occur or were less problematic. They focus clients' attention on exceptions to their problems. De Shazer (1985) and Walter and Peller (1992) have proposed beginning with exceptions to the problem, finding out when and how they occur, and having the client do more of what works.

Exceptions are powerful, in that their discovery by clients begins to lend hope that their situations can actually change. Initially, exceptions may be dismissed as flukes, accidents, insignificant or trivial events, but upon closer inspection they are often found to contain the seeds for new solutions. The literature on exceptions stresses that counselors search for exceptions to the problem as diligently as they formerly searched for problems. Useful phrases to elicit clients' exceptions are:

- You have been describing this problem in some detail. When is it not a problem?
- When doesn't this problem happen?
- There are always exceptions to any situation. What have been exceptions in this situation? (The assumption is that exceptions will be found.)
- When was the last time you thought the problem was going to happen but then it didn't?

- What is it that you do when you successfully overcome the urge to [the self-defeating pattern is inserted here]? (de Shazer, 1988).
- Tell me about those times when what you don't like doesn't happen. What are you doing at those times? How could you go about making those times happen just a little bit more?

When exceptions are discovered, counselors have clients engage in one simple task—do more of what previously worked. The proposed task is deliberately increasing one thing which has worked. In other cases, the task may involve increasing the doing of many parts that have worked in the past. The key to using exceptions is to build on the incidents of success that clients have already experienced in the problem area. In the following case the client and I discovered an important exception to his current pattern— he had not recognized the exception as important in realizing his goal.

When Are You Successful?

Paul had great plans for an exercise program. He wanted to walk for at least 30 minutes during his lunch hour. Despite his good intentions, Paul had actually gone walking only once or twice in the past month. At first Paul thought his problem was one of procrastination, because in examining his behavior he found that if the phone rang or someone came in with a question he invariably picked up the phone or talked with the person. He just couldn't turn down requests. At that point Paul began to conceptualize his problem as a lack of assertiveness.

I asked Paul to focus on exceptions by raising the question, "When in the past have you been able to go walking at noon regardless of anything else that was happening?"

Paul looked at me for a moment and then said, "In the past if I put on my walking shoes at noon then I would always go walking, regardless of whether the phone rang or someone wanted to talk." We co-authored Paul's statement into a small and powerful goal—"I will put on my walking shoes each and every noon at work." Paul's immediate reaction to his newly stated goal was one of relief and enthusiasm that he could achieve that goal. He gave up the "procrastinator" and "nonassertive person" labels and began to see his problem, as well as his solution, in a new light.

Finding exceptions can be challenging. People often have patterns from their previous experiences that may be useful in effectively dealing with the present but when asked they say, "I don't know." Sometimes they have sim-

ply forgotten them or failed to connect and apply them to the current situations. An example of forgotten resources that were quickly remembered is
illustrated in the following very brief (ten-minute) counseling session.

Texan Tough Love

At the end of one of my brief counseling workshops in Texas, Agatha asked
if I would listen to a story about problems she had with Marian, her daughter. Marian, now in her early twenties, had moved back home. Agatha related
how prior to the move she and Marian had discussed ground rules. However,
despite the ground rules, Marian had more than once taken off for several
days with no explanation; this pattern of going away without informing her
mother was very worrisome. Agatha also seriously objected to the fact that
Marian had brought home a man and was living with him in her home.
Marian's lifestyle was definitely unacceptable to Agatha. If her daughter wanted to live with a man, that was her daughter's decision, but Agatha was not
about to condone Marian's behavior by having her do so in her own home.

I asked Agatha what her goal was in this situation. She sighed and said,
"My goal is to forget that she is violating my moral standards in my home."

Agatha's frown and other nonverbal cues informed me that, while this
might sound good, it certainly didn't fit for Agatha. Therefore, I responded,
"I wouldn't accept that as a goal in our working together." Agatha looked
puzzled, so I added by way of explanation, "The goal that you just stated is
what you wouldn't be doing. What is it that you would be doing if you
reached your goal?"

Immediately Agatha replied, "I would be kicking her out if she kept
behaving the same way."

Sensing she was not finished I said, "Okay, but . . ."

She completed the sentence by adding, ". . . but I would feel I was being
too harsh."

Returning to the goal, I again asked her, in view of what she had just
said, what she wanted. In short order she said her new goal was, ". . . to
renegotiate the contract with my daughter and enforce it."

Attempting to access previous patterns of success, I asked her, "When in
the past have you enforced a contract?"

Agatha looked at me and smiled as she said, "I did it several years ago
when I had her first move out. I used a Tough Love approach and it was
successful." Her smile was one I often see when clients realize that they
have resources from the past that might be useful in the present. Still,
despite her newly remembered resource, Agatha looked worried.

I said only, "And."

Agatha continued in a hesitant voice, "I could use the same Tough Love approach again."

Again I said, "And."

With vigor in her voice this time, Agatha said, "I *will* use the Tough Love approach again. It worked before. I'll make it work again."

We finished our truly brief counseling session by designing some fun ways to reach her goal (see Chapter 9—*Acknowledging Fun*—for expansion on this theme). In this counseling situation I added, "I can even imagine you inviting some of your friends in to witness the contract being signed. Perhaps even having balloons floating around the room in celebration."

Agatha was aglow with enthusiasm and a renewed sense of power. We ended by talking about how she could return to the Tough Love pattern she had used before, but this time she could also see it as a celebration of her daughter's independence and as something that she could do to foster in her daughter more responsible behavior. Agatha also saw her Tough Love approach as a way of modeling for her daughter how she, the mother, was being responsible.

When eliciting exceptions we encounter clients who say, "I don't know" when asked about resources and strengths. This answer is particularly rampant among adolescents, who expertly deliver the lines based on continual practice with adults. When we hear "I don't know" we can take it as an accurate current condition, but one that reflects an incomplete memory search. A useful pattern to elicit prior resources is to use Egan's (1990) phrase, "If you did know, what would the answer be?" and then wait patiently. Despite the absurdity of the question, approximately 90% of the time clients respond by accessing useful information. This phrase has a way of relaxing clients by taking the pressure off getting the right answer, not unlike the useful directive, "Guess." Rick Raulston provided a short transcript illustrating the power of the phrase in the case below. Note how Rick paused long enough after asking the question to give his client, Lyle, a chance to think and to share some meaningful goals. Lyle even began to mirror Rick's use of silence as he answered his own question.

If You Did Know . . .

Lyle, a client in a halfway house, had been talking about how hard it was for him to bring other halfway house residents around to his way of thinking about how to approach working on the required tasks. Lyle said it was frustrating for him. Rick used Lyle's "I don't know" to begin the first steps of goal-setting with Lyle.

RICK: It sounds like you would like to get away from it for a while.

LYLE: I don't know, I don't know what I want anymore.

RICK: If you did know what you wanted, what would you want? *(seven-second silence)*

LYLE: If I did know what I wanted, what would I want? *(said with a confused expression on his face; eight seconds of silence elapsed before Lyle continued)* What I'd have is a family, kids, small town, nice church, nice job, just have a mediocre life, nothing real expensive, nothing real fancy, just a close-knit family to enjoy and keep company with. I don't want much out of life, just to be happy with a family. That's something I never had when I was a kid. I think all I want when I grow up is to have a family.

Many times when we are seeking possible exceptions, our clients, like Rick's, say some form of "I don't know." Brief counselors avoid agreeing with their clients in these circumstances because clients often do have exceptions, they just do not have speedy access to these memories. Trusting clients to know was a working assumption in Milton Erickson's repertoire. Erickson used a variation on the "If you did know . . . " technique while working with an adolescent for the first time. Erickson had asked a perfectly reasonable question for which he thought the young man should have an answer. The adolescent replied with a classic verbal pattern of youth, "I don't know." Erickson looked at him and in his gravelly voice slowly said, "Well, since you don't know me very well *(pause of several seconds)* lie." The young man laughed and provided the information; Erickson had spoke a language that made sense to his client.

By the time an aspect of life has become problematic, exceptions to the problem behavior may easily be overlooked. Brief counselors assist by making exceptions salient. Once exceptions are recognized, clients are encouraged to do more of what has worked, whether it be increasing or decreasing the doing of a behavioral pattern. The wonder of looking for exceptions is found in how frequently clients already have engaged in patterns that work—they have just not recognized that simple fact.

5. Ask Miracle Questions

A fifth powerful technique for creating hope is the miracle question. Family therapist Steve de Shazer (1988) modified Erickson's hypnotic and future-gazing use of the crystal ball. Instead of a crystal ball, the counselor asks, "Suppose that one night, while you were asleep, there was a miracle and this problem was solved. How would you know? What would be different?" (p. 5). The miracle question is a potent tool for accessing goals. When we begin with this question we can glide easily into solution-focused states. A most effective illustration of the miracle question in action was provided by my former student, Melissa DeRadcliffe.

Truly a Miracle Question

Melissa was counseling clients in a Baptist church. In a move that headed the session toward solutions and at the same time spoke the language of the client, Melissa asked, "If God changed your life with a miracle tonight, what would it be like tomorrow?"

De Shazer's miracle question is a secular one, while Melissa's miracle question incorporated the all-powerful doer of the miracle—God. Her modification of the miracle question is a notable example of how counselors may use a technique such as the miracle question and tailor it to a language that makes good sense for clients.

Miracle questions must fit the client. When working with children the miracle question may be asked so as to incorporate a magic wand. For example, "If a good fairy were to wave a magic wand tonight and . . . ." As in all counseling situations, we need to be aware of possible drawbacks to our interventions. There are some parents who may object to the use of counselor language that alludes to "New Age" concepts like "magic" and "fairies."

With adults the simple and straightforward approach is sometimes right on the mark. The counselor might ask the miracle question in the following ways:

- If you believed in miracles, what would be the miracle you would like to see happen in your life right now?
- Looking into the future can enhance our ability to achieve what we truly want. What would your future look like if you were successful?

The miracle question helps us avoid getting mired in problems before we know where clients want to go. Clients who know their destinations are more eager to participate in counseling than those who are lost in their problems.

6. Amplify Partial Resources

One approach for moving beyond a recitation of problems has been to focus on clients' attempted solutions (Fisch et al., 1982; Watzlawick et al., 1974).

While a focus on attempted solutions does place attention on what has not worked in clients' lives, it has the benefit of providing the counselor and client with information about what *not* to attempt as solutions. In addition, when attempted solutions are viewed as the problem, then goals can be formulated that do not follow the format of previously attempted solutions.

However, exploration with clients of their attempted solutions provides the most assistance when counselors and clients can build on patterns of attempted solutions that have been at least partially successful. One way of using partial patterns is to weave several together. Clients sometimes believe that if they have not been 100% successful in the past, then they have failed. Helping clients piece together parts of older patterns and recognizing that nothing will work 100% of the time takes the pressure off. I have used the phrase with clients, "What combination of things you have tried in the past would increase your odds of moving toward your goal?"

7. Elicit Latent Resources

At times it is necessary to create new patterns with clients, especially when previous patterns are not appropriate or available. Several methods are available. First, other people's patterns may be borrowed and tried to see whether they fit or may be modified to fit. Second, completely new patterns may be created (see the next section: Teach New Resources). In the next case a movie character provided a pattern that the client could incorporate into his repertoire.

The Terminator

Terry was once again in the high school counselor's office. Terry's social studies teacher, Mr. Murphy, had sent him there for being disrespectful. Terry's counselor, thinking like a brief counselor, asked herself, "Who has the problem?" She concluded that Terry did not have a problem except that he might not pass the course and thus not graduate. Terry was mostly upset and blamed Mr. Murphy. On the other hand, she concluded that Mr. Murphy was the one who had the complaint and therefore was the potential client. She also knew that Mr. Murphy wouldn't buy being a client or consultee—she had tried that route before.

Checking to see if Terry might be willing to modify his behavior to achieve a goal, the counselor rhetorically asked Terry if his goal was to graduate—Yes. Was his goal to pass the social studies class?—Yes. Would he like to be able to stay in the class and just get the work done?—Yes, but. Terry said he wanted to do all that but that Mr. Murphy picked on him all the time. What was the basis for this? Well, it seems Terry had a difficult time being respectful in Mr. Murphy's eyes.

What was Terry doing on those occasions?—"Once he wanted me to look at him and I did but I imitated the stupid expression on his face."

What else?—"Once I didn't look him in the eye. I stared at the floor. Oh, yeah, once I just looked right past him into space."

Would Terry be interested in learning how to stay in the classroom, be respectful, and do it in a way that made him a winner?—Yes, but he didn't see how. The counselor asked Terry if he would be interested in borrowing the Terminator's strategy. Terry could use it without the teacher's awareness and thus be upset but not get into trouble. Terry wanted to know more.

The counselor explained that the Terminator could remain outwardly calm while inside its head it could be getting an object in its sights. The Terminator could outwardly be respectful while inwardly expressing anger. After a few minutes of practice, Terry was able to borrow the Terminator's technique as a way to carry out his goal of being respectful in Mr. Murphy's eyes, passing social studies class, and graduating from high school.

The counselor received Terry's permission to talk to Mr. Murphy. She told him that Terry was going to be making some changes over the next week and that she would like to talk to Mr. Murphy at the end of the week to see what changes he had seen. At the end of the week Mr. Murphy told the counselor that she had done a great job because Terry was much more respectful in his class than ever before and that Terry looked at him when he spoke.

Terry's end-of-the-week report to the counselor indicated that Mr. Murphy wasn't on his case like he had been. Terry had even seen Mr. Murphy smile at him. Terry concluded that maybe Mr. Murphy wasn't as bad as he had thought.

This counselor helped her client borrow and adapt another's pattern. Care must be taken that borrowed patterns fit for the particular client. In addition, patterns must help clients achieve their goals without negative side effects. Employing the Terminator's pattern with clients who have acting-out tendencies or poor reality-testing could be a recipe for disaster.

8. Teach New Resources

Here is an example of creating a new resource. Kim, the counselor, relates how he helped his client, Luke, experience a new and useful pattern, rather than just talking about it. The case also illustrates how quickly clients can learn and use new patterns. Kim's observations are write-ups of the second and third sessions.

The Orange Baton

Second Session. Today is my second one-on-one session with Luke. Luke is a depressed ten-year-old who perceived himself as having no friends and little, if any, power to change unpleasant things in his life, such as the playground bullying to which he had been subjected daily. His parents had brought him in for counseling because lately he had been so melancholy. They were unaware as to how to help him get through this.

Luke continued to have a dull affect throughout the session. He related to me that he had just today gotten pushed off the jungle gym at school by a 4th grader. Luke had scratches and slight bruising on his arms and shins from the fall.

As we talked, I noticed an orange baton lying on a nearby table. I grabbed it, gave it to Luke, telling him it represented POWER! I informed him that, although it was his power represented in the baton, other people could take it from him if he allowed it. As I said this, I snatched the baton out of his hand and claimed it as my own.

He got this look of determination on his face as he said with a semi-forceful, almost daring voice, "Try that again." I repeated everything as I initially had, giving him his "power." I also repeated that, although it was his power, others could take it from him if he let them. I once more made the attempt to take the baton from him. However, this time he held on tenaciously, refusing to relinquish it to me.

I hollered a very excited, "YESSSSS!" and gave him a high-five. For good measure we played this scenario again. Luke was excited. His affect changed in literally a matter of seconds. The session was coming to a close so we agreed to continue next week. Luke walked out holding the orange baton.

Third Session. Luke returned to my office with his mom. He was smiling—a first excluding the final minutes of last week's session—and he had some life in his step. When I commented that I noticed a change from last week, he interrupted proudly and said, "Yeah! I'm smiling." He then told me how he had taken a stand against one of the playground bullies since our last meeting. Luke was manifesting some life. When I asked him what other changes I might be noticing he responded, "I'm cuter this week." Last week he was struggling with his personal appearance. He held onto the orange baton throughout most of this session. There had been a distinct change in Luke!

One of the topics covered in this session was the fact that I would be leaving this agency in about a month. When he asked whether he'd ever see me again, I told him I didn't know but I would bet he wouldn't NEED to see me. I then asked him why I might say that. He retorted, "Because I'll be able to do this stuff without talking to you every week." Again, the "YESSSSS!" and another high-five from me.

As his mom was walking out the door upon our closing this session, she smiled at me and whispered, "You're doing something. He's not the same." What a great way to end the session!

In many settings, Luke would not have been viewed as a prospective candidate for rapid change. Even Luke's mother was amazed at how fast change was occurring. Creating new patterns can be done quickly; when that occurs, the quickness itself engenders hope in clients that change can become a new reality.

Resourceful patterns are readily available. They may come from clients' pasts, be borrowed from other people, or be newly created. Brief counselors help clients identify and create patterns that will empower them. Rather than dwelling on clients' patterns that have not worked, brief counselors focus clients' attention on patterns that have or will work. Building clients' hope again is one of the most beneficial services counselors can provide. When our clients believe that their thumbs are in the middle of their hands, then accessing old patterns and/or creating new ones are simply two powerful ways to build hope.

9. Strengthen Existing Resources

Sometimes clients' existing resources require strengthening. The phrase "I can" needs to become "I will." I have found that combining warm humor when strengthening existing resources is an excellent way to help clients laugh at their own mistakes and begin the process of forgiving themselves for "screwing up." In the next case, a counseling practicum student and I focused on one of her resources that needed strengthening—her promise-keeping. We discovered that when that was strengthened she had all she needed to reach her goal.

A Promise Is a Promise

Wendy shared with our counseling practicum class that she was having a difficult time completing her thesis. She was near the end but she had stalled. I asked her what she had tried so far in her attempts to finish. Wendy said she had made a promise (and bet) with a friend that she would finish, but that the deadline had passed and she was now avoiding her friend. She had also told herself that she couldn't watch TV until her thesis was finished, but she hadn't followed her own advice—the soaps just couldn't be missed. Both of Wendy's attempted solutions involved promises that she wasn't keeping.

I asked Wendy how she sabotaged promises to herself. She looked a bit shocked at the word sabotage so I modified it by asking, "How do you make sure that despite your best intentions in making promises to yourself, you break those promises?" She answered with a sheepish grin, "I really know I'm not going to keep them, even as I make them. They just keep me from having to work on my thesis, which at this point I hate."

Wendy's meaningful goal was completing her thesis. Then I asked her what *one* thing she would never want to do as a penalty if she didn't finish her thesis. She immediately told the class, "Getting married again soon since I'm just recently divorced." I asked her if she would promise to remarry immediately if she didn't complete the thesis in a month. She thought about the promise, found it fascinating, and agreed. She said she took this promise seriously. We agreed it would up the ante on her promise-making resource. However, we decided that it was best if we made sure she would keep her promise.

I asked Al, an ordained minister in our class, if he would perform her wedding at the end of a month if she did not complete her thesis as promised. He heartily laughed and enthusiastically agreed. I asked Wendy who she would not want to marry if she didn't finish her thesis. She said there was a student in her dormitory who kept asking her to marry him so he could apply for U.S. citizenship. She said she liked the man as a friend but certainly not as a future husband. Looking pained, a bit scared, and totally energized, Wendy agreed to have the wedding in a month if she didn't complete her thesis. Other students in the class began making plans to have a small wedding cake, ice cream, and punch.

Within less than a week, Wendy phoned. She said, "I've kept my promise to finish my thesis. I've just given it to my major professor. You can cancel the wedding!" The only ones slightly disappointed with Wendy's success were the students who wanted wedding cake, ice cream, and punch, and naturally, the man seeking U.S. citizenship.

Wendy had the resource of "keeping promises" in her repertoire, which on most occasions worked fine but failed her when it was time to write her thesis. Strengthening the resource in a fun and yet serious manner permitted Wendy to use the resource to achieve her goal. Despite its lightness and brevity, the case contains all eight characteristics of brief counseling:

1. *Time-limited.* The single session lasted approximately 20 minutes while the follow-up lasted one minute.
2. *Solution-focused.* We focused on what Wendy wanted rather than on her problem.
3. *Action-based.* Wendy had the choice of two actions—writing or marrying.
4. *Socially interactive.* Wendy, the students, and the potential groom provided a rich array of characters, all with their parts.
5. *Detail-oriented.* The wedding cake, ice cream, and the wedding service received the most attention, while writing the thesis was skimmed over as something Wendy said she knew how to do.
6. *Humor-eliciting.* The "overkill" promise of getting married was definitely funny and highly motivating.
7. *Developmentally attentive.* Wendy was temporarily stuck and not getting her needs met. Strengthening her resource assisted her in moving past being stuck.
8. *Relationship-based.* I was empathic and caring even as we planned her premature wedding.

Historically, the counseling profession has focused on clients' strengths and resources as a means of inspiring their hopes about new possibilities. As counselors we often see clients whose hopes have been diminished as they struggle alone with their problems. In this chapter the nine methods of tapping clients' resources provide counselors with tools for eliciting resources and ensuring that clients begin to recognize the strengths they already possess. Clients deserve hope. Counselors can help them regain it—often rather quickly.

Do Something Different

1. Listen to your next several clients and observe how, given the chance, they discuss problems rather than solutions. Note how they are stuck to their problems and how inflexible they feel. What is the first method you will apply to loosen the problem orientation?
2. Observe how you occasionally find yourself thinking about your clients and wondering, Why can't they separate those

things out? If you become stuck, focus on how you would like the session to be different.

3. *Miracle Question.* To move toward solutions, ask the miracle question. Say, "If a miracle occurred tonight and when you woke up your life was how you would want it to be, what would that be like?"

4. When clients say, "I don't know," then gently add, "If you did know, what would the answer be?" BE SILENT— give them time to think and respond.

5. What percent of your time do you and your client spend on problems? goals? patterns that work? Change the ratio in favor of less time on problems and more on past and present solutions. Then change it even more, so that the bulk of the time is spent on what has worked and is working.

6. *Attempted Solutions.* Ask your client, "What have you tried so far?" Listen for those parts that have some degree of success.

7. *Exceptions.* Give the following directive, "Let's generate a list of all the times in your past that this hasn't been a problem or it didn't work out badly." Assume that there have been those times.

8. *Before We Begin.* With your next new client, begin the session by saying, "Before we begin, I'd like to know, if we were successful in helping you solve your problem, what would it be like for you?"

9. *First Session Opening Lines.* Begin a session with a new client by saying one or both of the following lines:

   • Before we begin today, I am wondering what you would say you really want to have changed by the time we finish?
   • Before we begin, what percentage of what you want to have happen have you already accomplished?

10. *Second Session Opening Lines.* Begin the second session by using one or both of the following lines:

    • What has changed since our last session that you are excited to tell me about?
    • I've been wondering since we last met, what will be the first thing you'll tell me today about how you are moving in the direction of your goal?

CHAPTER 7

Co-authoring
the Future

CLIENT: *We never did figure out what I really wanted.*

Co-authoring the future with clients is one of the most fascinating aspects of counseling. Unfortunately, the reputation of co-authoring the future, generally called goal-setting, is not enhanced when it is presented as a lifeless process that is lockstep and mechanical. I find most texts offer barely a hint of my favorite themes—fun, interest, or excitement—in their presentations of goal-setting. In this chapter I hope to offer an alternative to the bleak models of goal-setting generally used in training counselors.

In practice, brief counselors find goal-setting one of the most exciting and enjoyable aspects of counseling. The process of co-authoring challenges us to really listen, to exhibit flexibility, and to demonstrate innovative ideas. Co-authoring the future is important because it permits counselors and clients to know where clients want to go. Knowing where clients want to go avoids the dilemma posed by the title of Campbell's (1974) book, *If You Don't Know Where You're Going, You'll Probably End Up Somewhere Else*. Only when we know where clients want to go can we ethically provide ways to help them get there. Preoccupation with methods of travel before we know the destination is getting the process backwards.

When we know where we are going, then we are free to devise many different ways to get there. Wurman with Leifer (1992) shared a delightful story about a father who taught his son to tie his shoelaces in a very short period of time. Because the destination was clearly known, the father was able to assist the boy in getting there.

Tying Shoelaces

I know a man who taught his son to tie his shoe in five minutes. He tied the shoelace into a bow, then untied it one step at a time. He taught his son by doing it backwards. His son instantly grasped the relationship of each step to the tied bow. He showed his son the goal (the bow), then showed him the steps leading up to the goal. (p. 184)

Goal-setting and pursuit can be, on occasion, just that easy and intriguing. This chapter looks at a model that offers a stimulating way of co-authoring futures. The model is based on a method used by one of the greatest entertainers of this century—Walt Disney.

Walt Disney's Creative Strategy

Based on a search for outstanding examples of the creative process, Robert Dilts and his associates (Dilts with Bonissone, 1993; Dilts, Epstein, & Dilts, 1991) created a model of Walt Disney's creative strategy. Dilts proposed that Disney used three separate states in transforming that which did not yet exist into a present reality. Dilts labeled Disney's three states the Dreamer, the Realist, and the Critic. The Dreamer looks for possibilities that are desired. The Realist brings those possibilities into the present. The Critic examines what is being created and works to make it the best it can be.

Goal-setting as an activity can be conceptualized as a creative process involving the Dreamer, the Realist, and the Critic. We work with clients to envision what can be; we help translate their dreams into ones they can achieve; and together we critically examine what it would be like if their dreams were realized. The following sections elaborate on how we can guide our clients through the states of Dreamer, Realist, and Critic to facilitate co-authoring their futures.

The Dreamer

Stated in the Positive. The Dreamer state is a useful place to begin when we co-author the future with clients. In the Dreamer state clients can dwell on what they want, not on what they do not want. Most clients do not start with positive dreams. They need assistance because they initially tend to move away from imagined nightmares, as in:

I WON'T ALWAYS IMAGINE THE WORST WILL HAPPEN.

or

I WON'T FEEL GUILTY LIKE I NOW DO.

or

I WON'T CRITICIZE MY DAUGHTER SO MUCH.

These messages are what clients do not want to be thinking, feeling, and doing. Once we train our ears to hear goals that contain the word *not* in its various forms, such as *don't* and *won't,* these words cue us that the goal is being stated in terms of what is not wanted, rather than what is desired.

How do we help clients acquire the skill of positively stated dreams? A useful technique for changing negative statements into positive ones is through the use of the 180° flip. When clients make statements of what they do not want, I hold out the palm of my right hand and glance at it. I say, "This is what you don't want." Next I take my left hand and place in over my right hand. Then I move my left hand in a large arc with my left hand coming to rest palm-up about 18 inches from my right palm-up hand. My eyes follow my left hand to its new position while I say, "If that is what you don't want, what is it that you *do* want?"

We might expect clients to respond to the 180° flip with the opposite of what was initially stated. However, frequently their positively stated goals are not the polar opposites of what is not wanted. This lack of logic does not seem to bother them. If we do not check explicitly with our clients about what they want, we may fall into the trap of assuming that we and our clients both understand and are in agreement about what they want; that is, since we know their negatively stated goals, we therefore know what they want. Because we think we know what clients want, we are free to begin employing methods to help them reach their goals. Employing methods to reach goals before goals are stated in the positive is a recipe for disaster.

A typical example of employing methods before positively stating goals occurs when we work with tense clients. They state their goal as not wanting to be tense, and we assume their goal is to be relaxed. When we don't bother to check this out, we may choose tools such as relaxation exercises that turn out to be inappropriate. Results of the 180° flip have convinced me that I am a poor predictor of what tense clients will say they want. When we do the 180° flip, we might find that the tense client's goal is to be more assertive with a boss, to have a more peaceful household, or even to start a new business. The following case illustrates how sometimes the flip of a negatively stated goal is not the polar opposite.

Easy Rider

Jill wanted to attend and enjoy baseball games at which her boyfriend played. She used to love to go; however, at a recent game a baseball had appeared out of nowhere and hit her on the shoulder. She had lost her enjoyment of the game. Jill said she was scared to go back despite her desire to watch her boyfriend play ball.

Jill's first answer to what she wanted was to say, "I don't want to be tense at baseball games." Since this was what she didn't want, I used the 180° flip and asked her what she *did* want. I was expecting Jill to say, "I want to be relaxed at baseball games." She upended my expectations by saying, "I want to be very aware of what is happening in my peripheral vision." Clearly, Jill was authoring a goal that was stated in the positive, but certainly not what I would have said would be her message based on my own framework.

While I had been prepared to assist her with relaxation and then systematic desensitization, we shifted gears. I asked her when in her life she had had good peripheral vision. She said she did when riding her motorcycle at fast speeds down North Dakota highways. I had her assume a posture of riding her motorcycle and having good peripheral vision. When she had fully stepped into that state, I "anchored" her physiological state to her repeated word of "awareness" and my touch on her arm (Bandler & Grinder, 1979). Both her word and my touch were done as she was congruently into the physiological state of excellent peripheral vision. Repeating this exercise several times securely anchored her motorcycle state to her key word and my touch. We then generalized the arm touch so that she could touch her own arm while using her word and achieve the state of good peripheral vision.

Jill used her anchors during the following week at two baseball games, and she reported to me that she had enjoyed the games immensely. At first she had been conscious of using the anchors, but soon she found herself watching the game with the knowledge that if a baseball came her direction she would see it and be able to react fast enough to prevent herself from getting hurt.

Clients find it easier to dream new goals when counselors help them momentarily step into the future for the long view. Brief counseling can be conceptualized as a method of providing clients with new perspectives.

Brief counseling offers the long view through the building of multiple scenarios (Schwartz, 1991); it is a way of seeing the forest, despite all the trees. One way of providing a new perspective is to rise above the problem. Provide clients with the means to see their situation from a distance, to step out of their maze and see the overall picture. This also helps clients temporarily disassociate from the emotions of the moment, thus increasing their chances for optimal decision-making (Janis, 1983).

Views from helicopters, airplanes, hot air balloons, tall buildings, hilltops, and mountaintops are but a few of the many ways to get an aerial perspective—the big picture. Sometimes the new experience may be in vivo, while at other times it may be in the mind's eye. The following case illustrates how to provide an aerial view for a client. Exercise physiologist and counselor Scout Lee Gunn lives on a ranch in Oklahoma. Scout tells the story of a woman client who had driven out to Scout's ranch to see her for a counseling appointment.

This Is Your Life

In a previous session Scout's client had told about how depressed she was about her limited life. Scout was watching out her window and saw the client drive into the parking lot. Scout observed her client's "depressed" posture as she got out of her car. Wanting to avoid a repeat of the previous session, Scout appeared at her front door and called to the client to follow her. Scout started running toward a small hill in the distance, repeatedly calling back for the woman to follow. The client obliged.

Both finally arrived at the top of the hill, which commanded an impressive view of the countryside. The client was out of breath and had definitely shed her listless "depression" for exhilaration. Scout swung her arm around in a large arc and had the woman view the entire landscape. Scout said, "That is your life out there. How do you want it to be?"

Scout reported that the new sweeping vista combined with the change from the client's stuck posture in a counseling chair into a vibrant moving body produced a profound change. The woman began to "see" new possibilities and experience more energy. They sketched out new possibilities as the woman surveyed the landscape of her wide-open future.

Most of us do not have the luxury of a nearby hill where we can take clients for a new view of their lives. Fortunately, the power of clients' imaginations can be tapped. A hilltop can become a mountaintop in clients' minds. Clients occasionally describe making changes as an uphill battle. The goal seems so far away. And, in fact, when we start our counseling sessions with problem orientations, goals can seem to be on a far distant mountaintop. One brief counseling strategy is to begin on the mountaintop. Have clients describe what it is they want but have them assume they have already achieved their goals. Finally, have them step into their futures and congruently *be* there.

Focusing on problems is as different from this "having-arrived" experience as looking up from the base of the mountain to where one wants to go is from looking down to where one started—the latter experience has more energy and feelings of accomplishment. Many times, when clients experience beginning on the mountaintop, they are able to generate highly useful information about the steps they took that helped them to reach the apex. I have found the following phrasing useful in creating a new perspective for clients, especially when it is used in our first counseling session:

> We have been completely successful in helping you to reach your goal. It is like we have climbed a mountain and have reached the top. In view of how you wanted your life to be, you have achieved it. I would like you to experience what that feels like. What do you see around you? What internal picture do you make? What are you saying about yourself? What are others saying? As you look down the mountain to where you first began, what was the very first step you took to begin to get to where we are now? What was the second step?

Changing clients' physiology is another powerful tool for helping clients dream new goals for their futures. Both running to the literal hilltop and standing on the imaginary mountaintop emphasize physiological change as a means of achieving greater perspective. Physiological changes assist clients who are stuck in undesired feeling states and have a difficult time imagining what they want. These clients find the future just that, the future. They find it easier to state what they do not want in the here-and-now than what they want in the to-be. Directives to change physiology can be as simple as, "Sit in a way that embodies dignity" (Kabat-Zinn, 1994, p. 107).

The Realist

Once clients have begun to state their dreams in the form of positively stated messages, the next step is to assist them in translating their dreams into realistic plans; clients enter the Realist state. Counselors are concerned with transforming the positive but still vague dreams of the Dreamer into more specific statements of what clients want to achieve and/or be. When helping clients develop their stated goals I use four criteria. The goals should be:

(1) under the clients' control, (2) specific and concrete, (3) short-term versus long-term, and (4) small. In the following case, Anna and I co-authored a future that met these four criteria of the Realist state.

Orange Crates

I met Anna at one of my brief counseling workshops. Because I like to have people see and hear what brief counseling is like, I invite people to volunteer with issues or concerns that are real and meaningful to them and that they would be willing to talk about in a public setting. Because the volunteer and I will not be working together for more than a single session, I preface my request for volunteers with these instructions:

> If you are planning a divorce this weekend, I would rather that you didn't volunteer. However, if your dentist has been telling you for some time now that you should be dental flossing each and every day, but you haven't yet acquired the habit, then come forward. Or perhaps you find yourself procrastinating on some task that you want to complete; something like that would be appropriate.

Anna volunteered; she stated that her problem was procrastinating. When I asked what she wanted, she said she wanted to begin clearing out of her house things she and her husband didn't need anymore. She said she and her husband had lived in the same home for thirty years and she wanted to clean so they could move. Anna went on to say that she wanted to move but he did not. Not only was he unwilling to help her clean house but he was also unable to help because of a disability that prevented him from going to the second floor where she wanted to begin.

Employing the four-step framework originated at the Mental Research Institute (see Figure 1, p. 14), I asked what steps she had taken so far. She said, "Up to this point, I have only looked in one drawer to begin throwing things away, but then I quickly closed it. That was it." We both agreed that she had certainly taken a small step, a very small one, but that the incident had helped her see more clearly the challenge ahead.

As we continued to stand in front of the workshop participants, we briefly discussed her relationship with her husband and their disagreement about moving. She wanted to move within a couple of years while he wanted to live the rest of his life in the house. I said that moving was a major transition after living in the same house for all those years and raising a family there. She agreed. We talked for a short time about the thirty years of memories and the meaning those possessions had for her.

The complex issues we had touched on and many ideas about relationships and transitions and meaning were running through my head, but Anna wanted none of them. When I asked her what her goal was she said in a straightforward yet joking way, "I want to be able to walk across my basement." We both laughed, as did the workshop participants.

Anna and I began to explore aspects of this concrete and specific goal. I asked her, "What is the smallest possible goal you might work on that would be meaningful to you, and yet if you began moving in the direction of this goal you would know that you were on the right track toward achieving a larger and perhaps more important goal?"

With this question I was continuing to define a goal that met the following criteria: (1) under the client's control, (2) specific and concrete, (3) short-term versus long-term, and (4) small (de Shazer, 1991). Anna and I eventually mutually negotiated and agreed upon an even more specific goal than walking through the basement. She said, "My new goal is to fill two orange crates with things to give away or throw away by Friday of next week." She said that if she were able to accomplish this goal she would be on her way. She added that the goal was doable and that it didn't overwhelm her.

Moving from a statement of her goal to ways of achieving it, we discussed possible actions. She said that just setting a goal was already very helpful because before we began talking she had felt overwhelmed with how much there was to do. Now, just starting the task, which she had experienced as overwhelming, was no longer so. We discussed what to do with the things she was putting in the orange crates. Giving them to her children and grandchildren when they visited was one option. A second option was just throwing some of the stuff away because it was just plain junk. As we ended our short demonstration, I asked Anna if she had any questions about filling the two orange crates. She said she felt satisfied that she knew how to reach her goal.

Immediately after the demonstration, I provided an opportunity for workshop participants to ask questions and provide their perspectives. Several participants mentioned that they would have dealt with the bigger issues. One representative of this point of view was quite troubled because I had not dealt with the "real and complex issues" that Anna had raised. Anna was still standing beside me so I said to her, "My hunch is that these things the workshop participants just mentioned—the relationship with your husband, the important transition in your life, and the meaning of the things you are cleaning out—are issues you will be working on in the process of filling those two orange crates. Would you be willing to change your goal to one of these 'larger' issues?"

Anna looked at me and congruently said, "You are right. I will be thinking of those other issues. But no, I don't want to change my goal. I just want to fill those two orange crates."

Small Goals. The case of "Orange Crates" illustrates the application of several co-authoring criteria as the client and I converted her dreams into actions. In particular, this case demonstrates how setting a small goal served to get Anna started in the direction she wanted to go. Anna had viewed her task as very large, and her response had been to be overwhelmed and discouraged. The small goal allowed her to experience success. Overcoming inertia and discouragement are two of the biggest problems clients face, especially if their previous attempted solutions have not resolved an issue.

Clients often believe when they enter counseling that they will be required to make big changes in their lives. Since we can assume that small goals are less frightening than big ones, one way to reduce clients' fears is to co-author the smallest possible goal that will make a meaningful difference. Theoretically, small goals imply small changes; however, as de Shazer's (1985) remarks, ". . . no matter how awful or how complex the situation, a small change in one person's behavior can make profound and far-reaching differences in the behavior of all persons concerned" (p. 16). Anna and I worked together to co-author a goal. We succeeded in making her goal so small as to be easily achievable. Small goals, even though they may seem insignificant in light of numerous obstacles, serve to focus clients' attention on what is doable and so raise their hopes and motivation.

Goals Under Client's Control. The case also demonstrates how goals work best when they are under the client's control, rather than the control of others. Anna's goal could be achieved independent of others' involvement. If she had stated her goal as, "Getting my husband to cooperate in cleaning the house," I might have said something like this:

> I believe in helping people achieve the goals they think are important. At the same time I want you to have a good chance of achieving your goals. Let me check. Do you have control over your husband so that you can make him cooperate in this house cleaning? I know you can influence him to help, but I suspect that it's outside of your direct control. How could we have the goal be within only your control?

Many clients initially state goals that include other people making changes. When we point out that they have more control over their outcome if they do not add the expectation that others will change, they choose goals that are more empowering.

Concrete and Specific Goals. Neither Anna nor I was under the illusion that life is reducible to the concreteness of two filled orange crates. However, the workshop participant who vigorously objected to our concrete and specific goal seemed to have made the following assumption: Global goals, such as addressing the developmental issue of making transitions, are more important and meaningful than concrete and specific ones. In brief counseling we accept that clients and their worlds may be conceptualized in concrete, specific terms. We also believe counselors must be very aware of clients' developmental stages, issues, crises, etc. It is not that these issues are not important; it is simply that clients are not, for the most part, asking us to help them with developmental issues. Rather, they want help with immediate decisions, specific stuck points, and current discomfort/pain. Anna had not asked for my help in dealing with the transitional issues the workshop participant thought Anna and I "should" be working on. In fact, Anna was quite explicit that she wanted help with her procrastination, not with other issues. I work from this assumption: Trust the client unless you have strong evidence to the contrary. I believed Anna had the ability to choose the level of intervention that would be helpful to her. Concrete and specific goals seemed to fit quite well for her.

Short-term Goals. Even when clients frame their issues in long-term and abstract language, we often find upon closer examination that they are struggling with one small part that is preventing them from moving on. Short-term goals assist clients at the level where they are stuck, rather than at a level where we as counselors think they should be working. Our counseling and developmental theories are tools for understanding; however, they should not be used to impose complexity that is not required. Many times short-term goals fit well with what clients seek to change. In classical mythology, Procrustes amputated the legs of travelers who were too long for his bed; he stretched those travelers who were too short. Anna did not present her predicament in a language of long-term developmental issues; her goal did not require stretching to fit that framework. In a like manner, not all clients present their predicaments in short-term ways; their goals should not suffer by being compacted unless it is a framework that is equally acceptable. Effective brief counselors help find goals that work for their clients.

The Critic

Effective critics are ones who examine the strengths and weaknesses of something. They alert us to aspects we might overlook. They deliver the message, "Pay attention to this. Don't overlook that. That part needs more work. Don't mess with that part; it's working nicely." The best critics offer, in ways that can be easily heard, constructive feedback—literally, ways to construct something in a better way.

After we and our clients have explored the future and translated the dreams into doable "realities," we enter the Critic state. Our clients' goals can be reviewed for answers to the following questions:

- If you reached your goal, how would that affect you and others?
- What do you want to make sure that you keep from the past?
- What new skills might you have to learn to deal with the changes?
- Who will be supportive of the changes you are making?
- Who will you have to deal with as you move toward your goal?

The following case illustrates what happened when I overlooked my role as a Critic in preparing my client, Suzy, for possible consequences of changing—in particular, not preparing her to handle other people's reactions.

Fear of Heights (and "Friends")

Fears often have a strong social component. Years ago, I worked with a client in North Dakota. Suzy had a fear of heights. We were using in vivo desensitization as a way of helping her overcome her fear. The building where we met had an outside metal fire escape, and we chose that as a test of her newfound courage.

The day was warm and pleasant. Suzy and I had begun walking up the fire escape and together we had reached the first floor landing just half a flight up. Suzy was doing fine and we talked about her resources in staying calm. Next, we walked up until we reached the second floor landing. We had one floor to go.

The second floor housed the Department of Psychology and as we reached the landing outside the second floor, one of Suzy's psychology professors, whom she considered a friend, appeared in the open doorway. He asked what we were doing and Suzy explained how she was overcoming her fear of heights. Wearing a mischievous smile, her professor quipped, "Golly, Suzy, if you look down between the bars of the metal grate you're standing on, you can see all the way to the ground far below." Suzy's fear suddenly and massively reinforced, she escaped into the building as quickly as possible. Our in vivo desensitization session was over—the professor had reinforced the fear using the reverse of my technique. He had employed in vivo sensitization.

In the role of Critic, we assess the impact of other people on our clients' abilities to acquire and maintain new behaviors. In addition, we help our clients assess the impact of others' reactions, both harmful and helpful, to their chances of changing. But beyond assessment, brief counselors as Critics help clients build social support for their changes. Often clients try to go it alone and fail to realize the potential life-supporting and life-enhancing environment surrounding them. There is considerable support for the idea that other people can enhance the change process (Prochaska, Norcross & DiClemente, 1994). With Kara Sanford, I investigated the effects of social support in single-session counseling (Sanford & Littrell, 1997). We discovered that brief counseling with social support was more effective than brief counseling without social support. As a result of our investigation, we routinely help our clients identify and utilize the people in their environment who can be supportive. Many times people are there who would help, but our clients have not thought to ask them for support or have been too afraid to ask. When, with our encouragement, they do ask, they almost always find others highly supportive and encouraging.

As Critics and as teachers of how to be in the Critic state, we are instrumental in checking that clients' goals include a future perspective. This role provides a proactive perspective that increases clients' social support. We perform a protective function in helping to minimize possible negative effects associated with change.

Summary

Co-creating clients' futures is an exhilarating process. It opens up new possibilities. Many times as we help clients into the states of Dreamer, Realist, and Critic, we find that the process of co-authoring clients' futures has been very therapeutic. For some clients clarifying what they want is the most important activity of counseling. Once they know what they want, they are done. They know what they now need to do and they have the skills to do it.

Counselors can introduce clients to the process of goal-setting by employing a Disney strategy (i.e., Dreamer, Realist, and Critic) or by traditional methods. Some clients find that neither of these approaches to goal-setting fits them. In that case, brief counselors avoid these two approaches and search for others that do fit. We need to be flexible. Brief counselors have their favorite ways to clarify goals, yet they remain open to doing what works for their clients. Using clients' frames for defining what they want is often considerably faster than teaching clients the favorites from our stock repertoire.

Co-authoring possible futures is a means of clarifying what clients want, but some clients, even after the clarification, express doubts about how to get there. That is when counseling methods and techniques to help clients achieve goals become important. In presenting ideas about brief counseling to thousands of workshop participants, the most challenging task I have faced is convincing professional helpers that we need to know clients' goals before we apply the means to get there. We have an ethical obligation as professionals to use counseling methods and techniques responsibly. Only when our clients' desired states are clarified are we justified in employing the powerful tools of our counseling trade.

Do Something Different

1. Conceptualizing goal-setting as co-authoring is but one way of taking what is often considered a boring and routine activity and making it more interesting. If co-authoring roles work for you, use them. On the other hand, you may have a way of conceptualizing the process that works better for you. Again, use what works. Brief counseling is not prescriptive of what you have to do; it follows Milton Erickson's approach of finding what works and then doing it.
2. Think about a professional future you would like for yourself. Become a creator of your future state by sequentially putting on the hats of the Dreamer, the Realist, and the Critic.
3. With your next several clients, begin by determining what futures they want. Do not be surprised if a few of them "forget" to backtrack and tell you about their problems in excruciating detail. When clients are headed for the future, they sometimes have no need to backtrack and talk about what did not work.

CHAPTER 8

Encouraging Action

CLIENT: *I just wanted to be doing something—anything.*

After clients and counselors have mutually decided where clients want to go and have set goals that meet the criteria listed in Chapter 7, then it is incumbent on counselors to help them reach their goals. An underlying principle of brief counseling is to inaugurate clients, as well as counselors, into doing something different—this chapter explains how. This doing may range from one end of the 7-point continuum to the other on what I have termed the Carl Scale.[2]

1	:	:	:	:	:	:	7

mild   flamboyant

Carl Rogers[3]   Carl Whitaker[4]

manner   flair

The many tools available in counselors' repertoires become useful in helping clients achieve their desired outcomes. There are no limits set, beyond legal and ethical ones, on the strategies, methods, techniques, and

---

[2] Reliability and validity data unavailable.
[3] A gentle, predicable grandfather-type therapist.
[4] A teasing, unpredictable uncle-type therapist.

"The first thing we want to do, Mrs. Jeffries, is to start feeling better about ourselves, so I'm prescribing a pair of these wonderful cowboy boots."

ideas that brief counselors might employ to assist clients in reaching their goals, provided the goals meet the criteria enumerated in the last chapter. And if the client's goal is specific, a brief counselor might prescribe an enjoyable way of getting there.

There are innumerable ways to help people reach their goals. For example, clients may generally state their goal as being more relaxed at work. Given that goal, there are countless way to assist clients. Sometimes relaxation training may be precisely the technique that will help. At other times, assertiveness training that helps clients say "no" to unreasonable requests will be useful. In some cases, clients might benefit from taking part in a group of people struggling with similar types of concerns. When working from a brief counseling framework, counselors recognize that many methods may be appropriate in helping clients. No method is categorically ruled out.

However, while brief counselors are trained to know a variety of methods, they do not assume responsibility for coming up with specific methods. They believe that they share responsibility with clients for generating new options. Therefore, brief counselors do not assume that they will work harder than their clients when generating possible solutions.

While counselors may have large repertoires of standardized methods for reaching goals, even these are viewed as only a fraction of the possibilities. Part of the art of counseling is tailoring methods to clients and to their specific goals. Because each client is unique, general methods are selected that will work best for the person, and these are then tailored to fit the specific client.

The most general method available for helping clients reach their goals is to have them do something different from what they are currently doing (de Shazer, 1985). In and of itself, doing something different will not necessarily move clients in the direction of their goals, but it does have the advantage of breaking patterns that are keeping people stuck. Our clients do not intentionally remain stuck. Many times they repeat the same patterns because at one point the pattern worked. The hope remains that the pattern will work again. This hope is illustrated in the following ancient Chinese story attributed to Han Fei Zi (1985) entitled, "Waiting for More Rabbits to Bump into the Tree."

Waiting for More Rabbits to Bump into the Tree

One day, a farmer of Song was working in the fields, when he noticed a rabbit run by very fast and bump into a big tree by his field. The rabbit broke its neck and died beneath the tree. With very little effort, the farmer picked up the rabbit and took it home.

After the experience of picking up the rabbit, the farmer laid down his hoe and just sat under that big tree, hugging his knees, waiting for the next rabbit. But not a single rabbit ever came to bump into the tree again. (p. 61)

To be successful, the farmer of Song needed to be doing something different than sitting under a tree waiting. Our clients need to move beyond their repetition of patterns that do not work. We assist our clients when we co-design and co-monitor doing of something that moves clients in the direction of their goals. When I work with clients I give the generic task of doing something different after I have reiterated the goal and given the client a compliment. I often phrase it this way:

We have identified your goal as [insert restatement of goal here]. I would like to say that I have been very impressed with your willingness to work hard at understanding and clarifying what you want [a compliment]. As a way of moving in the direction of your goal, I would like you to do something different. It can be fun, interesting, and exciting, or it can be ordinary and regular, or it can even be difficult and challenging—it all depends on what would work best for you. The most important thing is that you do something different as you head toward your new goal. Together let's brainstorm three, four, or five possibilities.

Doing something different is a pattern breaker. It encourages clients to explore new ways of thinking, feeling, and acting. Clients often are stuck in a pattern that they repeat without variation, despite lack of success. The task to "do something different" is given in the context of doing something that will increase the probability that clients will head toward their goals. It is not simply given to modify clients' behavior haphazardly.

Our experience in working with clients of all ages is that, when they are asked to do something different as a way of moving in the direction of their goals, some get expressions on their faces that seem to say, "Have I got some great ideas." Unfortunately, some of these great ideas are also not in the best interest of the clients or others. Therefore, we have learned to add the following phrase when giving the directive to do something different: "However, what you do cannot be illegal, immoral, or hurt yourself or others." We have been surprised to note how many clients offer a knowing smile, what the Adlerians would call a smile of recognition. As counselors we often function as permission givers; we need to be aware of what we are permitting. The added qualification is a safeguard to unbridled permission-giving.

In the case examples in this chapter, the clients were encouraged to generate new options by doing something different. I am constantly amazed by the resourcefulness of clients when we give them permission to try new patterns. Their cleverness and resourcefulness in generating different patterns are amazing, as is the way they personalize the generic task of doing something different.

The two major sections in this chapter focus on how clients can do something different as a way of moving in the direction of their goals. In the first section, I present cases of clients who wanted to enhance relationships with other people. In the second section, clients are coping with negative relationships and doing their best to protect themselves. These clients did not want to work on enhancing their relationship with another person. They preferred to defend themselves and regain peace of mind.

Enhancing Positive Relationships

Social relationships are prime breeding grounds for the repetition of patterns that do not work. Parent-child relationships thrive on repetitious patterns that may have worked at one point in a relationship but have outlived their usefulness. In the following story, the mother worked with me to improve her relationship with her daughter.

Bear with Me, My Daughter

I met with only the mother, since her daughter, Jodi, was studying abroad. The mother wanted to treat Jodi as though she were younger than her 19 years. Letting go was difficult for the mother, and she acknowledged that she nagged Jodi about her clothes, her weight, and numerous other things. Jodi had one response to her mother's constant nagging—she withdrew. Jodi's backing away had simply increased the mother's desire to intervene.

The mother and I explored alternative methods of communicating with Jodi. In response to my directive to communicate in a new manner, the mother wrote a letter to her daughter. This letter is not without faults. The mother has changed from a more intrusive demanding style to a more subtle one. The story metaphor is less demanding. However, the mother is still pumping Jodi for information and gently reminding her to watch her weight. On the other hand, the mother was responsible for the clever metaphor and was delighted that she had found a new way of communicating with her daughter. The letter is as follows:

> Dearest Jodi,
> I'd like to share this excerpt with you. It's taken from the February 1989 *Reader's Digest*. It goes this way.
>
>> We were discussing reincarnation, and most of us were thinking of coming back as doctors, lawyers and actresses. Then one friend broke the trend, "I'd like to come back as a bear," she said. "Why?" we asked. "I would finally have a fur coat. I could sleep all winter, and I wouldn't have to worry about my waistline."
>
> Isn't it nice not to be worried about our waistlines and to be able to gobble up the eucalyptus leaves or sweet, juicy bamboo shoots? And, as animal lovers, and you, in particular, an adorer of both the koala and panda bears, it would be just fantastic not only to look at them, but BE THEM—to live, lumber around, and roll about in your fur coat.
> However, bears growl and don't sing as sweetly as you do. Can you imagine a Panda singing soprano or tapping away at the drum set in church? Try fantasizing this scene: Mama Bear (me) wobbles and reads, the growling Jodi Bear bangs at the drums and Daddy Bear thumps on the piano all on a beautiful sunny Sunday. It'll be fun, won't it?
> But since we don't believe in reincarnation and we have to, unfortu-

nately, go on and shop for our clothes, it'll be better to watch our waist-lines. What do you think?

I also like the recent photos you sent me. You look very sweet and pretty—as though you've slimmed down a bit. It was also good of you to send your dad and me information about your checking account and your test results. They really reveal that you are getting disciplined in the way you spend your money and in your studies as well.

Soon you'll be twenty. That's really an exciting age. Your dad and I wish you all of God's best as you reach towards graduation in a year's time. Have a blessed birthday—your first really independent one—and in a beautiful snowy country in the winter. Perhaps we do need fur coats after all.

XXXX Love,
Ma

The mother's letter to Jodi was her first attempt at doing something different as a method for improving her relationship with her daughter. The mother was very proud of her attempt and believed that writing it in this way was much better than her previous attempts. I was pleased that the mother's efforts were a substantial improvement over her previous way of treating her daughter. However, there were parts of the letter that I thought might be read by the daughter as still interfering too much in her life. The mother responded to my concerns about these parts of the letter, and she subsequently modified them before sending it.

The next case also involves letter writing as a means of doing something different. Sheri was struggling with the end of a relationship with a man with whom she wanted to remain friends. She found that doing something different was a means to open up new ways of relating to her former boyfriend. Also noteworthy in the case is the Sheri's use of social support as a way of checking out her use of a new method of communicating. The case is presented in her own words.

A Friend-ly Letter

I've done a lot of thinking about my situation and I did brief counseling—or more solution-focused therapy—on myself. Guess you call it self-solution focused. I realized that during and since my breakup with Karl I'd done nothing but focus on the problems I saw us having. I switched modes and looked at what I liked about the relationship with him, and I looked at what I (we) were doing when the relationship was going well. I then looked at what I wanted to continue to do.

Since this is a relationship issue the only control that I have is what I do. When we parted Karl said he wanted to remain friends, so I looked at my friendship and what I do with friends and the things we continue to do because I realized that with friends we rarely do things that cause disagreements.

So at first I wrote Karl a letter stating what I was doing and thinking; that is, being more solution-focused about us and not problem-focused. I then related the various things that I wanted to continue to do in regards to him (e.g., write and talk as before). After I wrote the letter I called a friend and asked her response to the letter I had just written. She asked me what my goal or underlying motive was in what I had said in the letter. I said it was to let Karl know that I am ready to handle being friends. Sure, there's the hope that we'd get back together = underlying motive.

My friend had me think about how I would respond to such a letter. I looked at what I would do in response. Then I realized that it wasn't a letter I'd send to a friend; rather, it was a contract or almost a plea to be friends. Suddenly I remembered the following quote from our church bulletin:

I WENT OUT TO FIND A FRIEND AND COULD NOT FIND ONE THERE;
I WENT OUT TO BE A FRIEND AND FOUND THEM EVERYWHERE.

To have a friend, you must be a friend first. So I stuffed the letter away and began to think about what I write to all my friends—for each friend I share different aspects of my life. My goal now is to write a letter and share those things I want to share. What an eye opener! I definitely had an "Aha!" experience.

There is nothing unique about the client's discovery that "to have a friend, you must be a friend first," except the client was stuck in a pattern and had not yet discovered what she already knew. When we as counselors prescribe "do something different" to our clients, we are giving them permission to explore new patterns. When delivered by someone whom clients perceive as having expertise, trustworthiness, and interpersonal attractiveness, permission is a powerful tool for change.

When counselors choose to assign tasks of doing something different to help clients reach goals, they may choose from two major categories: ordeal and non-ordeal. Jay Haley (1984) provided helpers with the definitive text on ordeals that can be assigned to help clients reach their goals. Ordeal tasks challenge clients to engage in actions that are by their very nature difficult, arduous, and uncomfortable or unpleasant. Haley, with tongue in cheek, suggests that counseling/therapy is in of itself an ordeal and that clients are "cured" to the extent that they decide that counseling/ therapy is in some ways more of an ordeal than changing.

The following case lasted one session with several short phone calls to check on progress. Haley's ideas on ordeal therapy were fresh in my mind as I began working with the family. There is a phrase in folk wisdom, "Give a child a hammer and suddenly everything is a nail." I suspect that my choice of an ordeal in this case was in keeping with the wisdom of the folk saying.

Poisoned Snow

I had the opportunity several years ago to work with a father, mother and their son, aged eight. The boy had suddenly developed a fear that his food could have poison in it. He was driving his parents to the brink of insanity by constantly seeking their reassurance that the food he was being fed was not poisoned. They responded to his requests for reassurance by doing what most parents do—they sought to reassure him that the food was perfectly safe. Their efforts to comfort him were in vain and, paradoxically, had the opposite effect. The more they reassured, the more worried he became. Thinking of this problem from the Mental Research Institute's (Fisch et al., 1982; Watzlawick et al., 1974) frame of reference, the parents and child were engaged in a more-of-the-same pattern. The more the parents reassured, the more reassurance the child sought. The parents were at a loss as to how to break the pattern.

When I inquired about the beginning of the problem, I was told that it began in early December when the parents and child were visiting the grandparents' farm. The boy and his friend were in the barnyard playing as children often do during the first snowfall of the year—they were scooping up snow and eating it. Unfortunately (in retrospect), the boy's grandmother looked out the window and saw what they were doing. She yelled out to them, "Don't eat that snow! It has poison in it." From that point on the child generalized the grandmother's warning to include all types of things that could be placed in his mouth.

The mother and father were conscientious parents and had the snow checked. It did not contain fertilizers as the grandmother had feared. This fact was pointed out to their son but to no avail. The more rational the parents were, the less rational their son became.

Because I had recently read Cloé Madanes' *Behind the One-Way Mirror*, in which she employed an ordeal task, I chose that type of task as a way to help the family reach their goal of eating meals in peace (i.e., without being constantly asked whether the food was poisoned). I told the parents that I had a task that I thought would be helpful in moving them in the direction of their goal, and I asked if they were willing to do it. They were desperate enough to agree to the assigned task before knowing what it was; I call this signing a blank check.[5]

My task to the parents was as follows: Each and every time your son comes to you seeking reassurance about the safety of food, you are to hand him crayons and paper and have him draw a picture of his fear. As parents, you are to alternately take turns going into the back yard with him while he digs a hole and buries the crumpled-up drawing.

The parents proved themselves worthy of the arduousness of this ordeal when their son awakened them on Christmas morning at 2:00 A.M. He was expressing fears about eating some of the Christmas candy later that day. The father got out of bed, had the boy draw a picture of his fears, and together the two headed into the back yard. The boy's ordeal proved to be challenging since the ground had frozen and digging a hole was no easy task.

I met with the boy and his mother in early January. She reported that since Christmas morning the child had not reported any fears. She said that she and her husband were no longer having to constantly reassure their son. In fact, she reported that it was almost as if a miracle had occurred. The boy had discussed the possibility of food being poisoned on several occasions, but before the parents had a chance to intervene, he had added that he used to believe that it might have been poisoned but now he knew this wasn't true. The parents were pleased to report that their son now reassured himself with precisely the same types of phrases they had previously used.

A six-month follow-up inadvertently occurred in a supermarket when I met the mother while grocery shopping. I inquired how she, her husband, and their son were. She said that from Christmas morning on their son had no longer sought their constant reassurance and that the problem no longer appeared to be a problem. Because I tend to be curious about how clients make changes in their own personalized way, I asked what she believed accounted for the change. I would have preferred to hear, "John, it was your brilliant ordeal that changed our lives." Instead, she said, "John, you urged us to be firm and consistent with him and not to let him rule our lives. That really helped. The other thing I think really helped is we did a lot of praying together as a family."

---

[5] See *Change* (Watzlawick et al., 1974, pp.154-157) for a discussion of this strategy, which they labeled the "Devil's Pact." Given the current counseling climate, in which the title "Devil's Pact" might give rise to charges of satanism, I prefer to reframe this technique as "signing a blank check." The intent is the same: the client is expressing trust that the counselor can be trusted to do what is in the best interests of the client. I suspect the same cannot be said of the devil, since the devil supposedly has ulterior motives—claiming the pact-signer's soul.

As I later reflected on my client's answer, I thought possibly I could take a small amount of credit for my suggestion of a parental united front so as not to be bullied by their son. However, I don't remember stating it quite as boldly as she apparently had heard. I sadly realized that the "brilliant" ordeal I had designed had gone unacknowledged and unappreciated, despite their use of it. Finally, I distinctly remember that we did not discuss prayer as a change strategy. The point of my reflecting on my client's recollections is to emphasize that, while designing, tailoring, and assigning tasks, we must constantly remind ourselves that it is often not the specific task assigned but the fact that our clients are doing something different that makes a difference.

While counseling may be an ordeal, brief counselors ordinarily do not conceptualize it in that way. They prefer to view counseling as an opportunity to learn new ways to deal with what they perceive as problems and new ways to reach goals. In other words, brief counselors reframe counseling as a time for new learning, a time for increasing options, and a time to explore new ways of being in the world.

Coping with Negative Relationships

Clients do not always seek to enhance relationships. Sometimes they are quite willing to avoid contact with others or, barring that option, to have minimal interactions in which they protect themselves. Brief counseling may prove quite effective in helping clients learn new responses to employ in unpleasant situations. The final two cases were single sessions; the first lasted 5 minutes, while the second took longer—15 minutes.

In the first case I listened to Darlene describe a work situation in which she felt sexually harassed. Darlene wanted a solution she could use to deal with a salesman's unwanted statements; she was not asking for long-term counseling. In this case I suggested a specific strategy she could employ. In contrast, in the second case I spent more time designing with the client an intervention that came from her frame of reference. I have noticed that, when I suggest a specific intervention as a way of moving in the direction of the client's goal, I must exercise special care. I can get wrapped up in my own ideas of what might work or become so enamored of my cleverness in designing a task that I fail to really hear or understand my client.

Would You Repeat That?

Darlene approached me during the break of a workshop I was presenting and said she had a problem at work. One of the salesmen who worked in her office was constantly making suggestive remarks to her. Several attempted solutions had been tried to no avail. She had told him to stop but he hadn't. She had threatened to tell the supervisor but he had just smiled. Like many people who are being abused, Darlene did not want to get the man in trouble, yet his statements were particularly troublesome.

I sensed that Darlene might be giving the salesman an ambiguous message by not being firm enough in her demand that he stop immediately. I asked Darlene if she was truly invested in having the man stop. Very congruently, she said she was. Based on her goal, I made the following suggestion:

> You are to get a small, battery-operated tape recorder and keep it in your purse. If the salesman makes any remark to you that you consider inappropriate or sexual in nature, you are to reach into your purse, remove the tape recorder, and say to him. "Would you please repeat that into my tape recorder?"

In a six-month follow-up, Darlene said that she had used her line only once, but the man immediately stopped the type of talk she found objectionable. He had made no offensive remarks since her intervention. Darlene learned what she needed within minutes; she used her learning almost immediately. Teaching Darlene assertiveness skills may have proven equally effective, but the teaching would have taken longer. Brief counselors seek the minimum interventions that will be effective.

The next case took only slightly longer but once again demonstrated that many clients have tremendous resources to change patterns when provided with a context that grants them permission to do so and to do so quickly.

Mental Tap Dancing

Because of terms in her divorce settlement, it was necessary for Marilyn to occasionally communicate by phone with her ex-husband. Marilyn hated these calls. During the phone calls and for some time after, she was tense and irritable. Marilyn wanted relief. She wanted ways to be on the phone with him and still feel good about herself.

I checked about previous situations in which Marilyn had felt in control of herself and her emotions, despite adverse circumstances. She immediately said that when she danced she felt centered. When she danced she handled stress and pressure in ways that she liked. I asked Marilyn the following question:

> Bearing in mind what you have said about dancing and if you were to do something different when you and your husband talk on the phone,

what would be something really different that you could do that would move you in the direction of feeling in control and confident?

Marilyn paused for a few moment and said, "When I talk with him on the phone, I need to dance." I asked for details, and she said she would be imagining herself in a dance outfit and she would be dancing around the room as she talked with him on the cordless phone. In response to my questions, she named the music she would be dancing to and how she would stay in her dancing frame of mind.

Several days after we finished, I sent a follow-up card showing several women dressed in dance outfits and dancing. Marilyn informed me six months later that the dancing card had been useful for a while but that she had needed to do other things when her ex-husband changed his tactics and started to become more belligerent.

No solution works forever. Marilyn's dancing frame of mind was effective until circumstances changed. We need to remind clients that solutions are only good for the situation for which they were designed. When problems change then solutions need to change. Nadler and Hibino with Farrell (1995) have proposed that we help people apply the solution-after-next principle, in which we "look beyond the immediate problem and its solution to future needs" (p. 302). If I had used the solution-after-next principle with Marilyn, we might have anticipated solutions to her ex-husband's escalation of the problem.

Life is in a state of constant flux and people can easily get trapped into patterns that have worked in the past but no longer work in the present. Like the farmer in the short story, "Waiting for More Rabbits to Bump into the Tree," people often repeat the formerly successful pattern or limit their responses to their typical ones. "Do something different" is a pattern interrupter. Used as a general directive it can be useful in creating new options. However, "do something different" is most powerful when combined with the phrase, "To move in the direction of your goal." When the goal is explicit, the directive to "do something different" takes on a direction. The directive is not random but is used in the service of assisting clients in reaching their goals.

Do Something Different

---

1. After clarifying with clients what their goals are, give the following directive:

As a way of moving in the direction of your goal, I believe that it is important that you do something quite different from what you are currently doing. What are some new things that you could be doing that would be really different from what you are currently doing and at the same time would begin to move you in the direction of your goal? Let's brainstorm some possibilities. [At this point wait and allow clients to have some thinking time.]

2. Simply having clients do something different is not sufficient if the "difference" does not move clients in the directions of their goals. Check to make sure that doing something different is a goal-directed step.

Part III

Speeding Up
the Action

Acknowledging Fun

CLIENT: *My counselor was always so serious. I felt guilty when
I enjoyed making changes.*

Mickey Mouse is a cultural icon of fun in the U.S. and around the world.
People respond to Mickey with smiles. The big-eared, bulbed-nose, squeaky-
voiced, thin-tailed rodent tickles our funny bones. Mickey reminds us that life,
including work, can be taken far too seriously. Glen and Rosie Walter (personal communication, December 1992) wrote two equations that define the relationship of work and play, and with which Mickey's creator, Walt Disney,
might have concurred. Their first tongue-in-cheek equation is about play:

$$A(IW)ITL = P$$
Anything, including work, if taken lightly = PLAY

The Walters' first equation reminds us that the work of counseling,
despite its seriousness of purpose, can be play when approached in that way.
Their second equation is the flip side of the first but addresses the dangers
inherent in too much emphasis on play. It reads:

$$A(IP)T2S = W$$
Anything, including play, taken too seriously = WORK

If we err as counselors, I believe it is because we are inclined to take the
play of counseling and make it work. When we are "working" with clients

to assist them with life's difficulties, we have a tendency to become remarkably serious. Clients present their problems with mirthless expressions so we extrapolate from their seriousness and reason that the solution phase of counseling should match their serious demeanors.

However, in brief counseling, we question the assumed necessary relationship between the seriousness of problems and the seriousness of solutions. In brief counseling we notice that when clients focus on solutions they possess more energy, display more optimism, and exhibit a sense of playfulness. During solution-focused times, clients often experience flow, "the state in which people are so involved in an activity that nothing else seems to matter; the experience itself is so enjoyable that people will do it even at great cost, for the sheer sake of doing it" (Csikszentmihalyi, 1990, p. 4). When my clients are engaged in solution-focused counseling, they tend to exhibit the following dimensions that Csikszentmihalyi (1993) says define the state of flow: (1) unambiguous goals with swift feedback, (2) personal skills are matched to challenges, (3) action and awareness become unified, (4) strong concentration on the task at hand, (5) a feeling of potential control, (6) self-consciousness vanishes, (7) time passes more swiftly, and (8) what one does becomes worth doing for its own sake (pp. 178-179).

Humor and laughter are two ways of introducing flow into the search for solutions. Flow, when experienced by both the counselor and client, can lead to more rapid change while avoiding a grind-it-out approach (Fletcher, 1993). In this chapter I will demonstrate how laughter can be used as a tranquilizer and as a rapport builder. I will describe fun actions that facilitate change and methods of tapping clients' sense of humor. I will conclude with some life-enhancing metaphors.

Laughter as Tranquilizer

Humor with its resulting laughter can significantly lighten clients' burdens. A wonderful characteristic of laughter was identified by Arnold Glasow, who said, "Laughter is a tranquilizer with no side effects" (Peter, 1977, p. 286). Laughter as a tranquilizer offers clients time to relax. The reduction in stress allows for more effective thinking and decision-making. Janis (1983) identified one characteristic of effective decision-making as an optimal level of stress. Too little stress was associated with lack of sufficient motivation to change, while too much interfered with making effective decisions. I find most clients are overstressed, rather than under-stressed. Laughter, that tranquilizer with no side effects, helps reduce stress and contributes to better decision-making.

My clients and I experience greater use of humor and more laughter now that I am working in a brief counseling framework focused on solutions in life, rather than dwelling on life's problems. A solution-focused approach encourages less reliance on habitual ways of viewing life and more on new ways of being. Just as enumerating problems often stimulates the production of more problems, so the generation of new solutions generates additional solutions. Dreaming up new solutions is often a time of joint laughter. My clients and I are fascinated by the juxtaposition of new behaviors, new thoughts, and new feelings as marvelous replacements for older ones. Our laughter reminds my clients that they have an ally—someone with whom they face the future. In the following case, Sandy and I enjoyed the opportunity to use humor from the past to deal with an annoying problem in the present.

Like Barney

Sandy expressed concern about her landlord who was, she said, "driving her crazy." When asked to describe him, she made a face and told how he was short, skinny, and ever so self-centered. The man would drop by her rented house to work on leaky faucets and a sometimes non-functioning furnace. Sandy believed he was harmless, but she found his manner irritated her to the point of distraction.

I asked her who the landlord reminded her of. She thought for just a moment, laughed, and said, "He's just like Barney, you know, Barney Fife from *The Andy Griffith Show*." After Sandy realized the association between her landlord and Barney, we proceeded to compare the two in greater detail. She kept shaking her head at the many ways the two men were similar. She was also laughing.

As we continued, we arrived at a goal of increasing her behavioral repertoire in dealing with the landlord, or Barney as we now called him. We explored possible solutions. I asked Sandy a question that opened up some amazing possibilities about how to handle her Barney. I asked, "How did Andy Griffith handle Barney when Barney was being so compulsive and strange and irritating?"

Sandy thought for a little while and then began listing ways that Andy remained cool in the face of Barney's irrational behavior. She said Andy let Barney's irritating remarks and obnoxious behavior just roll off him without taking Barney too seriously. A second way that Andy handled Barney when he was excessively agitated while in possession of his gun and his one bullet was to say to Barney, "Okay, Barney, give me the bullet. Give me the bullet, Barn."

I believe role models can be useful in helping clients learn new behaviors. I asked Sandy if she could locate any old episodes of *The Andy Griffith*

Show so she could observe Andy's handling of Barney in more detail. To my surprise Sandy answered that she already had videotapes of the show at home. I said, "That's great! They can be a useful resource." I thought, "What a strange coincidence."

In a follow-up several months later, Sandy said she had been using some of Andy's strategies, but occasionally she just gets tired of her landlord "Barney" and she tells him to leave in a more direct fashion. She added, "I could hurt his feelings so easily by squashing him emotionally and intellectually, but I'd feel so guilty later. It's a real release to use the how-Andy-handles-Barney way of thinking when he's around. He's such a fool but the new ways of acting give me relief and satisfaction."

Several months after the follow-up I received a small gift from Sandy. Appropriately enough, it was a videocassette with three episodes from *The Andy Griffith Show*. As I watched them I was reminded of how irritating Barney could be at times and how Andy had been a most helpful role model for Sandy.

Searching for humor in situations often results in finding it, just as the search for seriousness leads to finding seriousness. With minimal guidance, clients such as Sandy can be quite resourceful in identifying the humor of their predicaments and in finding ways of laughing at them. As is typical of Sandy's experience, clients often have the ability to step back and laugh and to see the absurdity of the patterns they are caught in. As counselors we can assist clients in accessing a playful quality both while focusing on stuck patterns and while generating new options.

Building Rapport in an Exciting Way

Establishing rapport may be accomplished in many ways. In brief counseling the counselor explores ways to speed up rapport building. My friend Lorrie Young loves working with adolescents because she finds they enjoy excitement. In the following case, Lorrie created a humorous situation to entice Gina, a 16-year-old client who was very distrustful of counseling, into freely participating. In using humor and surprise, Lorrie was following a tradition that endorses a lively therapeutic climate for adolescents (Selekman, 1993).

The Incredible Hunk

Lorrie asked Gina what would make her want to participate in counseling with Gina's mother and Lorrie. Gina replied with her standard response: "I don't know." Lorrie proposed several conventional ideas, such as keeping the time very short and doing a practice session so that Gina could evaluate Lorrie's approach. Gina immediately turned down these ideas.

Lorrie recognized that Gina was, in the mother's description, "boy crazy." Lorrie said, "Look, if I got a gorgeous hunk of a man to come here next week and sit here with you while I'm talking to your mother, would you willingly participate in counseling?" Lorrie reported that the girl's face turned red. Lorrie continued to ask related questions such as, "If he were a guy you'd dream about as a perfect date and if he were really good looking, would you be willing to participate?" The girl's reply was, "You wouldn't really bring a guy like that in here." Lorrie came back with, "Oh yes, I would." Gina said she'd come next week but she refused to believe that Lorrie would follow through.

The next week Lorrie had followed through. Gina sat in the waiting room while Lorrie was seeing her mother. Gina shared the room with an extremely good-looking man in his early twenties. He talked with Gina about her interests, and he told her how he knew Lorrie and what a wonderful person Lorrie was. Lorrie reported that from that day on the girl was very cooperative in working with Lorrie and the mother in making change.

Lorrie told me later that when she works with people she likes to build rapport as quickly as possible. She has found that carrying through on what she says she will do is one of the fastest ways to convince people that she can be trusted. Lorrie added that she tries to make counseling interesting and exciting for her clients. "Boring" is not in Lorrie's counseling vocabulary. She extends this same attitude to rapport building. Eliciting clients' sense of humor and wonderment is an excellent way to engage clients and build rapport.

Fun Action

Plunging clients into fun, interesting, and/or exciting situations is yet another way of speeding up counseling. Doing something with humor, rather than just talking about it, changes the situation in encouraging ways. In the next two cases, fun actions provided within our sessions and given as homework assignments helped clients quickly learn new ways of responding.

Madonna

"How do you do your anxiety?" was the basic question I asked my client when she talked about how nervous she became while waiting for the results of a licensing exam. Upon first hearing this question she looked at me with a puzzled expression. Her reply was a question, "What do you mean?" I responded with a question and a directive, "I mean, what do you look like, sound like, and feel like when you do nervousness? Show me right here and now."

In response, she moved very little and she complained a bit as she described butterflies in her stomach. With a twinkle in my eye and because we had rapport, my response was to indicate that she wasn't being very original in how she did her nervousness. I pointed out that she could have so much more fun being nervous if she were only more dramatic. I asked her, "Who are your favorite singers and actresses?" She looked at me and said, "Madonna and Meryl Streep." Again I asked a question and gave a directive, "How would Meryl Streep do nervousness? Show me."

She practiced how Streep would do nervousness in a very sophisticated manner. "Now, how would Madonna do nervousness?" I modeled for her a brash, self-centered, I-don't-care-what-the-world-thinks-of-me, flamboyant version of "I'm nervous."

Her immediate reaction was to laugh. Then she tried doing her nervousness as Madonna might do it. She said that her kids would get a kick out of this version because they were all so tired of how she typically did it. We talked about how she could practice doing nervousness as Meryl Streep or Madonna, but she could also choose to do it as other people if she wished.

Getting clients to do new activities is facilitated when they are having fun. Directing my client to act like Madonna and Meryl Streep upended her expectations about what a problem is and how to solve it. My unexpected directive to step outside of her nervousness and play her stuck pattern in new ways provided acknowledgment that she had constructed her original nervousness and that she could construct alternatives. The fun action provided her with more options, so that she was not superglued to her problem.

As I did with my client in the previous case, my friends Glen and Rosie Walter also plunge their clients into fun actions. The Walters present programs entitled TA DA for elementary and secondary school children. TA DA is expressed by throwing one's arms out, making an expressive face and saying "TA DA!" The Walters get their self-esteem messages across by a willingness to take risks of being seen as silly and enthusiastic and full of energy. The Walters have students practice giving each other standing ovations, during which half of the group surrounds the other half and applauds for several minutes. Accompanying the loud and continuous hand clapping are whistles, shouts of "Oh yeah!" and foot stomping. The people on the receiving end are at first pleased with the response, then they seem to go through a period of embarrassment that it is lasting so long, and finally they just beam with delight.

As Glen and Rosie point out, very seldom are we really appreciated for just being. People are sometimes rewarded for their accomplishments if they are accomplishers, but if they are not accomplishers they are out of luck. On *Mr. Rogers' Neighborhood*, Fred Rogers' message to young children is consistent, "I like you just the way you are." Rogers does not put preconditions of accomplishment on children; he acknowledges them just for being, not for what they can do.

When Glen and Rosie have students give each other standing ovations, they are not rewarding accomplishment; they are acknowledging that being, in and of itself, is a wonderful state. Glen and Rosie find that "TA DA" gives way repeatedly to "Ha Ha." Their friend David Pitner adds that the third step in the sequence is frequently "Ah Ha"—the opening up of new insights and options.

I attended a workshop that Glen and Rosie held for professional counselors. They had us do standing ovations for each other. The energy and warmth in the room were unbelievable. The Walters are comfortable sharing their energy with the students and adults they work with. For them it is not a risk to do what they do, but for some of us it is.

Recently, I was telling a class of counselors about the Walters and how their standing ovations were such a powerful tool. Suddenly it occurred to me that I was talking about the experience, but my students were not really having the electrifying experience of doing it. Next to our classroom was a class in educational philosophy. We walked next door and surrounded the educational philosophy instructor and students and began giving them a standing ovation. We continued for more than a minute. The instructor told me later that our ovation had been one of the most fascinating and moving experiences he had ever had with a class—they all loved it.

The next case is an extended example of the power of designing fun, interesting, and exciting ways to help people change. The client was Rosie Walter, one-half of the TA DA team described above. The case is described in her words.

The Road to Physical Fitness Is Rocky

In December 1991, I went to a brief counselor training workshop at Winthrop College. My presenting problem was I felt guilty about exercising in the afternoons when I got home from school where I was a counselor because I had a young son, Cary. At that time Cary was one-and-a-half years old. I also had other children who were there, and I felt like it just really interfered for me to take time out to do my exercising. My goal was to be able to run and to exercise in the afternoon, which was to run five days a week without feeling guilty. [Note that her "without feeling guilty" is stated in the negative—what she does not want.]

To me this is an example of brief counseling because it was a little problem that we worked out in a very short matter of time. John helped me see that there are solutions to every problem that can be fun and innovative and they don't have to be the regular run-of-the-mill way of solving problems. What we decided to do was the following: I got an audiotape of *Rocky* music, and I put it on, and right before I would go out to run I would get Cary to help me and we would put our arms up in the air and jump up and down like Rocky did at the end of the Rocky movie. We would jump up and down while I was warming up to get ready to go outside and run. Then I would go out the front door and my husband Glen and Cary would stand at the window (really it was mostly Cary) and watch me run off and we would both be shooting our arms up into the air. And it worked! It really worked!

After that I really didn't think about the guilt anymore. I was thinking about just having fun with Cary and having him help send me off. And we did this together. What was really funny though, after that, he still, to this day, and he's three, asks to hear the Rocky tape and unfortunately I don't know where it is—I've lost it. Anyway, I need to get another one.

It was really amazing to me how that changed my feelings from feeling guilty to feeling that Cary was helping me and I wasn't leaving him anymore. I was using him to help him help me. Help him send me off or help him see me doing something good for myself. And then I really didn't feel guilty anymore. I didn't hesitate to do any running after that. It was sort of like I got out there and I knew what I had to do and I did it and I got Cary in there and it was time to go and we'd do our little exercise and he would put his hands in the air and I would too and I'd take off. As I ran it was just a very freeing feeling so I know that the changes in myself and my thoughts and feelings came because I freed myself.

What did I like the best about brief counseling? It was very quick and it works if the person is willing for it to work. It worked because I really found something that would work for me. Applying this to my work with kids at school, they've really got to find something that works for them because I've found that my ideas don't work for them, they have to have their own ideas. In summary, I wouldn't change a thing if I had to do it over.

Rosie's experience is an example of how clients are highly resourceful when their creativity is released by doing fun, interesting, and exciting things. Milton Erickson used to knock clients off guard when they held strongly to a belief that wasn't helpful—he threw a rock at them. The rock was make of Styrofoam and light as a feather. Erickson's atrocious pun was, "Don't take things for granite." There is hope for the rest of us when a therapist of Erickson's stature can indulge in this type of play with clients. Better yet, there is hope for clients.

Tapping Clients' Sense of Humor

Humor can be used in several different ways. My preference is for clients to use their sense of humor to break old patterns and create new ones. Therefore, I encourage clients to explore how they can use their own sense of humor to create new ways to move in the directions of their goals. The following case illustrates how one client took it upon herself to design a task that guaranteed that she would achieve her goal. Upon hearing of her unique solution to a specific problem, I requested that Diana write it up. She warned me that, while her problem might appear somewhat frivolous to others, it was in fact a serious problem for her. Diana wrote the following.

My Sally Complex

I had a problem with ordering food. It took me a long time to order and when I did finally order I had all these crazy specifications on how the food was to be prepared. That's why I named my problem, "My Sally Complex" (after the character Sally in the movie, *When Harry Met Sally*). Sally was always being picky about what she ordered in restaurants.

After a counseling class one evening, Dr. Littrell suggested that I try something outrageous to help me overcome my problem and move me toward my goal. Well, I thought it would be pretty appropriate to envision that I was indeed Sally the next time I ordered food in a restaurant. If I did not order food in one minute flat, then I was going to embarrass myself and my dining companion by doing an imitation of Sally doing "the orgasm scene." [The movie includes a hilarious scene where Sally pretends to have an orgasm while seated opposite Harry in a crowded restaurant.] Well, needless to say, I never had to do that and I have never had a problem ordering food since! My friends are also much happier now that I have changed my behavior.

Encouraging clients to do things in fun, interesting, and exciting ways as they move in the direction of their goals is a form of permission-giving.

Clients such as Diana use our permission to expand their options. Approaching difficult tasks in fun, interesting, and exciting ways increases clients' willingness to act. At brief counseling workshops I conduct an informal poll of participants. I ask, "How many of you knew you would have to pay additional federal income taxes by April 15 of last year?" Usually half the hands go up. Then I ask, "How many of you who raised your hands chose to file your returns early?" Usually, no hands remain up. Next, I ask, "How many of you knew far in advance that you would be receiving a federal income tax refund last year?" The other half of the participants raise their hands. "Of those who anticipated a refund, how many of you filed considerably before April 15?" The number of hands remaining up is a large percentage. I ask these questions to show that people tend to do those things that are pleasant and delay those things that are not. When this pattern is applied to counseling tasks, the obvious syllogism is:

- Clients like fun, interesting and exciting tasks.
- Clients avoid serious, uninteresting, and dull tasks.
- Therefore, unless the client is a masochist or a grind-it-out type of person, give pleasant tasks.

The following case illustrates how a task assigned by the counselor was perceived by the counselor, but not the client, as humorous. Despite the counselor's intent, the client perceived the task as an ordeal. Fortunately, the task served to bounce the client into doing something that made much more sense in her world. The case occurred in a group counseling setting and illustrates how resources of the group may be utilized.

Driving and Smoking

Rita had been very successful on her own in becoming a nonsmoker, but she was acutely aware that when she drove long distances in her car she returned to being a smoker. Her job necessitated her commuting. As we examined Rita's attempted solutions to the problem, she discovered that she did not smoke if there were a passenger in her car. The mere presence of another person was a powerful reason for not smoking. We worked together to get a mutually-agreed-upon goal that was stated in the positive. She decided her goal was to be the driver of her smoke-free car.

We began the intervention stage of brief counseling and started brainstorming about how she could complete this final leg of her journey to be smoke-free. Rita was stuck about what to do differently instead of smoking. Finally, I asked her, "Will you agree to do my task if by next week you have not thought of something better that will work for you and be compatible with who you are?" She agreed that she would do as I said unless she thought of something better. As I assigned her the following task her eyes got big and she began to blush: "You are to go to a store that sells life-size, inflatable, plastic, human-looking dolls. You are to buy the doll and install it with a seat belt on the passenger side of your car. When you feel the urge to smoke you are to keep your eyes on the road, but you are to hold a conversation with the doll. On the other hand, when you think of a better idea before next week, you can use that instead of my task as a way of moving in the direction of your goal."

I turned to the group and asked who knew where Rita could find the type of doll I was describing. After considerable nervous laughter, several people said that they knew of a store in town that sold the type of doll I was referring to and that they would be willing to go with her to buy it. I thanked the group members and returned to Rita. Again, I stressed the fact that she certainly had choices and that if she thought of a way of driving a smoke-free car that fit who she was better than my idea then she could use that instead.

Rita did not wait until the next week to contact me. At the end of the meeting Rita approached me and said, "John, I've thought of something that I'm willing to do that is much better than your idea and also much less embarrassing. For several years I've been wanting to learn Spanish. I've decided to buy some Spanish lesson audiotapes and keep them in the car. When I feel the urge to smoke I'm going to practice my Spanish." I congratulated Rita on her wonderful idea.

Humor is in the eyes of the beholder, and my attempt at levity did not fit Rita's definition. I just about destroyed the rapport we had. Laughter must be *with* clients, not at their expense. We need to exhibit care in using humor, just as we do with any other aspect of counseling. Attempting to justify my humor by saying it worked successfully in helping Rita reach her goal is to miss the point—the end does not justify the means, in particular if the means may prove harmful.

Life-enhancing Metaphors

Metaphors are subtle but powerful influences on our actions (Combs & Freedman, 1990). As we listen to our clients, we often find that they employ metaphors that are not life-enhancing. In a similar fashion, we as counselors may have employed metaphors that deny the role of fun, interesting, and exciting ways of viewing problems and solutions. Humor and laughter are methods of lubricating the movement from old ways of thinking to new ones. In brief counseling, fun, interesting, and exciting metaphors are preferred.

The field of counseling has been rather depressing in its choice of metaphors. For example, Bergman (1985) offered the metaphor of counseling as *Fishing for Barracuda.* This metaphor leaves the counselor at the mercy of vicious, flesh-eating predators—definitely not a metaphor that enhances the desire to go to work everyday. In the world of Freudian terminology, Ray Lowe, an Adlerian, once offered at a counseling conference a Far Side-like definition of the superego, id, and ego. He said that it was like a spinster lady locked in perpetual deadly combat with a sex-crazed monkey in a dark cellar, the battle being refereed by a rather nervous bank clerk. This metaphor was improved upon only slightly when the child ego state in Transactional Analysis was given a part called the *little professor.* On the other hand, Perls (1969b) found therapy going to the dogs as Gestalt therapists helped clients with their topdogs and underdogs.

In distinct contrast to serious and problem-oriented metaphors, one way to enhance people's lives is to find metaphors that are full of life—fun, interesting, and exciting. Clients' metaphors for their problematic situations seldom fit the bill. Their metaphors are inevitably dreary, boring, painful, and restricting. They are metaphors that have clients reduced to being acted upon, rather than being actors (deCharms, 1968). Their metaphors stress (often quite literally) how things do not work, rather than how they work, and how hopeless their situations really are, rather than how hopeful.

People who seek our help as clients are not the only ones who choose metaphors of doom and gloom. I have noted that graduate students in counseling, a field devoted to proactive and developmentally enhancing views of life, frequently live their graduate school years with stupefying metaphors. Students who view graduate school as a series of hoops, each one higher than the next, spend their time doing a lot of jumping. In master's degree programs, some counselor trainees see courses in statistics and/or the thesis as the highest hoops; in doctoral programs, the prelim exams, research courses, and dissertation. The hoops get too high for some trainees; they quit, convinced that their inability to jump high enough, or not wanting to continually jump, is either their own fault (e.g., "I'm just not smart enough in math") or the fault of the people requiring them to jump (e.g., "Those *@#*% teachers get sadistic pleasure in making me jump higher and higher"). Unfortunately, the hoop metaphor for graduate school affords three options—serious jump, half-hearted jump, or no jump—and three outcomes—a successful jump, a failed jump, or no jump (a failure). Those students who enjoy jumping and are good at it find the hoop metaphor a useful one. Then there are the students who do not enjoy jumping and/or are not good at it. Jumping hoops becomes a necessary evil to be endured until the degree is granted.

A second popular metaphor that students use to describe graduate school is that of a tunnel. They talk about not seeing the light at the end of it. The tunnel metaphor is oppressive, claustrophobic, and loathsome. The light becomes visible only as graduation nears.

I have solicited alternative metaphors from those students who metaphorically jump hoops and scurry down inky-black tunnels. As they create more positive metaphors to describe their experiences, laughter ensues and smiles break out across their faces. Josh Billings' (Henry Wheeler Shaw) quip describes their new reactions, "Laughter is the sensation of feeling good all over and showing it principally in one place" (Peter, 1977, p. 286). One amusing metaphor for some students is to view graduate school as a golf course, as in the following description:

> Graduate school can be like a golf course. There are certain challenges along the way. Just like some holes on the golf course are more demanding than others, some of the courses and professors are more difficult and odious than others. Part of the success on a golf course comes from natural talent but much of it comes from learning the fundamentals so thoroughly that the game presents lively challenges. Ultimately, the game is a game played against/with/for yourself as a way of learning more about who you are as a person.
>
> On a golf course, in contrast to a dark tunnel, you can look ahead and plan what is coming next. Certain holes are more difficult, so you can take some time to figure out the best approach. While it is true that thunderstorms may approach, you can head to the club house for advice and refreshment. You know what needs to be done (either 9 or 18 holes) and you can plan accordingly. You can seek out those who have played the course before and get their expert opinion about how to play the various holes. You can select the necessary clubs (tools, skills, resources) for the level of difficulty inherent in each hole. Finally, just as in golf, perfection doesn't exist. Nobody has ever shot a hole-in-one on every hole; only a small number of play-

ers ever shot a hole-in-one in a lifetime of play. Doing one's best, given the difficulty of the course and the level of one's abilities, is the thing that matters.

Our clients often hold onto metaphors that present them as few options as do the students' metaphors of hoops and tunnels. It is not our responsibility to provide clients with more life-enhancing metaphors but we can explore, challenge, help modify, and encourage the use of new metaphors that will free them from ones that bog them down instead of empowering them.

Using Humor

Brief counseling can be conducted in ways that are fun for both the counselor and the client. If you are inclined to believe that counseling must be a very serious undertaking, I would insist upon seeing you in person, throw Erickson's Styrofoam rock at you, and say, "Don't take things for granite." Brief counseling heartily endorses the role of humor and laughter within counseling. A modified Walters' equation applied to brief counseling reads:

$$A(IBC)ITL = P$$
Anything, including brief counseling, if taken lightly = PLAY

This new equation ties how we approach brief counseling to how we approach life. Plato wrote, "What then, is the right way of living? Life must be lived as play." When we use our own sense of humor and elicit that of our clients, changes will occur more quickly—and we and our clients will have a more interesting time.

Do Something Different

1. By definition, spontaneous acts cannot be prescribed. Telling a depressed person to cheer up is not likely to be effective. However, the prescription to do something different in a fun, interesting, or exciting way differs, since it does not involve prescribing an internal state. Rather, this prescription is for new behavior, the creation of new ways of doing and being. In the process of doing something different, clients discover that the internal states change so as to match the exterior one. During your next counseling session, do something different

in a fun, interesting, or exciting way so that you open up more choices for yourself.

2. Standing ovations are for all of us—students, teachers, clients, counselors, and other colleagues. Organize standing ovations for those who have never received them. Do not wait until they retire.

3. Challenge your clients to find fascinating ways of moving toward their goals. Invite them to have a fun, interesting, and exciting time as they do. Model the behavior you are asking for.

●
●
●
●
●
●
●
●
●

CHAPTER 10

Scaling Problems to Size

CLIENT: *Am I moving in the direction of my goal?*

Scales are used to measure things. They assist us in knowing the relationship of one thing to another. In the field of counseling, scales have been the exclusive domain of test makers, who have determined the scales' content and psychometric properties. Until recently, clients and counselors did not co-create scales to fit clients' frames of reference. This is changing. We now have counselors and clients working together to construct scales that are tailored to clients' experiences (Berg & de Shazer, 1993; de Shazer, 1994). The following case provides several examples of how scaling techniques prove useful in counseling.

A Sure Cure

Kevin and I met for a single session about a problem that was bothering him. He began by telling me that several weeks earlier he had quit a job, but he was still saying goodbye to the people in that work setting. Kevin had also begun a new job. He expressed an interest in meeting more new people at his new job and in feeling more contact with them. He stated that he left his new job in the late afternoons feeling quite tense and sometimes with the beginnings of a headache. His tenseness lasted all the way home and into the evening.

As I listened to Kevin, I had few clues about what "quite tense" meant for him. I decided to employ a scaling technique as a useful way to talk about what Kevin wanted and how he would know when he arrived (Berg & de Shazer, 1993). I modeled our scale after those used by therapists at the Milwaukee Brief Family Therapy Center (Berg & Miller, 1992; de Shazer, 1994). Together, Kevin and I constructed a "tenseness" scale for his behaviors that produced the tension headaches. Ten on the scale was "totally debilitating," while 0 was a "couch potato with no worries." Typically, I help clients label the end points of the scale with exaggerated phrases. The extreme end points tend to normalize the behaviors of the client. They also increase the number of options between the polar extremes.

Kevin said that occasionally he went home doing an 8 on the tension scale. At these times he experienced a tension headache. As I typically do when clients provide verbal descriptions that are vague, I had him demonstrate for me how he did his tension. What exactly did he look like and sound like when he arrived home? O'Hanlon and Wilk (1987) refer to this as obtaining a video description; they stress how useful specific details can be for the counselor and the client. Kevin proceeded to wrinkle his brow and to hunch his shoulders so that they headed toward his ears. We both laughingly agreed that he could produce an excellent tension headache doing what he was doing.

I employed a qualitative scale to add a fun way to assess his expertise in producing tension. The proficiency of karate practitioners can be recognized by the color of their belts; belts range from white to black. I asked Kevin to tell me the color of his belt when he was producing an 8 on the tension scale. Kevin believed at those times he wore a karate black belt. Again he laughed and told me that he was really quite good at being tense on some days. We agreed that a black belt indicated that he had considerable expertise in producing headaches.

Returning to the tension scale, we explored where Kevin currently was and where he wanted to be. Kevin gave himself an 8 when he returned home doing a tension headache. On a typical day he returned home doing a 5 or 6. His goal was to do a 2. I had Kevin show me how relaxed he would be if he were doing a 2 on the scale. Although Kevin noticeably relaxed on his own, I prompted him to do so even more as he sat in front of me. I had him check his shoulders for tension and to relax any tension that he was doing. I asked him what else he would be doing if he were more relaxed. Kevin replied that he would loosen his tie and uncross his legs. Since we were both wearing ties, I began to loosen my tie as a way of showing him what he could do. We both uncrossed our legs. Was he wearing a smile when he was more relaxed? Would he be willing right now to smile a genuine 2 smile? He smiled and reported that he felt more like a 2 on his tension scale.

Usefulness of Scaling

The scaling technique is useful to the counselor and client in numerous ways. First, scales aid in clarifying clients' vague complaints. When Kevin first spoke of being tense, I had little understanding of what that meant for him. The use of the scale began to clarify how at different times he had varying degrees of tenseness. My directive to show me what the various tension states looked and sounded like resulted in more concrete and specific information and grounded the scale in rather distinct physiological states. To the extent that a client's particular scale allows, I find that having the client demonstrate right there in the session the various physiological states provides both of us with valuable information.

The use of a scale also pointed Kevin in the direction of a goal. Implied in the scale is a place where Kevin would like to be. In Kevin's case, he identified 2 as a desirable place. Again, having him demonstrate what this goal would look and sound like anchored and made more explicit where Kevin eventually wanted to be. The scale helped in transforming Kevin's initial negatively stated goal ("I don't want to be tense") into a positive statement of what he wanted ("I want to be a 2 on the scale"). Anchoring the 2 to a physiological state provided a tangible goal toward which to aim.

Third, to the extent that Kevin's scale indicated a goal he wanted to reach, the numbers along the way from an 8 to a 2 supplied steps that served as subgoals along the way to his final goal. As Kevin moved in the direction of his overall goal, he would also be continuing to reach mini-goals along the way.

When clients initially conceptualize their options in "either/or" terms or in "black/white" ways, they miss opportunities to see small steps as progress. The technique of scaling allows them to conceptualize a range of possible options (Walter & Peller, 1992). While Kevin's thinking was neither "either/or" nor "black/white," the scales did appear to open up a broader range of possibilities for him.

Another benefit of scaling is seen in how it served to motivate and encourage Kevin (Berg & de Shazer, 1993). The concreteness of the scale served to translate vague abstract goals into more immediate and meaningful ones. This translation inspired Kevin to believe that what he was seeking was more possible to achieve than he had previously believed.

Finally, the scaling technique allowed the two of us to assess Kevin's progress toward his goal. The scale was Kevin's, in that he had labeled the points on the scale, and he knew both cognitively and physiologically what the numbers stood for. The numbers became a shorthand for discussing his progress toward his goal.

A Sure Cure Continued . . .

Kevin and I agreed that his goal was to average 2 on his tension scale in his work setting, driving home, and at home immediately following work. Next we proceeded to find ways for Kevin to reach this goal. Steve de Shazer and Insoo Kim Berg typically emphasize taking small steps toward the goal, e.g., "So, now you are at 6. How will you know when you have reached 5½?" Since Kevin had already demonstrated 2 in our session, we proceeded as though he could make large changes. Several times in telling about his problem situation, Kevin had mentioned wanting to be more sure of himself in his new job and around his new colleagues. I asked him to tell me about a time when he had been in a new group and had been more sure of himself. Kevin recalled a recent gathering where, though he had not previously known the people, he had introduced himself and felt relatively sure of himself.

In the course of our working together, Kevin used the word "sure" several times, and I had pointedly let him know that I had heard the word. In brief counseling the use of the client's language, rather than the counselor's language, is one way to speed up the process of change. Clients should not have to learn a new vocabulary—they already have one with which they are familiar, their own. In my mind the word "sure" conjured up the image of the deodorant Sure. I shared with Kevin that because he wanted to be more sure of himself, and therefore more relaxed, I could imagine that he might remind himself of this goal by having a can of Sure deodorant on his desk at work, but out of other people's sight. Kevin and I laughed about how the Sure would help him remember to be more "sure" of himself, as he had been in the previous group situation with other new people. When I asked if the Sure reminder would help him access that more desired state, he said, "Sure."

Less than two weeks from the time of our single-session counseling, I called Kevin and asked him how he was moving in the direction of his goal. He said that following our session he had purchased a can of Sure deodorant. The first day back at work following our session, he placed the can of Sure in his office so that he could see it but the people he worked with could not. Kevin reported that he had felt good that day and had joked around at work. He had been averaging a 3 to 4 on the tension scale. I asked Kevin if he were more "sure" of himself in his new job, and he answered, "I sure am."

While he had alluded to his previous job and saying goodbye to his former colleagues, we had not spent time in our only session addressing this issue. However, when I talked to Kevin about his new job, he added that our mentioning the old job in our session had started him thinking about what to do about that situation. He said, "I remembered something about rituals being important to people so I came up with the following: I purchased a gift for the people at my former job—something they will remember me by. It's a calendar with quotes that have helped me." I congratulated Kevin on his progress toward his goal and said I too was "sure" he was moving in the right direction.

Qualitative Scaling

Quantitative scaling is a relatively easy technique to employ. As illustrated in the case of Kevin, scaling functions in various ways that are compatible with helping clients identify and move in the direction of their goals. While many clients may find quantitative scaling techniques fit their ways of thinking, others either do not think numerically or have an aversion to applying numbers to their lives. The latter find numbers cold and dehumanizing, as do a few counselors I know.

While quantitative scaling was compatible with Kevin's way of thinking, I had also employed a scaling technique that did not use numbers—the karate colored-belt scale, a qualitative scale. Clients are often intrigued by the colored belts used in karate. I even had a client tell me that his belt in his self-defeating behavior was not just black, it was ebony. Here are four other possible qualitative scales that might be used with clients' concerns:

1. **Solar System Scaling** is for a shy person who wants to warm up to people. A planet scale from Mercury to Pluto (i.e., Mercury, Venus, Earth, Mars, Jupiter, Saturn, Uranus, Neptune, and Pluto) is one way of presenting emotional warmth. Earth is an optimal temperature for being with other people. Mercury and Venus are too emotionally hot and people get burned. Pluto is so distant that it is perceived of as frigid cold and the ultimate in being remote. Jupiter is at least visible but too icy.

   Draw or obtain an illustration of the solar system and have clients indicate what planet they are currently on. Do they want to head toward Earth? If clients are on distant planets, what planets are their next steps? Suggest clients streak toward Earth in a rocket. (Note that a rocket is a metaphor for rapid change.)

Linear thinkers may prefer their solar system illustrations to show the sun and planets in a straight line. Non-linear thinkers may prefer a more three-dimensional illustration. Children of all ages find the solar system fascinating.

2. **Road Map Scaling** is a handy terrain guide for a client with low self-esteem. Draw a map and have clients identify where they once were, where they are now, and where they want to be. Treat the distances visually, rather than in units. Have clients choose their mode of transportation and identify the first stop on their way to their destination. What will clients notice about themselves at the first stop that is different from where they are now?

3. **Color Scaling** is applicable for clients who have suffered loss. What color are they feeling inside? What is the progression of colors the clients will feel as they move toward the point of feeling they have dealt with the loss? What would be helpful to begin moving to the next color? How would they know they are experiencing a new color? How soon will the colors of their clothes begin to reflect the changes they are experiencing?

4. **Car Talk Scaling** fits clients who happen to be boys (ages 5 to 100). Are they moving through life in a Yugo or a Jaguar? How fast do they want to move? Are their tanks filled with regular or premium? Are their tanks empty or full? Are we talking about a tune-up or a major overhaul?

Applications of Scaling

As with any tool that counselors use, the client is always more important than the technique. Scaling must be done with sensitivity to how well it works for the client. If the scaling technique is not working, do what brief counselors would suggest—*do something different.*

Stating the scaling in positive terms offers several advantages. In retrospect, I wish in my work with Kevin I had not labeled it a tension scale, because when Kevin thinks about the scale he will first have to access a tense state. More effective would have been a relaxing scale that would have had Kevin access a more relaxing state. In addition, a relaxing scale would also change the word "tension," a static and inflexible concept, into the word "relaxing," a more process and flexible concept.

Some clients tend to aim for perfection. For instance, if Kevin had wanted to be a 0 (perfect) on the tension scale, I would have negotiated with him, since I find that a goal of being perfect is impossible to achieve and sets clients up for defeat. An easy negotiating stance is:

> I'm not comfortable with helping you be perfect because I prefer to help clients be more like Mary Poppins, that is, practically perfect. Would you settle for a goal of 2 on the scale?

Both quantitative (numerical) and qualitative (non-numerical) scales assist clients to talk a common language with the counselor, to clarify their goals, and to see the various steps along the way toward their goals. They motivate clients in an interesting manner and provide a means of assessing movement toward a goal. The proposed qualitative scaling technique adds greater flexibility by providing an alternative or supplement to numerical scaling.

Do Something Different

1. As you have read chapters in this book, hopefully you found yourself wanting to increase your proficiency in doing brief counseling. Practice scaling the same experience both quantitatively and qualitatively.

   Quantitative Scaling. On a scale from 0 to 10 where 0 = No Proficiency and 10 = Master Brief Counselor, at what number would you currently place yourself? What is the number you would like to be at in (choose a time frame of months or years)? Once you have a number and a time frame, specify what would you be doing differently with clients than what you are doing now. What would an observer see and hear you doing that you are not currently doing?

   Qualitative Scaling. Follow the directions for quantitative scaling above but this time choose a non-numerical framework. Possible qualitative images are:

   - Songs
   - Species of animal (e.g., types of dogs, cats)
   - Fruits
   - Mythical characters
   - Type of book (e.g., mystery, romance novel, summer reading)

- Weather
- Famous Americans

2. Take a few minutes with your next client to use a scaling technique. Ask the client to identify a word or phrase to sum up one aspect of her life. If it is stated in the negative, ask what the positive phrase would be. Propose a scale from 1 to 10 and have the client identify the end points. Have her pick a number where she currently is. Where does she reasonably want to be? What would be her first step toward getting there? If the scale is helpful to the client, continue to use it so as to assess her progress in the direction of the goal. On the other hand, check if qualitative scaling with images would work better for your client. If so, use that approach.

CHAPTER 11

Viewing Feelings in Perspective

CLIENT: *All we talked about were my feelings—ad nauseum.*

We in the counseling profession have aptitude in the social domain (Gardner, 1983; Holland, 1985). We pride ourselves on our skills in relating to people and being sensitive to their feelings. In graduate classes and workshops, we expand our feeling vocabularies by mastering the nuances of affective expressions. Over time we begin to believe that feelings are the royal road to therapeutic success. We wonder how anyone could not endorse the following postulates and respective corollaries about feelings:

I. Experience (get in touch with) your real feelings—especially your deepest ones.
   A. There are feelings and there are real feelings.
   B. Real feelings are deep, not surface.
   C. Real feelings are sometimes buried inside and wait to be expressed (see the "Phantom of the Oprah" cartoon).
II. Express your feelings.
   A. You need a good feeling vocabulary.
   B. Let others know your feelings.
   C. It is harmful to bury your feelings and not express them.

These postulates and respective corollaries are often held so strongly that we begin to treat them as "shoulds." However, when Milton Erickson worked

with clients who expressed strongly-held beliefs that might be working against them, Erickson would challenge his clients by saying, "Don't be so sure." In a similar manner, this chapter has as its guiding principle the phrase "don't be so sure" as a antidote to an overemphasis on feelings at the expense of focusing on clients' thoughts, behaviors, and the meanings they construct.

Benjamin (1974) once addressed the role of questions in counseling. He concluded by saying, "I meant to dethrone it [The Question] but not to drive it out of the palace" (p. 90). In a similar fashion, my intent in this chapter is not to deny, minimize, or bury feelings (some would contend that people already do too much of the latter) but to provide a perspective in which feelings are viewed as an integral, but not dominant, part of counseling. To the extent we as counselors can increase our awareness of the benefits and drawbacks of feelings, we have the choice of not imposing feeling-language requirements on clients whose own language is quite rich, certainly not deprived or lacking.

Feelings in Perspective

The following two cases illustrate ideas about how feelings are understood and employed in brief counseling. Then we will clarify the roles and uses of feelings within a counseling context by focusing on three themes: (1) acknowledging and validating clients' feelings, (2) using clients' feeling vocabularies, and (3) focusing on creating new contexts in which clients have control.

Socially Acceptable Revenge

Marva, an elementary school counselor, was, in her own words, "angry" and "upset." According to Marva, her school principal made her so upset that she dreaded going to work. Despite the fact that only seven weeks remained in the school year and that Marva was transferring to a new school next year, she felt very stuck in her feelings toward the principal. Marva even attributed a malicious intent to the principal, whom she saw as somehow actively working to make her life miserable.

As we talked, Marva formulated her goal as trying to forget the principal. As we worked to have the goal meet the criteria of well-formed goals as defined in Chapter 7, Marva remembered that the students were her real reason for being a counselor. She realized that she had lost track of them because she was so upset with the principal. Marva's revised goal was to increase her focus on the students she worked with each day.

Together Marva and I explored avenues for reaching her goal; she identified several that made sense to her and that she was willing to follow. Marva said that she was really pleased with focusing on the students again, but she still felt angry and upset with the principal. Acknowledging that these feelings would continue to make work unpleasant and stand in the way of reaching her goal with students, we focused on how to deal with them. Marva felt it was too risky to express her feelings to the principal in a direct fashion—she feared retaliation. Based on her report, I believe she well may have been right. We explored assertiveness as a way to create a win-win situation, but Marva decided against it. She didn't want to waste her time having to work it out, especially since she was leaving the school soon and didn't consider the principal worth her time.

Occasionally, I tell stories about other clients' solutions in the hopes of seeding new possibilities that might blossom into new options for my current clients. I chose to tell Marva about an elementary school teacher I knew who had felt very upset with another teacher, but for safety reasons had chosen not to tell the other person in a direct fashion. The teacher in my story had taken a classroom puppet and taped a picture of the other teacher's face to the puppet. When the teacher got angry with the other teacher, she would go to the locked file where she kept the puppet and take it out. She would then punch it, pinch it, pound it, and stick pins into it like a voodoo doll.

As I told Marva the voodoo doll story, she began to smile and laugh and said that this solution felt good. Her major goal was to focus on the students, but she also wanted an effective method for dealing with her angry and vengeful feelings. Taking them out on the puppet served her purpose of acknowledging her feelings while not dwelling on them.

I employed a variation on "Socially Acceptable Revenge" in working with a college professor. Not having a drawerful of puppets like the elementary school counselor, the professor modified the puppet motif to fit her circumstances.

Voodoo Cow

Dr. Freedmeyer, a college professor, told me of her dissatisfaction, irritation, and total exasperation with an administrator with whom she was forced to work. I told her the story about the voodoo puppet. Dr. Freedmeyer immediately replied, "Actually, I think of this administrator as a cow. I'm going to start looking for a cloth cow that I can keep in my office for those times when I'm really upset." I did a follow-up to our talk by sending Dr. Freedmeyer a postcard of a field of cows along with a message of support about her overall goal—distancing herself psychologically from the administrator.

Use Clients' Feeling Vocabularies

"Socially Acceptable Revenge" and "Voodoo Cow" demonstrate various functions that feelings play in brief counseling. Marva was well acquainted with teaching about feelings to students in her classroom guidance activities, but when it came to expressing her own feelings about the situation in which she found herself she narrowed her vocabulary to words like "disgusted" and "angry." Marva was typical of many clients who stick with basic feeling words to express themselves.

As counselors we can spend our time teaching clients an expanded feeling vocabulary. However, many clients find it difficult or undesirable to engage in language lessons, whether French or feelings. It takes considerable time and effort to learn the vocabulary, let alone practice and eventually acquire proficiency in its use. While some people have the ability to learn new languages relatively quickly, others take a lifetime or never learn.

In brief counseling it is considered a better use of counseling time to use clients' vocabularies rather than become feeling-language teachers. Clients' vocabularies are deemed sufficiently large to cope with situations. Sensitivity is needed on counselors' parts to recognize that feelings are often implied rather than directly stated. For example, a male client may, with "no" facial emotion and "flat" affect, say, "Every day my boss gives me twice the amount of work he knows I can get done." Some schools of counseling would assume that the client is not dealing with his feelings. Attempts would be made to have the client get "in touch" with his anger and possible other emotions (e.g., irritation, rage, deep sadness). His inability or unwillingness to engage in this search would indicate that the client was resisting getting to the real issues.

In brief counseling the man's statement might be responded to in one of the following possible, but certainly not exhaustive, ways:

- "Every day the boss heaps it on you. You want to shove it up his—."

  [The counselor responds with a paraphrase followed by a collo-quial expression that contains no feeling words but does indicate an action motivated by anger. The use here of "adult" language by the counselor assumes that the client would not be offended.]

- "God, if I had a boss who did that to me, I would really be pissed."

  [The counselor engages in a self-disclosure to model a feeling state not found on most feeling-word lists.]

- "How do you stand it? How do you stop yourself from telling the guy how you feel about the situation?"

  ["How" questions get at the man's thoughts and actions. The second question simply assumes that there are feelings associated with the situation. The issue is not to coerce the man to acknowledge or own his feelings. The issue is that feelings are but one aspect of who people are; not everyone "feels" comfortable or has the desire to talk about them.]

The client with "no" facial emotion and "flat" affect is not coached to learn a new vocabulary in order to express his innermost feelings. His statement is considered quite sufficient because it is his code for a state that he is experiencing. To correct him by implying that his vocabulary is not sufficiently large is to play the role of a feeling-language teacher. Brief counselors simply assume that the clients' words are meaningful terms for them and thus avoid imposing a new vocabulary.

Acknowledge and Validate Clients' Feelings

In "Socially Acceptable Revenge," I attempted to acknowledge and validate Marva's feelings. Since feelings are an integral part of Marva's identity, to acknowledge and validate her feelings is to acknowledge some of who she is. On the other hand, I did not dwell on Marva's feelings but simply let her know that I had heard them. Sometimes I will use my own words as a way of checking if I have understood accurately. Placing feeling words in the context of a paraphrase allows them to be integrated, rather than treated as having an existence independent of the rest of the person and context. In the following case I worked with Elizabeth, a woman in her late fifties. Validating her feelings was key to the therapeutic process.

To Be or To Do

Elizabeth was contemplating retirement. There was so much she wanted to do when she retired and she sensed that time was running out. At the same time, she still loved her job. The pull in both directions was confusing. Twice as we talked, Elizabeth's eyes began to tear. The second time followed my self-disclosure about a mid-life crisis. I had talked about how Levinson's *Seasons of a Man's Life* had clarified my increased awareness of my own mortality and subsequent discomfort and how the book provided me more choices. I said to Elizabeth, "As I look at you, I see sadness."

Elizabeth replied, "I'm just remembering as we talked about my retirement and my feeling that time is running out that I'm still grieving my mother's death, which was just five months ago."

I asked her what the meaning of that was for her in this context and she said, "I need to give myself more time and not rush into making a decision about retirement. What I need to do is just be in my grief when I need to."

When I asked Elizabeth if she knew how to just *be,* she said that she did. She said she often went to a peaceful place where she found it comforting to grieve and remember her mother. I asked her what more we had to do and she answered, "Nothing." Our session had lasted 20 minutes.

A reader of this manuscript commented that he would have thought the counseling had just begun at the end of the 20 minutes, rather than ending as the client and I had. His comment makes salient the differences between brief counseling and other forms of counseling. The acknowledgment and validation of feelings are important for both, but in brief counseling feelings are not explored independent of clients' issues. Elizabeth had not requested counseling to assist her in grieving her mother's death. In fact, Elizabeth already had an effective way of grieving. The counseling was brief in that it allowed Elizabeth to remember to take time for grieving and not race into making changes before she was ready. Elizabeth said she was done—I believed her. Subsequent correspondence with Elizabeth confirmed my trust in her was well founded. She wrote me the following:

> You might like to know that you were on target to believe me. Amazing as it may seem to "non-believers," that brief, focused session worked. I simply needed to make the connection between my sense of urgency to retire and my mother's recent death—a heightened

sense of my own mortality and a fevered sense of not much time left. This connected awareness and solution—to just be with my grief when it comes—has put me where I needed to be. Now, I go on as before, enjoying my life, but grieving as needed. It's amazing to me how much joy has returned.

Acknowledging and validating feelings are powerful therapeutic tools. They often free clients so that they can deal with the changes that would be useful in their lives. My acknowledging and validating Elizabeth's feelings freed her to think in new ways—"to make the connection between my sense of urgency to retire and my mother's recent death." Sometimes acknowledgment and validation of clients' feelings are sufficient as an intervention; in these situations, counseling may be very brief.

Focus on What Can Be Controlled

A parallel to the brief counseling approach to feelings is found in the three themes of Morita Therapy (Reynolds, 1995). Its purposes are stated in plain language for clients: "to accept your feelings, know your purpose, and do what needs doing" (Reynolds, 1984, p. 26). As in Morita Therapy, feelings in brief counseling are accepted for what they are, but the primary work of counseling is on setting goals ("know your purpose") and doing new things to reach goals ("do what needs to be done").

Brief counselors understand feelings as learned physiological responses to complex social situations. Often, clients perceive they have little control over their feelings. Rather than attempting to convince clients otherwise, brief counselors assist clients in doing things they perceive they have control over—their behaviors and their thoughts.

People in Alcoholics Anonymous recite the Serenity Prayer—"Grant me the strength to change the things I can change, the strength to accept the things I cannot change, and the wisdom to know the difference." In AA, the things that cannot be changed are feelings and thoughts; only behavior is considered something the client has control over. Brief counselors would accept that feelings cannot be changed in a direct fashion, but they would contend that changing behaviors and/or thoughts will result in changing feelings. Assisting clients to have new experiences (both behaviors and thoughts) is a way of creating new context with new meaning. Heading directly toward changes in behavior and thoughts is faster than attempting to change feelings.

For instance, Marva did not believe that she could easily change her feelings or thoughts about her principal. She clearly held the opinion that the principal was making her feel bad despite her awareness that from a

Rational Emotive Therapy framework this thought was clearly irrational. While the "irrationality" of the causation was obvious, Marva was still angry. Focusing on changing her behavior allowed her to change her feelings.

Sinetar (1987) wrote a book entitled, *Do What You Love, the Money Will Follow*. The conceptualization of feelings in brief counseling follows the same format: focus on changing behaviors and thoughts, the feelings will follow. More broadly stated, if I as the counselor can assist my clients in changing what they see and hear, both internally and externally, then their feelings will change in response to the "new" environments in which they find themselves. This conceptualization is exemplified in the case that follows.

Deadly Hallucinations

Jan's fear of heights was not incapacitating, but she found it hampered her enjoyment of situations with others. Even being near a window in a tall building set her on edge. We changed her negative self-talk and provided her with new resources, such as a hefty imaginary rope around her waist to keep her from falling. After we had worked to help her add more positive resources to overcome the fear situation, we were set to check their effectiveness. Curtiss Hall at Iowa State University is an old three-story building. Its rotunda provides a view from the third floor all the way to the basement. A four-foot high, sturdy railing provides safety for people on each floor.

Prior to beginning our work, Jan could only walk within several feet of the railing before her heart would begin pounding. With her new resources Jan approached the railing. She rested her arms on it and looked down. Suddenly she exclaimed, "There are people walking down there on the basement-level floor!" This did not strike me as astonishing, since there were often people walking about the basement level. I inquired about why she had become so excited. She said, "In the past when I've looked down to the basement level, I've always seen my own body splattered there."

Jan's image of herself splattered on the basement floor triggered a powerful feeling response. In brief counseling we do not attempt to directly modify a powerful emotional response; rather, we look to transform the old context so that new and more acceptable feelings are triggered. When Jan's perception of new resources provided a context in which she believed she had more control, her response to a previous fear-inducing context was radically changed. While Jan's image of herself had evoked a powerful emotional response, thoughts can have the same effect. Years ago, while working at a psychiatric hospital, I witnessed a rather unusual illustration of this idea.

When I was working at the Children's Psychiatric Hospital at the University of Michigan, there was on the floor where I worked a seven-year-old boy who had been diagnosed as borderline schizophrenic. Tommy was getting more and more terrified as his birthday approached. The staff worked with him to let him know that birthdays were fun times, not times to be scared. Despite their efforts at reassurance, Tommy remained unconvinced.

Finally, one staff member figured it out. Tommy was scared to death because in Tommy's literal world he had heard and had believed one of the staff members who had told him, "Tommy, it won't be long before you're eight." Tommy had not heard "eight"; he had heard "ate." Naturally enough, Tommy wanted nothing of that fate, regardless of how excited everyone else was and however much they tried to convince him that it was good.

Tommy's feelings were a logical extension of his thoughts. His belief that he would be eaten led to his terror. Our clients hold belief systems and thoughts that lead directly to emotional states. While the emotions can be acknowledged and validated, which will result in increased rapport, the work of counseling proceeds by understanding and changing the behaviors and thoughts that trigger the undesired emotions.

Summary

The final case in this chapter pulls together the key elements in a brief counseling approach to feelings: (1) the use of the client's feeling vocabulary, (2) the acknowledgment and validation of the client's feelings, and (3) a focus on what the client can control. In this case, the client, Gloria, learned new ways to deal with painful feelings.

Heart of the Matter

Gloria, a woman in her late twenties, had suffered a minor heart attack 11 months earlier. In recent weeks she had been experiencing several problems—worry about another heart attack, shortness of breath, trouble sleeping, withdrawal from friends, and inability to concentrate on her work at the office. Gloria told me that these problems were combining to make her life miserable. I acknowledged and validated her feelings using her own words—"worried," "miserable," and "scared."

She had been to her physician. After a thorough exam the physician informed her that she was highly anxious but that her heart was doing fine.

The physician had given her a verbal prescription—relax more. Gloria had tried to follow the doctor's orders. Paradoxically, the more she drove herself to relax, the less relaxed she felt. Her attempted solution, forcing relaxation, became the problem. I speculated that if Gloria's goal continued to be reaching a relaxed state, it would be necessary for Gloria to do something different from her attempted solution of forcing relaxation.

I had attended a seminar by Evan Imber-Black in which she had demonstrated the powerful impact of ritual, and I had read her *Rituals for Our Times* (Imber-Black & Roberts, 1992). I was particularly impressed by how her clients were able to make smoother transitions when they employed rituals. Deciding to use ritual as a means of helping Gloria reach her goal, I asked her if she had already started making plans to celebrate the first anniversary of her heart attack. She looked puzzled and answered that she hadn't.

I asked if she celebrated her birthday each year. She said yes. I asked if she celebrated Christmas and Thanksgiving. Again, yes. I then told her that one way to reach her goal of relaxing more was to celebrate the anniversary of her heart attack. She looked intrigued.

I asked numerous questions: Who would be on her celebration list? What would she serve her guests? A cake with a single candle? How would she make it a relaxing and enjoyable time surrounded by people she loved and cared about and who loved and cared about her? Would she choose to tell her guests the true purpose of the party or would she choose to celebrate secretly?

As Gloria answered my questions she became fascinated with her heart attack anniversary. Having others around on that day made good sense to her. Giving, celebrating, and having fun on the anniversary made infinitely more sense than sitting home by herself and being worried sick about the possibility of another heart attack. Gloria agreed to carry out the arrangements we made for her heart attack celebration/remembrance.

In a short follow-up a week after the heart attack anniversary, Gloria told me that the party had been a wonderful success. She had served angel food cake and no-fat sherbet (not ice cream). While she and her friends ate, they shared stories about her experience of a year ago. Gloria also reported that since we had met that one time, she had been sleeping much more soundly, she was much more relaxed, and she was able to concentrate at work. We briefly discussed how she could celebrate each year if that continued to be a useful celebration/remembrance ritual for her.

In my work with Gloria I did three things. I acknowledged and validated her feelings, used her feeling vocabulary, and focused on creating a new context in which Gloria had control. Her "new" feelings were considerably more useful than her previous responses. The new ritual created a new context that helped her deal with her feelings in a way that was under her control.

Freud believed that dreams were the royal road to the unconscious. More recently, acknowledgment and expression of feelings have been championed as the royal road to therapeutic success. Brief counselors would argue that feelings are an integral aspect of who humans are, but that feelings are only one aspect, not the most important aspect. Those of us who practice brief counseling do not postulate deep and buried feelings that harm people if they are not expressed; rather, we view feelings as yet another expression of what it means to be human in specific contexts. Creating new contexts is an important therapeutic act. Acknowledging and validating clients' feelings are also therapeutic acts. Insisting that clients explore their feelings, and dwelling on them when they do, is to become a feeling-language teacher; that is a role brief counselors avoid.

Do Something Different

1. To what extent do you impose feeling-language restrictions on clients? As one gauge of this, answer the following questions:

   - How sorry do you feel for people who have less feeling-language proficiency than you do?
   - What names do you have for clients who do not seem to be as in touch with their feelings as you would like them to be?
   - How much more do you value feeling-oriented clients than those who are not?

2. Think of a counseling situation in which the client had a small feeling vocabulary. What did you do to "help" the client increase his/her vocabulary?

3. Many clients express feelings in metaphorical or implied ways. For example, in neither of the following phrases is there a feeling word—"I'm really down," or "I feel that nobody listens to me." Listen for clients' feelings expressed metaphorically or in implied ways. Resist the urge to be a feelings-language teacher. Use the client's own language.

CHAPTER 12

Staying on Track

CLIENT: *We talked about my past, my goals, relationships, etc. It was a hodge-podge, a multiplicity, but my counselor kept telling me it was all relevant.*

If counselors and clients have agreed upon a brief counseling framework, it is usually advantageous to stick with it. Occasionally, we work with clients who, despite our framework agreement, push our formerly learned theoretical buttons. Clients' words and phrases trigger in us responses in line with the therapeutic theories on which we were nurtured. Quite often we are not consciously aware until after the fact that this has happened. We only become aware when we recognize that we have spent the last 15 minutes of the session (or even the last several sessions) talking about a client's past and/or relationships in excruciating detail. We remain perplexed about how it all relates to the client's goal.

Switching to a brief counseling framework entails learning how to be effective, consistent, and comfortable with a new set of assumptions as well as a new way of doing counseling. As with any recently acquired learning, an older pattern may interfere with a newer pattern because the older pattern quietly occurs without our awareness, causing us to be derailed from the brief counseling track.

The focus in this chapter is how and when prior learned theories may take us off on side tracks or derail us from helping our clients reach their goals. Knowing how and when we are susceptible to derailing helps us remain alert. A case I supervised illustrates how my supervisee, Chico, was derailed to a formerly learned psychodynamic framework by his client's passing reference to her mother.

Derailed and Detained

Chico had been working with Maria, a client with an 11-month-old child. Chico and Maria were setting some goals related to her work. Without even being aware of what had happened, Chico responded to a comment Maria made about her mother and together Chico and Maria meandered off in the direction of exploring in detail Maria's relationship with her mother. The dialogue was as follows:

MARIA: I get so tired and yet I want to do it all. We recently adopted an 11-month-old girl and we love her so much. She's brought new happiness into our lives. At the same time I feel I'm not carrying my own weight at work. You know, at times I'm just like my mother.

CHICO: Just like your mother?
[Minimal encourager; focus on other person—the mother]

MARIA: Yes, and that is really scary because I see how she led her life of always wanting to sacrifice for us as kids and she never had a life for herself. I'm afraid I'm becoming just like her.

CHICO: Being like her is scary.
[Reflection of feeling; focus on client]

MARIA: Damn right. I've struggled most of my adult life and to think of ending up like her is a very scary thought.

As Chico and I listened to the tape of his counseling session, we discussed how just hearing the word "mother" had pushed his psychodynamic button. The familiar focus on the past mother/daughter relationship practically guaranteed that he and Maria would be exploring for quite some time the intricacies of how Maria and her mother got along, what Maria learned from her mother, and how this learning influenced Maria's current choices.

As we reviewed the tape, it was obvious to both of us that Chico and Maria's ensuing discussion had explored many interesting facts and resulted in some interesting insights. However, the overall effect had been to sidetrack joint movement toward work-related goals and some eventual solutions to Maria's concerns. In fact, the discussion about Maria's relationship with her mother resulted only in additional counseling time.

In our supervision session, Chico and I explored alternative methods for handling material that might be potentially useful without getting derailed or temporarily shunted onto a different conceptual track. We explored three choices we have as counselors. The first is to simply ignore what the client has just said and stay on the brief counseling track. A second is to temporarily take a side track with the intent of soon returning to the brief counseling track. A third choice is for the counselor to deliberately change theoretical tracks with the awareness that a brief counseling track is not the most appropriate one. The remainder of this chapter will provide rationale, methods, and examples of these choices along with the strategies and skills involved in implementing each.

Theoretically Deaf

When should we deliberately not respond to clients' words and phrases? Several situations seem reasonable. First, we can choose not to respond when we suspect that our clients are telling us things that they think they "should" be talking about. On the old TV sitcom, Bob Newhart played the part of the psychologist, Dr. Robert Hartley. His clients inevitably and incessantly talked about how other people did not understand or like them. Since nothing ever changed for Hartley's clients, one might suspect that his clients talked about the topics they did because that was what they thought they should talk about. Brief counselors would note that goal-setting was not a prominent feature of Dr. Hartley's counseling sessions.

A second time we may choose not to respond to clients' words and phrases is when clients are preoccupied with their pasts. Sometimes this occurs because our clients have been watching old Freudian-based movies on late night TV. In Alfred Hitchcock's *Marie*, the main character is finally helped by uncovering her past memories and working them through. This characterization of how people with problems receive "real" help forms the basis for many media presentations of counseling/therapy and as such influences many people's ideas of what should happen when they talk to a counselor. In short, they believe that the best way to receive help is to talk about their pasts. Brief counselors know that, unless clients are very young or have amnesia, clients' pasts are not brief. Brief counselors prefer to focus on what is currently happening and what can happen in clients' lives in the future.

A final time when we do not respond to clients' words and phrases is when clients are experiencing spontaneous and unprompted free association. In the case "Derailed and Detained," Maria mentioned a new child. Her association to the phrase "a new child" may have been "mother." In other words, Maria made an associative connection when she said, "I get so tired and yet I want to do it all. We recently adopted an 11-month-old girl and we love her so much. She's brought new happiness into our lives. At the same time I feel I'm not carrying my own weight at work. At times I'm just like my mother."

Counselors are trained to pay attention to what clients talk about; conversely, clients talk about what counselors pay attention to. Given this circularity of topic generation and extinction, one strategy when clients are heading off the brief counseling track is to ignore aspects of what the client says—a strategy consistent with actual counseling practice. We constantly ignore aspects of what clients tell us, and we make those choices guided by explicit or implied theoretical frameworks. When Chico responded to the mother-daughter relationship, he simultaneously ignored certain aspects of Maria's statement that had ended with, "I'm just like my mother." For example, he did not respond to any or all of the following:

- Maria's tiredness
- the impact of the adopted 11-month-old girl on Maria's life (and sleep patterns)
- the new happiness that Maria and her husband have recently experienced
- Maria's perception that she is not doing her fair share at work
- the possible metaphorical reference to weight (i.e., not carrying her weight at work)

It is not a question of whether we should ignore aspects of what a client is telling us, because we ignore, consciously and unconsciously, aspects of clients' stories all the time. Rather, the question is, "What aspects of the story are we going to pay attention to and then acknowledge or not acknowledge?" Brief counselors attempt to find a major focus for their sessions. In this situation, Chico and Maria were focused on her work situation. The following dialogue shows how Chico might have kept the focus on Maria's talk about her job, rather than being derailed.

MARIA: I get so tired and yet I want to do it all. We recently adopted an 11-month-old girl and we love her so much. She's brought new happiness into our lives. At the same time I feel I'm not carrying my own weight at work. At times I'm just like my mother.

CHICO: Given the major change in your life and your drive to do it all, what would be some realistic work-related goals you might set?

When working with parent-child conflicts, counselors often help mothers to recognize that their children have become "mother deaf." In other words, the child has learned to ignore the mother until the mother has repeated the same message countless times and raised her voice. One possibility when

Maria brought up the phrase, "I'm just like my mother," would have been for Chico to become "theoretically deaf"—not to all theories, but to those that led away without sufficient justification from the brief counseling one.

Following are some words and phrases counselors have found derailed them from the brief counseling track or shunted them onto other theoretical tracks:

- mother
- my brother(s)
- parents were strict (or inconsistent)
- struggle with my weight
- inner child
- unhappy
- my husband (wife) doesn't understand me

- father
- my sister(s)
- growing up
- not liking myself
- codependent
- depressed
- my childhood

This is but a very short list of possible words and phrases that clients may say that send us leaping the brief counseling tracks. In learning and practicing a brief counseling approach, increased awareness of words and phrases that clients use that trigger other theoretical frameworks is essential.

Responding in a Limited Fashion

Some circumstances would justify a counselor's responding in a limited fashion to the phrase, "I'm just like my mother." There is the possibility that the phrase offers information that may prove valuable in moving toward clients' solutions. Ignoring the phrase may result in lost opportunities to help.

We can choose to respond the first time a client mentions words and phrases that push our other theoretically-oriented buttons. However, our mere acknowledgment of the word or phrase indicates that we have heard it and thus, by inference, believe it must be important; otherwise, why would we have responded as we did? Hence, our eagerness to respond may ensure that our clients will continue to produce more phrases related to the same or similar topics. A moderate strategy is: If the word or phrase is said only one or two times, treat it as a chance occurrence and ignore it unless it is accompanied by a significant expression of affect. Thus, we mentally note the occurrence of the word or phrase but deliberately do not share this recognition with the client. In this strategy we wait for further references before we overtly acknowledge what we have heard. In this way we avoid prompting the client to tell us more when we have no need to hear more.

A second strategy is to overtly acknowledge the phrase and use it as a way to open up more options. For example, the following dialogue illustrates how a counselor might use the client's reference to her mother to focus on the client's strengths and resources.

MARIA: I get so tired and yet I want to do it all. We recently adopted an 11-month-old girl and we love her so much. She's brought new happiness into our lives. At the same time I feel I'm not carrying my own weight at work. At times I'm just like my mother.

CHICO: You just mentioned your mother. How are the lives of you and your mother really alike and how are they really different?
[Here Chico focuses on similarities and differences to assist the client in differentiating herself from her mother. Chico's choice of "really alike" and "really different" establishes polar extremes, leaving room for greater intentionality on Maria's part.]

MARIA: We're really alike in that we both worry about things a lot.

Chico: How good a worrier is she and how good are you?
[Reframe of worry as a skill that requires some proficiency.]

MARIA: I can worry a lot at times but she is considerably better than I am.

CHICO: So you still have time as her daughter to have your mother teach you how to become a better worrier. [Maria and Chico both enjoy a good laugh at this point.]

MARIA: I don't think I'm going to have her give me lessons because I don't ever want to be as good at worrying as she is.

CHICO: So you share some similarities about worrying but not completely.
[Chico acknowledges that even with supposed similarities there are differences.]
How are you two a lot different?

MARIA: I'm more gregarious, more outgoing, and I have more fun.

CHICO: So you are more gregarious, more outgoing, and you have more fun. Any chance you might teach your mother how to be more like you? Those qualities of gregariousness, more outgoing, and having fun seem like useful qualities that you might use to help you reach some solutions to the difficulties you initially discussed. More specifically, how might you use gregariousness, outgoingness, and having more fun as ways to reach your goals?
[Chico deliberately repeats Maria's words so as to acknowledge them and stress them, especially since they seem to be aspects of Maria that she identifies as positive. He then proceeds deliberately to tie her perceived strengths to her work-related goal.]

Changing Theoretical Frameworks

Brief counseling is not for all clients and for all concerns. Short-term approaches can be the wrong choice under two conditions. First, the client strongly prefers a longer-term approach and is unwilling to adapt to a shorter one. Second, longer-term treatment is essential.

Clients come with many agendas. One agenda may be for a long-term therapeutic relationship. Another may be for extended in-depth exploration of the psyche. Recently I talked with a woman who had spent eight years in psychoanalysis. My descriptions of brief counseling struck her as utterly lacking in the focus and long-term security she wanted and sought from therapy. She told me how she loved to explore her past and determine how it played itself out in her life. For this woman, brief counseling would not have provided the essential elements she was seeking in therapy; however, her longer-term self-exploration seemed to provide her with help that short-term approaches would not.

If I have the skills and inclination to be of assistance to the client who is asking for these types of counseling agendas, then one option is for me to shift theoretical frameworks and provide a match between the client's request for a longer-term approach and my preferred way of working. On the other hand, if I cannot in good faith provide the type of theoretical framework the client is asking for, then I have an ethical obligation to refer the client to a colleague who does.

Sometimes clients seek short-term approaches when they are not appropriate. In writing about single-session therapy, Talmon (1990) proposed that certain clients will not benefit from very short approaches. He ruled out (a) clients requiring inpatient psychiatric care (e.g., suicidal, psychotic), (b) clients who are suffering from conditions that suggest strong genetic, bio-logical, or chemical components (e.g., bipolar depression, schizophrenia), and (c) clients with anorexia nervosa, bulimia nervosa, or attention deficit disorder. Clients seeking brief counseling for the conditions listed by Talmon need to be provided with realistic information about the limits of shorter approaches. As I have stated repeatedly in this book, brief counsel-ing is not the treatment of choice for everyone.

Counselors' Choices

Clients' words and phrases constantly remind us of our previously learned theoretical frameworks. At times we hear clients use "child" voices (Transactional Analysis) and engage in self-talk resembling "topdog and underdog" dialogues (gestalt therapy). We see them act out with irresponsible behavior (Reality Therapy). Clients employ many other patterns of thoughts, feelings, and actions that trigger our excursions into diverse theoretical frameworks.

As a framework, brief counseling is intended to increase our options as counselors, not diminish them. Therefore, the recognition of words and phrases that can be conceptualized from different frameworks is desired. What is undesired is being derailed or shunted onto another theoretical framework, especially at the expense of clients seeking our help. Under three conditions I need to get my counseling back on a consistent theoretical track: (1) My theoretical agenda is determined unconsciously (e.g., I revert without awareness to a Rational Emotive Therapy framework); (2) my theoretical agenda is determined by my curiosity (e.g., I am intrigued theoretically or personally, rather than therapeutically); or (3) my theoretical agenda is determined haphazardly (e.g., I flit from one theoretical framework to another unguided by reason).

The bottom line in brief counseling and any other form of counseling is that we help clients. Clients are not helped when we fail to realize we are shifting from one theoretical framework to another. Clients' words and phrases that derail us into other theoretical frameworks are subtle. They sneak up on us; before we know it our theoretical train is off the track. A train engineer is constantly alert so as to keep the train on the track. A brief counselor also needs to be constantly alert in keeping the brief counseling train on the theoretical track. Brief counselors actively avoid theoretical derailings.

Do Something Different

1. Old habits have a way of reappearing when we are learning new approaches. In addressing this issue, Dr. Dean Ornish (1993), the heart specialist, found that his patients with high cholesterol levels were more effective in lowering them when they made one profound change in their lifestyle rather than many incremental ones. Applying this to learning brief counseling, plunge into brief counseling as though it were the only way to do counseling. Do brief counseling in a consistent way. Take special precautions that you not be derailed by other theoretical frameworks. Realize as you are making this total conversion that brief counseling is not the one way to do counseling, but that the temporary conversion is a method of expediting your learning. You can always choose to return to other frameworks when they are appropriate.

2. What are the words and phrases that your clients use that serve to derail your theoretical train? Here are a few of the possibilities:

- mother
- my sister(s)
- parents were strict (or inconsistent)
- struggle with my weight
- my childhood

- father
- growing up
- not liking myself
- my inner child
- my husband (wife) doesn't understand me

- my brother(s)
- depressed
- unhappy
- codependent
- my dreams

During the next several weeks focus your attention on which of your former theoretical buttons clients tend to push. Given the options discussed in this chapter, occasionally ignore or minimally respond to those words or phrases that in the past you would have pursued.

CHAPTER 13

Learning to Interrupt

CLIENT: *Sometimes I just wanted my counselor to interrupt me and scream,*
"Do you have any clues about what you're saying?" Many times
I would have replied, "No."

I entered the field of counseling ill-prepared to interrupt clients. I had been reared to believe that interrupting an adult equaled rudeness. Interrupting was impolite and I was not supposed to do it. Equating interrupting with rudeness was not a natural gift I acquired at birth; rather, it was the product of continuous instruction.

How could I have learned otherwise considering that in the 1930s my father had been the Manners Chairman in his social fraternity? The message in our home was that it was bad manners to interrupt adults. My father had an ancient book about the Goops that he read on occasion to my brothers and me, *Goops and How to Be Them* (Burgess, 1968, original work published 1900). Goops were mischievous children who were immortalized in doggerel verse such as the following called "Interruption":

Don't interrupt your father when he's telling
funny jokes;
Don't interrupt your mother when she's
entertaining folks;
Don't interrupt the visitors when they have
come to call,—

In fact, it's generally wiser
not to interrupt at all.

Given my "dysfunctional" background related to interrupting, it is easy
to see why I was ill-prepared to deal with certain clients in my early training. A number of counseling sessions lasted longer because I allowed clients
to continue in patterns that were not in keeping with effective counseling.
Had I acquired the skills of interrupting respectfully and with finesse, we
would have saved countless hours.

Reframing Interrupting

Because the word "interrupting" is emotionally loaded, we avoid the act of
interrupting, even when it would be appropriate and useful. Reframing
interrupting in a positive manner serves to justify and encourage its use. Two
possible reframes, which arrive at the same outcome, are the following:

Taking Turns. Counseling is an interactive process. In brief counseling
we think that counselor head-nodding and minimal encouragers, important
as they may be, do not constitute sufficient counselor input. Counseling is a
sharing of ideas. Brief counselors engage clients in thinking about their
worlds. Taking turns helps ensure active participation of both parties.

Changing Monologues into Dialogues. A second way to reframe
interrupting is to understand it as the useful activity of changing client
monologues into dialogues. There are occasions when clients' monologues
are useful, but most of the time changing monologues into dialogues keeps
both counselors and clients engaged in the change process.

When to Interrupt

Over the years I have discovered that there are five specific situations where
counselors can use the skills of interrupting, hopefully with respect and
finesse. Understanding when I could interrupt clients was my first step in
helping clients use our counseling session time more productively.

War Stories. Clients who relish telling war stories love to find counselors who lack interrupting skills. These clients appreciate audiences who
seem required to listen endlessly. When they find a new listener, they have to
start at the beginning of their story, a story that may have already exhausted
multiple listeners. When heard for the first time, such war stories can sometimes be quite entertaining; in fact, counselors may be reluctant to interrupt

because at least the client is talking and the stories are new. It may take counselors a while to realize that the stories are never going to stop. In my experience, the true masters of war stories are eighth grade girls with perfect auditory memories. They can repeat every detail of every interaction over the past week, especially as it relates to who is currently liked and not liked.

Monologues. Closely related to clients who tell war stories are clients who engage in monologues. One factor distinguishing monologues from war stories is that monologues result in counselors becoming bored much more quickly. These clients are often seeking professional friends. The cheaper the counselors' rates, the better bargains these clients obtain.

A technique used by clients doing monologues is to make their stories seamless through the use of the word "and" and by appearing not to breathe. These clients do not use periods in their speech patterns, and they do not stop for a breath before plunging on. The flow from one story to another is seamless. Once counselors hear how clients use "and" and realize they *are* breathing, there is a technique that can be used to intervene.

Stuck Emotional States. Crying because of pain is one thing. Endless crying is another. When clients continually experience heightened emotional states to the exclusion of new thinking and new behaviors, it is time for counselors to interrupt and break the state so as to allow new options.

Irrelevant Material. Virginia Satir (1972) described irrelevant clients as those who go in many different directions at the same time. Their talk seems to go nowhere and have no point. Irrelevant clients differ from those who tell war stories and engage in monologues in that their talk has no direction. When clients continually recount irrelevant stories, it is time for counselors to intervene by focusing the direction of counseling.

Restricted Focusing. Clients who focus exclusively on others guarantee that they will not have to explore their own thoughts, feelings, and actions. When others are the focus, the client is not. In contrast, clients sometimes focus only on themselves, to the exclusion of other people, topics, counselor and client relationship, and cultural/environmental issues (Ivey, 1994). Some who focus on themselves pick only their feelings or thoughts or actions to discuss. Counselors benefit their clients when they interrupt to assist them in increasing their range of focus.

Techniques for Interrupting Respectfully and with Finesse

Training for counselors focuses almost exclusively on being respectful to clients by letting them talk, not by interrupting them. However, as demonstrated in the above five situations, there are appropriate times for interrupting—times for increased sharing and dialogue. Thus, I have come to view not interrupting clients in the above situations as showing considerable disrespect. The following techniques are ways of interrupting respectfully and with finesse in appropriate situations.

The Eyes Have It. The first technique is borrowed from Harry Stack Sullivan. I begin with it not because I endorse its use but because it illustrates a very indirect approach to interrupting clients. My own preference is for more direct, less subtle approaches. Therefore, I do not recommend Sullivan's technique for general use, even though I cite it first.

Sullivan perfected his technique in the days of classical psychoanalysis. Direct interruptions signaled countertransference on the therapist's part and were viewed as nontherapeutic. The patient was supposed to be allowed to explore without interruption. On those occasions when Sullivan was convinced that the patient was wandering off in unproductive ways, he would maintain eye contact with the patient but ever so slowly close his eyes. When they were half shut he would open them, only to have them again begin slowly to droop. Sullivan reported that when he used this technique his patients tended to switch to more productive topics.

Everyone Has to Breathe. An effective interruption technique for clients who go on and on without apparently breathing is to force them to breathe so that the counselor notices. One way to do this is to interrupt their talk with a visual motion. When I think interrupting is appropriate, I simultaneously (1) lean forward, (2) move my hand away from my body with my index finger pointed up, (3) say, "Excuse me. Let me check if I'm really hearing what you have to say," and (4) proceed to intervene (e.g., change the focus of the interview, without pausing after what I have done in #3).

I once watched Dr. Richard Fisch at the Mental Research Institute interrupt a client with respect and finesse. He raised his left hand to a position above his head, gently patted his hair, and then brought his hand down almost guillotine fashion while warmly smiling at the client. The client momentarily stopped talking and Dr. Fisch used the occasion to ask a question.

Clarifying Our Roles. Clarifying the roles of the counselor and client can aid in changing the nature of the counseling session from a client monologue into a dialogue between counselor and client. I begin counseling sessions with a short introduction to the ground rules about our respective roles, but occasionally clients need to be reminded to play by the rules. If necessary, I add,

When we first met, I mentioned some ideas about how to get the most out of counseling. You've been telling me lots of information about your situation. I need my turn to make sure I'm really understanding what you have to say. I'm sure you'll understand that when I stop you so as to clarify and sometimes challenge you to look at your situation in different ways, what I'm really doing is providing the best help I can.

I have found that most clients are understanding because they wish to receive the maximum benefit from counseling.

Relevancy Challenge. Clients who wander into seemingly irrelevant stories and examples and constantly flit to new topics may benefit from counselors' posing relevancy challenges (McMaster & Grinder, 1980). A relevancy challenge is a method for determining if what the client is saying is pertinent to the themes and issues at hand. It is particularly powerful when the counselor challenges the relevance of the current topic to the client's goals. For example,

Jim, I'm sorry that I'm getting a bit confused. You're talking right now about your uncle's motorcycle. I'm wondering how that relates to your goal of getting a job so you can work your way through college.

Frequently, clients discover that what they are talking about bears no relationship to their goal or any other aspect of why they are in counseling. They just happen to have drifted into the new topic. The relevancy challenge draws them back to more germane talk.

Clients know more about their worlds than we as counselors will ever know. In the past, I have offered relevancy challenges with the certainty that the current talk was totally irrelevant, only to have clients convince me otherwise. When they linked the current topic to their goals, my understanding of their worlds increased.

Soft Interrupting. In one of my classes we watched a film of Fritz Perls doing Gestalt Therapy. After the film we were discussing Perl's use of confrontation and I mentioned that, while Perls was very direct and forceful in confronting, one could achieve the same outcome using a less direct and forceful approach. The students asked me to show them an example and I did. When I finished one student said, "I think I see the difference. Fritz Perls' approach is hard like brick ice cream. Your approach is soft and mushy like a Dairy Queen." Interrupting can be done hard like brick ice cream or soft and mushy like a Dairy Queen. My preference is for the latter because I find it results in clients' not defending their position but, rather, looking at what they are doing.

At the same time, interrupting done in a faltering fashion is ineffective with forceful clients. While students saw my interrupting as a Dairy Queen-like style, I prefer another metaphor—a velvet glove over a steel fist. The velvet glove is what clients see, but the forcefulness comes from knowing that my intent is serious and my persistence will be unbending. The words I use are soft while my nonverbal manner is intense. I truly intend to have my turn, so I say the soft words in a polite but forceful manner. Examples of soft words are:

- Excuse me, Carlos. I'm wondering . . .
- Trudi, perhaps you can help me understand . . .
- Vern, I'm puzzled. You are telling me about how Sarah sees the situation. How do you see it? What are your thoughts?

Emotional State Interrupters. Continuation in any given emotional state by clients may slow counseling down considerably. If a client is constantly crying, it is not possible to do much work. Therefore, interrupting stuck emotional states is occasionally necessary. Verbal methods are not as effective as nonverbal ones. One method for breaking stuck states involves making physiological changes. Clients become accustomed to sitting in the same chair and associate the chair with certain emotional states. Changing chairs or standing up and moving around may help in shifting clients out of stuck positions in ways we may not anticipate. In workshops, Richard Bandler has related how he would anticipate his clients' stuck emotional states and not even let them enter them. He would meet his clients at the door and say, "Before we begin, tell me how will we know when you are successful?" This move to envision a desired state often precluded clients' getting stuck in unpleasant emotional states.

As counselors we need to be aware that we may be the ones who are influencing clients to stay stuck. Continuous reflection of feelings may leave the client wallowing in emotional states. The following story illustrates how the counselor's nonverbal behavior acted as a powerful determiner of client behavior and how the physiological changes benefited both counselor and client.

Musical Chairs

Cindy, a women in her mid-twenties, was a counseling practicum student at a halfway house for ex-psychiatric patients. I was supervising Cindy, and we were listening to one of her audiotapes. Cindy was working very hard at trying to get Jim, an 18-year-old male, to open up; she was having little success. As the going continued to be rough, Cindy had fallen into the trap of asking closed questions. Jim was responding with minimal discouragers such as "yes" and "no."

Because we did not have the interview on videotape, I asked Cindy to describe the room arrangement. She said Jim sat on a large overstuffed sofa and she sat on a chair in front of him. I had her pretend that I was Jim seated on the couch. Then I asked Cindy to pull her chair over and show me the distance she and Jim sat from each other. Cindy moved her chair toward me until our knees were practically touching. It was then I confirmed my hypothesis:

> Jim was an 18-year-old with minimal social skills, especially around members of the opposite sex. Cindy was an attractive and vivacious young woman who liked to be in touch with people. Jim was overwhelmed by a woman who was invading his personal space. His response was to close down. Cindy's response when she wasn't getting a response was to move closer to be more in touch.

I shared my hypothesis with Cindy and she thought it plausible. I gave her a task to carry out during the next session with Jim. She was to enter the room first and sit on the sofa, thus leaving the chair to Jim. Because the sofa was enormously heavy, Cindy would not be able to move it toward Jim. On the other hand, Jim could move his chair to any distance from Cindy at which he felt comfortable.

The following week we listened to Cindy's tape of her latest counseling session with Jim. He was talking much more and Cindy was asking fewer questions. Cindy said that when she sat on the couch she could still lean forward but that the distance between them was now greater than previously. She added that Jim looked much more relaxed.

When I want to change clients' stuck states, I begin by saying, "I'd like you to stand up for just a little bit." I stand up myself to model what I want clients to do. If when clients stand they are still leaning over in a "depressed" posture, I direct them to stand up straight, throw their shoulders back, and take several deep breaths. If there is an open window, we walk over to it, and I have them look up and out and begin to see a future where things are the way they want them to be. The shift from a stuck emotional state in the present to visualizing the future helps clients change quickly. Once in a new state, clients can be taught how to move to that state by themselves.

Interrupting Because We Care

Using the time within a session in the most productive manner is a major way to make counseling briefer. When clients engage in behaviors that are counterproductive to their goals—such as telling war stories, getting lost in extraneous details, and becoming too stuck in a given state—it is time to interrupt. When there is a sound therapeutic reason, it is not rude to interrupt if the interrupting is done respectfully and with finesse. Interrupting can serve to refocus the client on more productive themes, speed therapeutic movement, and make counseling a mutual, interactive process. The skills of interrupting are important ones that make counseling briefer. They also convey we care enough about our clients that we will not let them unwittingly waste their time in unproductive chatter.

Do Something Different

1. Practice nonverbal interrupting. Sit in front of a mirror so you can see your whole upper body. Experiment with various hand gestures, facial expressions, and body movements that would be interrupting but not annoying to clients. Practice until the nonverbal interrupting behaviors feel natural.

2. Practice verbal interrupting. Explore, either by writing it out or saying it orally, possible phrases you could use to interrupt clients. Make the phrases congruent with who you are—put them into your own words. Practice saying them respectfully and with a degree of finesse.

3. Choose a client you are working with who has a tendency to describe his or her problem in more detail than you can assimilate. Use a nonverbal gesture to momentarily interrupt the client's story. Verbally, with respect and finesse, let the client know that you want to check if you understand what the person has been saying. Summarize briefly. Evaluate the impact on your client.

CHAPTER 14

Addressing the Whole Person through Specific Solutions

CLIENT: *I kept asking my counselor, "What should I do?"*

Bread-making is an activity that incorporates varied aspects of what it is to be human—mental, physical, emotional, social, and spiritual. Bread-making involves us mentally in a series of decisions, some simple and some complex. After mastering the fundamentals of the craft, seasoned bakers find creative challenges in the advanced levels of bread-making. Bread-making involves us physically (albeit not in an aerobic fashion) through the measuring and the mixing of ingredients and eventually the kneading of the dough. Emotional aspects of ourselves may be engaged—we feel accomplishment, pride, and joy, or occasionally, when the bread does not rise, a sense of disappointment, irritation, and embarrassment. Bread-making can be a way of sharing communion with others. It connects us to other people through a long history of food preparation and the social ties surrounding it. In addition to occupying us mentally, physically, emotionally, and socially, bread-making highlights our spiritual selves. Making bread can be a time for centering and for renewal. It is a time of creating something marvelously whole from separate ingredients.

Like bread-making, brief counseling addresses the mental, physical, emotional, social, and spiritual dimensions of living. Moreover, both activities are grounded in the concrete and specific. The final product of making bread is a loaf of bread; the final product of brief counseling is a specific solution that solves a client's problem. Even as brief counselors help clients solve problems with specific solutions, we recognize that these problems involve the whole person. While brief counselors focus on the specific, we maintain awareness of mental, physical, emotional, social, and spiritual dimensions.

While I recognize that these aspects of clients' lives are intricately intertwined, I have separated them out in the following five sections. The cases presented demonstrate a small sample of the many techniques and strategies that brief counselors might employ to assist clients in generating concrete and specific solutions to problems involving numerous dimensions of their lives.

Mental Aspects

Mental dimensions of living involve engaging our minds to explore, understand, and plan new ways of living. Thinking about solutions to life's difficulties becomes more difficult under conditions of stress. In the case below, Pam began to think about her situation in new ways. As she discovered new solutions, she also touched emotional and social aspects of her life. The case is written by Pam about her experience in applying brief counseling to her own life.

Apples and Whale Blubber

During a class in brief counseling, another student and I were struggling to define my "problem" in positive terms and to come up with a goal. I had stated that my goal was to not become angry or upset with a friend's frequently irritating behavior. I wanted to "not let it bother me" because it was really "no big deal," but we couldn't seem to frame it in a positive way. Our teacher, John Littrell, joined us and listened for a few minutes; then he reframed my negatively stated goal in the positive, "So, your goal is to remember that it's no big deal."

"Yes, exactly," I said, amazed at how easy it was. John then asked me to think of something that reminded me of "no big deal." After some thought, I recalled a time in my childhood when I was walking home from school with some friends. We saw a tree full of big, red apples in a yard next to an old house. Many of the apples had fallen to the ground. As we each picked an apple from the tree, an angry old woman came out onto the porch of the house, waving her cane, and yelling at us to stop stealing her apples. I can remember thinking that "a couple of apples is no big deal." There were plenty of apples and no reason for her to get so upset with us.

I told John the story, and he suggested, "The next time you feel yourself becoming angry with your friend, you will notice an apple appear on his head. The apple will sprout leaves and branches and become a tree. Then the old woman will appear, waving her cane and yelling. You will see the whole scene and even hear background music like in a movie. And you will remember that 'it's no big deal.' " I laughed, thinking it was a pretty weird way to remember something, but I was willing to try it.

To my amazement, it worked. The next time I felt myself becoming angry with my friend, an apple appeared on his head and grew into a tree. The old woman appeared waving her cane and yelling, and I heard the background music from a scene in the movie *The Wizard of Oz* when Dorothy picks up an apple from an unfriendly apple tree. My friend was puzzled when I just smiled and walked away, but it definitely helped me feel better about the situation.

I have found the technique very useful and have adapted it for my own personal use in "remembering" other things. For example, to remember that greasy or sugary foods have high calories and low nutrition, I have the image of a chunk of whale blubber appear as I am about to eat any greasy or sugary food (except chocolate!). Although I have never seen whale blubber, I have a vivid imagination and it's a very effective way to curb my appetite for those foods.

While I prescribed the imagery of the apple tree growing out of her friend's head, it fit well enough for Pam that she used it. That success prompted her to explore the same type of approach to a problem of remembering that "greasy and sugary foods have high calories and low nutrition." Pam used her own imagination to generalize the imaging strategy to another problem situation.

Physical Aspects

Sometimes clients need to take action. Clients can talk and talk but often physically doing something provides, or is, the solution. In the next case, Kirk, a community college counselor, recognized that his colleague, Thomas, needed to do something, rather than just continue to talk. Kirk's intervention was short and to the point. It was a confrontation because Kirk implicitly identified a contradiction between what Thomas stated he wanted and what he was doing to achieve it. The following is Kirk's description.

You Can't Dance

Thomas was sitting in the library lamenting his future. He was stymied in his desire to do what he wanted to do. "I want to study dance therapy. I really do." He went on and on telling me what he wanted to do. My assessment of what was happening was that I was talking to a classic fence sitter, at least on this issue. Finally, feeling some frustration and yet wanting to be helpful, I looked Thomas in the eye and said, "You can't dance if you're sitting on your ass!" He looked at me and said, "Yeah. You're right."

Two days later Thomas showed up at my office with computer printouts of all the dance therapy schools in the country. He thanked me for giving him the best advice he had ever received. Later, I reframed my unadulterated advice-giving as a strategically planned "do something different" task.

Several weeks later Thomas appeared at my office with a catalog from a dance therapy program. Still later he arranged his job so that he could go and do the program. I consider this the briefest intervention I have ever done—and one of the most successful.

There is nothing remarkable about advice-giving. The therapeutic skill comes in delivering advice when clients are ready to attend and profit from it. While Kirk would be the first to admit that his intervention was driven in part by his own needs, it also assisted Thomas in moving from thinking to action. Unlike Carl Rogers, who had disdain for advice-giving, brief counselors do not categorically rule out any technique or strategy that may prove helpful. Kirk could have waited a long time for Thomas to assume responsibility on his own in this small career step. However, we should not assume that Thomas had been taught to look to others for motivation just because he did not initiate seeking the career information on this occasion. Perhaps metaphorically it means that Thomas's car was out of gas and Kirk supplied it. One would hardly anticipate that Thomas will from now on neglect to glance at his fuel gauge and simply rely on Kirk to supply gas.

Emotional Aspects

Dealing with emotions is difficult when the overriding emotion is fear. Gaining control of emotions rather than letting them control contributes to more effective living. Joshua's fear illustrates how emotional override may severely distort perceptions and how new resources may open a client's eyes to see what is truly there.

Joshua and the Fire Bell

In the late 1970s our family lived in Fargo, North Dakota, a state whose unofficial motto, "30° below keeps the riffraff out," acknowledges the brutal winter temperatures. Our son Joshua went to third grade at Roosevelt Elementary School, a monstrosity built in the early part of the 20th century. One winter morning as my wife Mary and I were eating breakfast with Joshua, he announced that he didn't want to go to school. When Mary asked why, he said that there was a very loud fire alarm bell in the school and that they were going to have another fire drill today. Further questioning by Mary revealed that Joshua hated the sound of the huge cast iron bell because it hurt his ears and scared him.

Mary listened carefully and did a wonderful job of paraphrasing and reflecting Joshua's feelings. Unfortunately, her empathic approach increased, rather than decreased, his fear and strengthened his initially stated plan of avoiding school. I noted that what was happening was not producing the results that we as parents wanted—Joshua going to school.

I asked Mary if I could try something different with Joshua; with a sigh of relief she quickly relinquished responsibility. I asked Joshua how loud the fire bell sounded. He said it was really loud. I asked if it were as loud as when he was outside playing. No, it was louder than that. I kept upping the ante until I finally said, "Is it as loud as the time you, Craig, and Martin were in the tree yelling, 'Monkey! Monkey! Monkey!'?" Joshua started to laugh a bit. From that point on I talked about "the boys in the tree yelling, 'Monkey! Monkey! Monkey!' I mean, when the fire bell rings." More laughter.

Next I asked Joshua how scared he was. He said he was really scared. I said, "If you were really afraid your body would be shaking. Shake your body to show me how scared you are when you three boys in the tree yelled, 'Monkey! Monkey! Monkey!' I mean, when the fire bell rings." Joshua sat in his chair and shook but now more with laughter than fear.

By this time Joshua didn't seem too scared anymore but I took it one last step. I said, "Joshua, if a kid is really scared, his hair stands on end." He sat in his chair looking at me for a moment; then he leaned his head over so that his face was upside down. In that position his long blond hair stood on end. Mary, Joshua, and I shared a good laugh at his cleverness in producing a really scared look.

I told Joshua that he could scare others in his class when the fire bell rang by shaking and having his hair stand on end. Soon all the kids in his class would be scared and then the fear would spread to all the kids in his school and then to other schools in Fargo, and then across the Red River to Morehead, Minnesota, and then on to Minneapolis.

Joshua headed off to school with no prompting, perhaps considering himself lucky to have escaped his father's off-beat sense of humor. On

Joshua's return home from school, I met him on our sidewalk and asked him how the fire bell had gone. He looked at me and said, "Dad, it's no big deal."

Joshua is not alone in having been inhibited in his life by powerful emotional responses. Many clients have experienced life situations that they have learned to associate with strong emotional reactions. Important aspects of life may be neglected when powerful emotions preclude positive social relationships and support. Brief counselors work with clients so that their emotions assist, rather than curtail, living life fully.

Social Aspects

People seem to be hardwired to need other people. Most counseling involves clients who are struggling to get along with others. Once relationship patterns are established it is often difficult to create new ones. In the following case, the work on solutions accessed the client's sense of playfulness and humor in a direct fashion. In working with Rita, I borrowed Richard Bandler's (1985) pattern interruption technique, and I also called upon Mickey Mouse because my client had said that Mickey always evoked a smile and warm feelings in her. Thus, Mickey Mouse, a master at inducing smiles, figured prominently in her solution.

Smile, and the Whole World Smiles with You

Rita worked at a nutrition center that specialized in helping people with weight loss, but lately she had found going to work less and less exciting. The staff at the nutrition center was small and that meant constant interaction with Betsy, a less-than-fun person who long ago had forgotten that smiles can be contagious. Rita was greeted at work each morning by Betsy's grumpiness and down-on-life attitude; for Rita encounters with Betsy precipitated a daily Excedrin headache. Rita had tried being pleasant but Rita's pleasantness did not elicit pleasantness from Betsy. Rita's reaction of discouragement was beginning to change into a what-the-hell attitude that Rita didn't like in herself. She had even reached the point of thinking about looking for a new job.

As Rita and I worked together we discussed what she had control over; Rita realized it was her thoughts, feelings, and actions—not Betsy's gloomy behavior. Rita agreed that she wanted to have some new options for herself; she wanted to be able to laugh at the absurdness of the situation by seeing Betsy in a new light. Her explicit goal became "to remain calm and relaxed in the presence of Betsy."

To accomplish her goal, I gave Rita the following pattern interruption task involving fun visualizations. I had her see a picture of Betsy in her mind's eye. Using Richard Bandler's Swish Pattern (Andreas & Andreas, 1987; Bandler, 1985), I asked Rita how she could change the picture so as to find the picture of Betsy funny enough to bring a smile to her face. Rita told me that if she were to visualize Betsy as Mickey Mouse that would really be funny. I had her add to the picture two huge black ears (I outlined the shape with my hands as I talked) and a round black bulb of a nose. I said if she looked at her Betsy's picture very carefully, she would notice that Betsy had a long, thin black tail coming from her derriere. We repeated the visualizations four or five times with Rita beginning with a picture of Betsy as she really was and then adding the nose, ears, and tail until they appeared automatically. Whenever Rita envisioned a picture of Betsy, she changed it immediately to a Mickey Mouse-like Betsy; each time Rita laughed.

The following week Rita reported that she had gone to work on the day following our session prepared to use the new visualizing techniques, but that Betsy, in contrast to her usual gloomy self, had smiled and been pleasant. In fact, Betsy had continued to be pleasant all week. Rita was puzzled as to what had caused Betsy to change so much.

As Rita and I examined the interaction, we reached the following conclusion. When Rita had walked in the door at work following our meeting, she had been prepared for Betsy. Rita was ready to visualize the nose, ears, and tail on her co-worker. Betsy's pleasantness had so surprised Rita that she hadn't realized that she herself had entered the office, not with her own face in a tight smile, but with a warm smile of good humor. We surmised that when Betsy saw Rita's genuine smile Betsy had felt good and smiled back. Rita had failed to notice that she had set in motion a "pleasant smile evoking a pleasant smile" feedback loop.

Most clients seek to be cooperative and are often irritated, puzzled, and discouraged when their best efforts do not elicit the same from others. Disrupting nonfunctional patterns and creating new ones is a major task. Brief counselors are quite willing to use a variety of means to break the hold of nonfunctional patterns. Finding innovative ways to accomplish that task means that counseling will never be dull.

Spiritual Aspects

Viktor Frankl (1959) was but one therapist who focused on clients' search for meaning. While these therapists' ways of questing for spiritual qualities are diverse, the underlying theme is a search for something beyond the person that will give life purpose. Career counseling is an area where people seek greater meaning in their lives. The following case is drawn from the life of my family. It focuses on our son Joshua's search for meaning in his schooling.

Do What You Love, the Money Will Follow

Several years ago our son Joshua was half through his junior year in college. When we talked with him about his major, communications, he said it was okay, but he showed little enthusiasm. At the end of a short January term studying English theater, Joshua was set to return to college for the spring semester. While Mary and I discussed Joshua's situation with each other, I was reminded of Marsha Sinetar's book, *Do What You Love, the Money Will Follow.*

One morning, as Mary and I left for our jobs, I said to him, "Joshua, when we return home tonight we would like to talk to you about what you are studying. What really gets you excited and what do you find fascinating? In other words, what do you really love?" When Mary returned home after five, Joshua began talking about how he had thought about the questions. He had a eureka experience—what he really loved was history. Joshua proceeded to tell Mary that his favorite book in third grade had been *A Child's History of the World.* He told about how the plays he had found most fascinating in England had been the historical ones. Joshua returned to college the next day and changed his major to history.

I consider my one-minute career counseling session with Joshua my fastest ever. Focusing on what he really loved clarified his goals more productively than the hours he had spent worrying about his future career. Career decision-making is a highly complex task, but sometimes the right framework allows the person to explore and use his or her potential and skills to explore in useful ways. When we assume that *complex* does not necessarily mean *longer*, then we can begin to explore how to help clients reach their goals more quickly.

One way to conceptualize Joshua's problem is to understand it as a spiritual search—a search for greater meaning in his life. By answering the question, "What do you really love?" he generated specific solutions. Many of our clients possess a longing for something beyond themselves. Brief counselors recognize that while the search for meaning is broad in scope, the answers are often in the details.

This chapter began by discussing bread-making. A loaf of bread is a specific solution that touches many aspects of your life. Translating the hard issues of life into tangible results means that brief counselors help clients look to the specific while remaining cognizant of the big picture. A brief counseling approach recognizes that many aspects of clients' lives are addressed in the process of helping them find specific solutions.

Do Something Different

1. Rather than helping clients see how they can deal with some aspects of their lives, reverse the process and generate how many different aspects can be met by any specific solution. This puts the emphasis on generating specific solutions that touch as many aspects of people's lives as possible, in contrast to having to find solutions for specific aspects.
2. As you and your clients assess the impact of the changes they have made, also evaluate the extent those changes have found expression in the mental, physical, emotional, social, and spiritual aspects of their lives.
3. Historically, physical and spiritual aspects of clients' lives have been overlooked or ignored by counselors. What can you do to be more attuned to the whole client?

Part IV

Backing Up
Brief Counselors' Claims

CHAPTER 15

Researching the Potential of Brief Counseling

CLIENT: *Yes, but is there any evidence to back up brief counseling's claims?*

In this chapter we will examine the brief counseling research to answer two questions: (1) Is there research support for the idea that we can significantly reduce the time to conduct effective counseling? (2) Is there research showing that we can extend the scope of our counseling models to help a greater number of people?

The first research question, which refers to reducing counseling time, has intrigued me ever since the mid-60s, when I participated in a group studying Carl Rogers' *On Becoming a Person* (1961). It was obvious from Rogers' approach that when facilitative conditions were provided by counselors, clients would eventually find the resources within themselves to more directly experience and accept their emotions. However, it appeared to me that real and meaningful change took a long time. For example, one case in Rogers' book lasted 39 sessions. I marveled at Rogers' patience as he facilitated and allowed the client's internal changes to occur. I questioned whether I could ever acquire that much patience.

Later I had an "Aha" experience after reading two of Fritz Perls' books—*Gestalt Therapy Verbatim* (1969a) and *In and Out the Garbage Pail* (1969b). Perls lacked the Rogers' patience, but he had another appealing quality—he was very proactive in creating therapeutic movement. Unlike Rogers, Perls refused to wait for clients to change on their own while

spending numerous sessions basking in a relationship characterized by facilitative conditions. If Perls had heard Rogers' client say, "The symptom
was—it was—just being very depressed" (Rogers, 1961, p. 134), then Perls
would have given a here-and-now directive, such as, "Say, 'I am very
depressed.' Now, say it again. Again!" Perls' clients complied with his directives and their sense of immediacy for problem-solving amplified. I remember being impressed with Perls in two ways. First, something as simple as a
pronoun change from *it* to *I* has the potential to generate a sudden and dramatic shift for a client. Second, counselors can dramatically accelerate the
counseling process. Easier and faster were exciting alternatives. Perls had
inspired me with evidence that counselors can speed up the process of
client change. Since the late 1960s, the foundation of my research program
has been the question: Can we significantly reduce the time to conduct
effective counseling?

The second question posed in this chapter is: Is there research support
for the idea that we can extend the scope of our counseling models to help
a greater number of people? This question is a more recent one for me and
has been inspired by the research studies of Prochaska et al. (1994) as well as
my current research on the counseling program of Claudia Vangstad, a child
development specialist in an elementary school.

Helping People Faster

Is there research support that we can we significantly reduce the time to
conduct effective counseling? The brief answer is yes. A longer but not
exhaustive answer will follow, but first we must address the issue of how we
determine if counseling is effective. Since the Mental Research Institute
(MRI) in Palo Alto first began its work in the late 1960s, the standard
method to ascertain if counseling/therapy has been beneficial has been to
ask the client. This method is based on the assumption that clients are the
ones with problems/complaints, and therefore they are in the best position
to judge if they still have problems/complaints. Five questions form the basis
for judging the success of brief counseling (Weakland, Fisch, Watzlawick, &
Bodin, 1974). They are paraphrased as:

1. Has your specified treatment goal been met?
2. What is the current status of your main complaint?
3. Have you sought additional therapy since we terminated?
4. Have any improvements occurred in areas not specifically dealt
   with during the therapy?
5. Have any new problems appeared?

Based on clients' answers to these questions, cases were rated by the MRI staff as: 2 = successful (complete relief of the presenting complaint); 1 = significantly improved (clear and considerable, but not complete relief of the complaint); and 0 = failure (little or no such change) (Weakland et al., 1974).

MRI Study. One "law" commonly recognized in organizations is that "meeting agendas will always expand to fill the scheduled amount of time." In a similar fashion, the number of sessions that counselors meet with clients seems to be a function of counselors' beliefs about how many sessions are needed. A formidable barrier to shorter counseling was breached by the MRI group in the late 1960s when they limited the number of counseling sessions to 10 (Watzlawick et al., 1974). Clients cooperated with the new limits by reaching their goals as effectively as they had with other forms of counseling with no set limits. Research results reported by Weakland et al. (1974) using the research methodology summarized above indicate that the 97 families, comprising 236 individuals, averaged 7 sessions. Success was achieved in 40% of the cases, while significant improvement was found in 32%. When MRI summed the clients who they rated as either "complete relief" or "clear and considerable improvement," they arrived at a 72% success rate.

BFTC Study. The Brief Family Therapy Clinic (BFTC) in Milwaukee pioneered the use of solution-focused counseling. De Shazer (1991) reported that in a study of follow-ups at BFTC using the same questions employed by MRI, they achieved the following results:

> . . . we found an 80.4% success rate (65.6% of the clients met their goal while 14.7% made significant improvement) within an average of 4.6 sessions. When recontacted at 18 months, the success rate had increased to 86%. (p. 161)

When they checked to see if new problems had developed, 77% of their clients reported no new problems. On the other hand, "67% reported improvements in other areas since the end of therapy " (de Shazer, 1991, p. 162). The Brief Family Therapy Clinic staff's breakdown of the data into number of sessions and success rate produces some intriguing findings:

> Interestingly, 51.8% were seen for three sessions or less and they reported a 69.4% success rate, while the 48.2% seen for four sessions or more reported a 91.14% success rate. Furthermore, when seen for three sessions or less 44.26% met a secondary goal, while of those seen for four sessions or more 61.29% met a secondary goal, a rather dramatic increase. (de Shazer, 1991, p. 162)

The average number of sessions reported by MRI was 7 with a success rate of 72%. BFTC reported an average number of sessions of 4.6 with a success rate of 80.4%. While comparing results from two separate studies with many uncontrolled variables is fraught with methodological problems, the most straightforward conclusion is that the BFTC's solution-focused approach is able to help clients in less time.

One- and Two-Session Counseling. Beginning in the early 1990s, several researchers with a fresh perspective approached the issue of the duration of counseling. We asked, What would be the least number of sessions counselors could meet with clients and still do an effective job? We proposed that researchers investigate how much could be accomplished if there were but one or two counseling sessions. Our results have upended counselors' expectations. To date, several research studies have suggested the power of very brief counseling. Even one or two sessions can be quite successful for a number of clients.

Based on a series of studies on single-session therapy (SST) that Moshe Talmon, Michael Hoyt, and Robert Rosenbaum conducted from 1987 to 1989 at Kaiser Permanente Medical Center, Talmon (1993) concluded:

> . . . we found that clients who were seen for a single interview have done as well as those who stayed for a longer course of therapy. The single-session clients did not face simpler problems. Among the SST clients were heavy drinkers, abusers of hard drugs, and people faced with severe and stressful events such as violence in the family, death, and recent divorce. (p. 14)

Based on findings from the single-session therapy studies, Hoyt (1994) proposed nine counselor attitudes that facilitate successful SST. Modified to fit counseling, these attitudes are:

1. View each session as a whole, potentially complete in itself. Expect change.
2. The power is in the client. Never underestimate your client's strength.
3. This is it. All you have is now.
4. The therapeutic process starts before the first session, and will continue long after.
5. The natural process of life is the main force of change.
6. You don't have to know everything in order to be effective.
7. You don't have to rush or reinvent the wheel.
8. More is not necessarily better. Better is better. A small step can make a big difference.

9. Helping people as quickly as possible is practical and ethical. It will encourage clients to return for help if they have other problems, and will also allow counselors to spend more time with clients who require longer treatments. (p. 143)

In the late 1980s, I began working with a team of graduate students at Iowa State University on a series of brief counseling research experiments. We sought answers to the question—How brief can brief be and still prove helpful to the client? Our experiments employed single- or two-session counseling with follow-up evaluations. As you will see below as we discuss the four studies, we expanded our research to include:

1. high school students with academic, career, and personal/social concerns,
2. college students offered brief counseling with and without additional social support,
3. Hispanic college students, and
4. high school students with learning disabilities.

Study #1. In our first study we hypothesized that single-session counseling might be a viable way to assist high school students to deal effectively with academic, career, and personal/social concerns. We trained four counselors in a large urban high school to use three different forms of brief counseling with their students: (1) *problem-focused brief counseling approach with a task* (MRI steps 1–4), (2) *problem-focused brief counseling approach without task* (MRI steps 1–3), and (3) *solution-focused brief counseling approach with task* (MRI steps 3–4). The problem-focused, single-session brief counseling was modeled on the MRI four-step model (see Figure 1 in Chapter 2; Watzlawick et al., 1974) with BFTC intervention tasks (de Shazer, 1985, 1988). The solution-focused brief counseling blended the final two steps of the MRI approach with BFTC intervention tasks. The intervention tasks involved the following:

. . . the counselor assigned the student one of the following three tasks by saying: "Between now and when we meet for the follow-up interview in two weeks, I want you to: (a) observe, so that you can describe to me, what happens in your life, family, relationship, school, etc., that you want to continue to have happen; (b) do something different, no matter how surprising or fun or enjoyable or off-the-wall what you do might seem; or (c) pay attention to what you do when you overcome the urge to overeat, procrastinate, be depressed, etc." Students were informed that what they did could not be illegal, immoral, or harmful to themselves or others. Upon providing this qualification, the counselors observed that "knowing" smiles often illuminated students' faces. (Littrell et al., 1995, p. 453)

Two meaningful conclusions can be drawn from the results of this first experimental test of single-session, problem-focused counseling (modeled on the MRI approach) and single-session, solution-focused counseling (modeled on the BFTC approach):

1. ... all three brief counseling approaches were successful in helping students move in the direction of their goals and in reducing uncomfortable feelings associated with their problems. The success is particularly striking when these effects were associated with only a single counseling session. ... (Littrell et al., 1995, p. 456)

2. The three brief counseling approaches (i.e., problem-focused with task, problem-focused without task, and solution-focused with task) did not differ among themselves in their effectiveness in alleviating students' concerns, moving them toward their goals, and decreasing the intensity of undesired feelings related to their concerns. This finding throws into question the claim of those who believe that a solution-focused approach is more effective than a problem-focused approach, at least when it comes to counseling that is of single-session duration. However, the time spent by counselors with students was shorter in the solution-focused approach than with the two problem-focused approaches. The solution-focused approach thus has the advantage of producing comparable results, but in less time. This would seem to be an important consideration for busy counselors. (Littrell et al., 1995, pp. 456–457)

In summary, the two problem-focused forms of brief counseling proved as effective as the solution-focused form of brief counseling. The advantage of solution-focused is that it reduced the time spent in counseling.

Study #2. Does the addition of social support, beyond that of the counselor, increase the effectiveness of single-session brief counseling? In a second study, Kara Sanford investigated the use of social support as an added element in single-session counseling with 79 students who were receiving tutoring and who voluntarily signed up for short-term counseling (Sanford & Littrell, 1997). Social support occurred when clients enlisted the help of one or more additional people, e.g., a friend or family member, in reaching their goals. Three groups each received one of the following experimental treatments: (1) single-session counseling without social support, (2) single-session counseling with social support, and (3) delayed single-session group counseling with social support. All single-session counseling was based on the MRI four-step problem-solving model.

All three groups showed a decrease in the perceived severity of the problem, with an especially sharp decrease in the single-session and single-session/social support groups. Students in the single-session and single-session/social support group rated their current problems as significantly less severe at the first follow-up than did students in the delayed treatment group. Overall, students in the single-session and single-session/social support groups demonstrated a sharp drop in reported emotional intensity at the first follow-up. This drop was sustained and decreased an additional amount at the second follow-up. In contrast, the feeling intensity reported by the delayed treatment control group decreased only slightly, and then decreased more sharply after meeting with a counselor. In the final analysis, the addition of social support did not result in significantly different outcomes for the three groups.

Study #3. Will counseling as short as two sessions work with Hispanic students? A third brief counseling study was conducted by Jeannette Cruz, who worked as an academic counselor/advisor in a university office serving Hispanic students as well as other multiculturally diverse groups. Jeannette, a native Puerto Rican, speaks Spanish as her first language. She worked with 16 Hispanic college students to assess the effectiveness of two-session brief counseling. Counseling sessions began in English and often ended in Spanish. The following descriptions are excerpts from Cruz and Littrell (in press).

> The first counseling session (second visit) lasted 45-60 minutes, while the second one (third visit), two weeks later, was 15-30 minutes. Both were audiotaped. The brief counseling session was modeled on a four-step counseling approach (Fisch et al., 1982; Watzlawick, 1974). Immediately following the sessions students completed rating forms.
>
> Concerns were rated using a 7-point Likert-type scale (1 = problem bothers me very little, 7 = problem bothers me very much). Following the first counseling session, the students reported very high ratings of concern; the overall mean was 6.5 (SD = .7, mode = 7). Following both counseling sessions, students reported an average severity rating of 4.1 (SD = 1.4, mode = 3).
>
> In addition to rating the severity of their concerns, students had selected two feeling/emotion words that best described their situation. The student-generated list included 34 words (21 different feeling/emotions). The most common feeling/emotion words were anxious, scared, and worried. The Likert-type rating scale for the

feeling/emotion words ranged from 1 = "very weak" to 5 = "very strong." After the first counseling session the feeling rating approached "very strong" (M = 4.5, SD = .8, mode = 5). After the second counseling session the feeling rating was considerably weaker (M = 2.6, SD = 1.0, mode = 2).

In contrast to other studies in which the first session resulted in a marked decrease in (a) how much the problem bothered clients, and (b) the severity of clients' emotions, the clients in this study showed high levels of concern and uncomfortable emotional states. The positive effects of the four-step counseling approach (Fisch et al., 1982; Watzlawick, 1974) did not appear until after the second counseling session and, while statistically significant, they are not as strong as in other studies. While the results of this study move in a positive direction, additional studies need to determine the optimal number of sessions for Hispanic clients using this particular model.

Rapport is essential in counseling and there are many ways to create it. Not all rapport-building occurs within the counseling session. Despite the fact that Jeannette was seeing clients for the brief time of two sessions, she was not a stranger to her clients because she actively participated in the Hispanic association on campus. While traditional counseling cautions against dual relationships, Jeannette saw her role in providing Hispanic leadership as a complementary way of empowering her clients. When Jeannette met with students in her office she was not a stranger because her clients recognized and identified with her. Jeannette worked to ensure that rapport occurred prior to counseling because she believed that brief counseling would not be as effective with Hispanic clients if more time were not devoted to building rapport first.

Study #4. Is brief counseling a viable tool for students with learning disabilities? Robert Thompson investigated the feasibility of using a four-step, solution-oriented counseling approach for two sessions with adolescents identified as having learning disabilities (Thompson & Littrell, in press). The study answered questions about the types of concerns adolescents with LDs bring to the counseling session, their progress toward goals, and their behavioral, cognitive, and affective changes. Information about the clients is as follows:

Twelve students from two small secondary schools in rural Iowa volunteered to participate in this study. The students' ages ranged from 16 to 18 years. All students reported their ethnicity as being white American. Nine students were male; three were female. According to Iowa guidelines (State of Iowa Department of Education, 1990), the students had been assessed as having learning disabilities. All students who participated in this study were receiving special education services in a resource room setting. Typically, students assigned to a resource program spend from a minimum of .5 hours to a maximum of 2.5 hours receiving academic support in a resource room. (Thompson & Littrell, in press)

Students worked on academic issues such as time management, homework completion, study strategies, and performance anxiety. They also worked on personal concerns or issues concerning relationships with family members and/or friends. The results of this study were consistent with the other three studies in that the brief counseling proved beneficial to the clients.

> . . . two-session solution-oriented brief counseling is an appropriate and useful counseling approach to use with adolescents ages 16–18 who had been identified as having learning disabilities. All students made progress toward their goals, with all but 1 of 12 reaching 90–100% of their goals. Students reported their situations as improving, and the intensity of aversive feelings associated with their concerns decreasing. Although goals involved significant changes in behavior, students also experienced positive changes in cognition and affect. All students experienced positive changes in affect and cognition even when 100% goal attainment was not reached. It appears that two-session solution-oriented brief counseling was effective regardless of type of concern or severity of concern presented in this study. (Thompson & Littrell, in press)

Across the SST studies and the four Iowa State studies reported above, one conclusion is indisputable: One- or two-session counseling demonstrated considerable benefit to many clients in helping them move in the direction of the goals they set. Qualitative data indicated that the solution-oriented focus on doing something, not just talking about it, was a very affirming feature of the brief approaches. A second conclusion is that very brief counseling can rather quickly result in significant decreases in negative client affect. Qualitative data indicate that clients appreciate the focus on the positive, which fills them with hope.

Helping More People

Research evidence is accumulating that counseling time with individuals can be reduced and still prove effective. A second major question focuses on helping more people: Is there research to support that we can extend the scope of our counseling models to help a greater number of people? Across three decades, proponents of the MRI school have consistently suggested that counselors seek application of their approach beyond the world of counseling/therapy. They have directed our attention to larger systems with the following statements:

> . . . we have tried to show that our approach to problem formation and resolution is by no means limited to clinical cases, but has much wider applicability in most areas of human interaction. (Watzlawick et al., 1974, p. 158)

> We view our approach as applicable to any kind of persistent problem involving human behavior, occurring in any sort or size of social-organizational context—immediately applicable in principle, and potentially applicable in practice. (Fisch et al., 1982, p. 289)

Drawing upon a different framework of change, Prochaska (1996) also directs our attention to working in larger systems. He faults counselors and psychotherapists' fascination with one-to-one counseling when its overall impact on the enormousness of the problems people struggle with is so small. Prochaska suggests that counselors raise their sights to design interventions that target populations, not just individuals. By way of example, he cites his work with the government health system of Great Britain. Typically, physicians would admonish their patients to stop smoking or lose weight only to have their well intentioned advice ignored. In the face of massive noncompliance with their interventions, many physicians simply quit trying to say anything about behaviors that led to serious health problems. When large numbers of physicians across Great Britain were instructed about how to intervene in ways that matched the stage their patients were in, patients began to listen more (see discussion of Prochaska et al.'s research on stages of readiness in Chapter 2). For example, if patients who smoked were in the precontemplation stage, then interventions were aimed only at helping patients move to the contemplation stage, not to the action stage of quitting. Not only were the patients much more receptive with this stage-matching approach but the physicians were also considerably happier. No longer were they caught in the role of delivering bad news. Their patients saw them as allies—people who understood that they first needed time to contemplate the pros and cons of smoking and who understood that even preparing to quit, let alone taking the action of actually quitting, could be very scary. Teaching a model of change to large numbers of people who can positively influence others is but one example of how counselors might intervene in a larger system so as to have greater impact.

The MRI team's written urgings and Prochaska's research-supported programs share the powerful idea of moving to larger systems where the therapeutic tools we possess as helpers can make significant differences for many more people than we could possibly assist as individual clients. Brief counselors have an array of powerful tools in their repertoires. A very potent next step would be to apply these tools in larger systems. One professional applying brief counseling to larger systems is Claudia Vangstad, a Child Development Specialist who works in an elementary school in Myrtle Creek, Oregon. Dr. Jean Peterson, a colleague from Truman State University, and I have been conducting an extensive qualitative case study of Vangstad's work (Littrell, 1996). Vangstad is a change agent who practices a modified MRI approach that is action-based, solution-focused, and highly socially interactive. She has done an exemplary job of expanding the target audience of the MRI brief counseling model from individual and family into one involving a whole elementary school of students, teachers, staff, and administrators.

As we have studied Claudia's work in her school, we have marveled at how she has been able to take the four-step MRI model and apply it with individuals, clubs, classrooms, and the whole school. As but one example, during a typical week Claudia runs approximately 20 clubs for one-half hour each. Students are "customers," in that they have to want to be in a club. Names of some clubs and their descriptions are as follows:

1. LemonAID—Learn to turn life's lemons into lemonade. For children of parents who are separated, divorced, or have experienced a death of someone close.
2. Colors of Invis-ABILITY—What we see is not what we get. Children come in many sizes and colors and often have invisible strengths. This group is for students who need time to be accepted for who they are and need the confidence to develop their own unique strengths.
3. Bear University Club—Some students can "bearly" pay attention! Attention deficit disorder (ADD) and attention deficit hyperactivity disorder (ADHD) students who are on or off medication would be appropriate for this club. Students learn how to use their minds to picture what they want to remember.
4. SIBS—"Stop It Before I Scream"—Some siblings seem to argue and tattle on each other most of the time. These students learn to solve problems differently instead of tattling to parents or teachers.

5. Achievers Club—Students who get everything done and want to do more. These students learn to develop their organizational skills and practice working together as a group. Each group organizes projects to help the school or community.
6. Bomb Squad—Some students hold everything in while others let everything out. Students learn to defuse their negative behavior and be more constructive in dealing with others. (Vangstad & Littrell, 1997).

The Bomb Squad has been one of Claudia's favorites. She runs this club, as she does the others, using an MRI-fashioned format. As Claudia states,

The goal of the Bomb Squad club focused on students learning how to defuse their negative behavior and be more constructive in dealing with others. This club was most appropriate for students who were: (1) word throwers of obscenities and angry words, (2) inappropriate movers and touchers, (3) tantrum throwers, (4) punchers, and (5) bullies. I established this club because when I arrived at the school we were having approximately 30 fights a month—the injury and blood types. We needed a Bomb Squad club so I set one up. The results have been phenomenal. After two years of Bomb Squad clubs, the number of fights dropped from 30 a month to two a month and these latter are of the pushing and shoving variety. (Vangstad & Littrell, 1997)

Regardless of whether children are attending clubs, in classrooms, or at recess, the MRI's problem-solving approach is ubiquitous. Problem-solving posters are displayed in all classes; there is even one on the principal's door. The posters include nine ideas to try if there is a conflict, e.g., wait and cool off, ignore it, tell them to stop. Students on duty during recess serve as problem-solving conflict managers. Teachers employ problem-solving strategies to deal with conflicts in their classrooms. The school is permeated so thoroughly with the problem-solving approach that teachers report that the culture of the school has changed. Claudia has successfully met the challenge of taking the MRI model and expanding its ideas and practices into a much broader system. Her work points to some exciting ways that we can maximize our potential as brief counselors by expanding the scope of our work to larger systems and thus help a greater number of people.

The findings presented in this chapter provide tangible research evidence to answer the first question: Is there research to support the idea that we can significantly reduce the time to conduct effective counseling? We have moved beyond using anecdotal evidence to buttress the claim that brief counseling is a viable alternative to longer-term counseling. Researchers now have empirically based findings from systematic investigations to guide counselors' actions. There remains the second question: Is there research to support the idea that we can extend the scope of our counseling models to help a greater number of people? Here we have emerging evidence that counselors using brief counseling approaches can reach out to help a greater number of people. Research to answer this second question more completely may lead us to discover additional ways to amplify the potential of brief counseling.

Do Something Different

1. First, establish a baseline of the average number of sessions you typically work with clients. Second, set a goal to decrease the average number of sessions while increasing the quality of your work. Third, move toward your goal by incorporating into your daily routine some of the brief counseling approaches and techniques presented in this book. Fourth, assess to what extent the quality of your sessions stays the same, improves, deteriorates. Fifth, determine the new average number of sessions. Finally, if needed, do something different to reach your goal.

2. Plan three new ways to extend your reach as a counselor beyond the number of clients you typically serve. Avoid burdening yourself with just another thing to do; make your new plan fun, interesting, and exciting. Write, call, fax or e-mail me to share your ideas and actions:

Dr. John M. Littrell
N221 Lagomarcino Hall
Iowa State University
Ames, IA 50011
ISU Telephone: (515) 294-5746
FAX: (515) 294-5746
E-mail: jlittrel@iastate.edu

Part V

•
•
•
•
•
•

Completing Counseling
in a
Single Session

CHAPTER 16

Case 1: Lights! Camera! Action!

CLIENT: *Nothing has worked so far. Why should brief counseling be any different?*

This part of the book contains three detailed cases of single-session counseling and adds to the growing literature about this phenomenon (Bandler, 1993; Bloom, 1981; Budman, Hoyt, & Friedman, 1992; Talmon, 1990, 1993). These detailed presentations allow for a clearer understanding of how the following elements interact: (a) the counselor's mindset in approaching counseling and how this is conveyed to clients, (b) the key steps in brief counseling and how they fluidly relate to one another, and (c) specific methods used to speed up action toward helping clients reach their goals. The case in this chapter, "Lights! Camera! Action!" (along with its embedded case "Instant Miracle"), supports my contention that brief counseling seriously challenges our traditional expectations about how counseling "should" proceed. The persistent emphasis on strengths, humor, what works, and speed combine to give the client a hopeful message—change can occur and it can occur rapidly.

The speed with which Gerald reached his goal was a challenge to his mindset about how long counseling would take. It was also a challenge to my own mindset. I did not begin the counseling with the idea that a single session would be sufficient. In fact, as I listened to Gerald's concerns, I was tempted to think that brief counseling would not be an appropriate treatment modality. Gerald's initial presentation had me thinking about long-term family therapy. As it turned out, Gerald surprised me by how quickly he resolved the problem and moved toward our mutually agreed upon goal. Frankly, I enjoy being surprised in this way. I find that this happens more and more often as I focus on clients' strengths rather than their deficits.

I met with Gerald alone even though I would have liked to have had his family present. As the session opened I attempted two things. First, I tried to demystify counseling by telling Gerald how I worked in a brief counseling manner and how I found that clients and I discovered solutions that worked. I provided structure to our time together by suggesting that we work together through a four-step brief counseling model: (1) description of the problem, (2) looking at attempted solutions, (3) setting a specific goal, and (4) looking at ways to reach the goal (Watzlawick et al., 1974). Gerald appeared receptive to this framework.

Second, I stated to Gerald in a straightforward manner that counseling might be over sooner than he might believe. The intent of this statement was to plant a seed of hope that change might occur much more quickly than expected. This statement also alerted Gerald to look for change sooner rather than later.

Gerald was in his late thirties. He was married to Irene, also in her late thirties; they had two daughters, Becky, 13, and Vickie, 10. Although Gerald had appeared alone for our session, it was quickly evident that he thought the client was not himself but his daughter Vickie. In a brief description of the problem situation, Gerald described the following home situation:

> Vickie is driving us all crazy. One or two mornings a week during this school year she throws a classic temper tantrum right in the middle of the kitchen floor. She puts us all on edge for the rest of the day. I drive to work just gripping the steering wheel because I'm so tense. The people at work know just from looking at me if it has been one of those mornings.

I acknowledged Gerald's thoughts and feelings through paraphrases, reflections of feelings, and summarizations. While trying to be empathic, I did not dwell on Gerald's feelings. Following Gerald's description of the problem situation, I had him tell me about the family's attempted solutions. He continued:

> So far, we have tried to ignore her tantrums. We have punished her. We have tried to reward her good behavior. Nothing has worked. Quite frankly, my wife and I are desperate for something that will work. To make matters worse, the teachers and the counselor at her school have told us that they would love to have Vickie as their

daughter because she is an eager learner, does extremely well in school, is very outgoing, and is popular with other kids. The counselor has as much as told us that we must be exaggerating because our story doesn't match the Vickie the school knows and loves.

Gerald was clearly discouraged as he finished his description of the current problem situation at home and the failed attempted solutions. Quite frankly, after listening to his recitation of the problem and what did not work, I caught some of Gerald's pessimism that nothing was going to work. Since this was not an effective response on my part, I looked for what was working in the family in connection with this situation. In other words, what were exceptions to the problem? One attempt to find exceptions was to reframe the situation so as to accent what was working rather than what was not working (Bandler & Grinder, 1982). I commented that it seemed to me that his family was 60% to 80% successful in dealing with the problem situation already. He looked at me in disbelief. I explained that one or two of the five school days each week would translate into 20% to 40% of the time there was a problem. Looked at from another perspective, the family was successful three to four times a week in having an acceptable morning, in other words, 60% to 80% successful. Gerald looked at me and smiled for the first time. He said that he had not looked at their situation in that way before. I believed him. Most clients are so focused on "the problem" that they do not see the parts that are "*not* the problem." When I reframed Gerald's situation in terms of strengths, he began for the first time in the session to show some hope.

Moving to the third step in counseling rather quickly, Gerald and I engaged in co-authoring the future through goal-setting. We tackled the questions: Where do you want to go? and How can we define that destination? rather than What is not working in your life? I asked Gerald what he wanted to be able to achieve as a result of our meeting together. He said he did not want to be so tense, and he wanted his daughter to stop her temper tantrums. I pointed out that both of these goals were stated in negative terms—as what he did *not* want. What did he *want*?

We worked to clarify a small and meaningful goal. If he were to reach this goal he would know that he was moving in the right direction. Eventually we arrived at a goal of having nine out of ten school day mornings be typical-family-of-four mornings, that is, okay mornings, but definitely not perfect. This meant that Vickie was allowed to have one tantrum during the ten-day period; this would translate into 90% success for the family. Gerald agreed that 90% was better than what they had. He was visibly enthusiastic about reaching this goal.

I prefer to work with clients whose ability to attain their goal is completely under their control. Therefore, I had some misgivings about the attainment of the goal, since it was not completely under Gerald's control. However, Gerald was a customer in that he was willing to do something different to move in the direction of his goal.

Once Gerald and I had negotiated a goal, we explored actions to help him reach his goal. However, as we moved into methods, he said he was not sure he knew how to get there. This is typical of many clients. As they move into new territory they need some guidance. Clients often move in the direction of their goals when they are having a sense of fun, excitement, and interest. Tasks and methods that are fun, interesting, and exciting are more likely to be completed than those that are not. Despite the difficulty of problems, humor can frequently assist clients in making needed changes.

I have found that telling stories is one useful way to stimulate clients to think in fun, interesting, and exciting ways (Combs & Freedman, 1990; Gordon, 1978). As a means of stimulating Gerald's thinking of ways to achieve his goal, I told him the following story about another client who had used her imagination and sense of fun to influence others to change.

Instant Miracle

I once worked with another client, Harriet, who had two adolescents—a boy and a girl. Every day when the mother came home from work her two kids were fighting over which TV station to watch. Countless other topics were grist for their arguing mill.

Harriet had resorted to all sorts of ways to stop the fighting, but she had been unsuccessful in bringing about a truce. She had even begun to suspect that they didn't fight when she was gone—they saved their energy until they heard her car turn into the driveway.

I challenged the mother to do something different—something that was much more fun, interesting and exciting as a way of moving in the direction of her goal. As we discussed possible new actions, she told me the following plan for doing something different. She said,

> I know what I'm going to do. I'm going to get out our tape recorder. When my son and daughter are fighting I will go into the room where they are, place the tape recorder on the table in front of them, turn it on, and say, "You are both very special to me and one of these days you will be grown up and moved out of the house. Then I am going to be very lonely even though you will come back to visit on holidays. Therefore, I want you both to communicate in the typical way you do when I come home and I will record it. That way in my old age when the two of you are not around I can play my tape and

remember fondly the way you two communicated with each other. Would you do this so your mother can have a tape of memories for her old age?

I thought her new plan was marvelous and told her so. However, Harriet didn't need much cheerleading from me because she was almost looking forward to her kids' not cooperating so that she could try her new solution.

The following week Harriet told me that she had carried out what she had said she was going to do and that a miracle had occurred. Her most uncooperative adolescents had instantly learned the skills of cooperation. Later, she told me that when her son and daughter "forgot" their newfound cooperation, she didn't say a word; she simply brought the tape recorder into the room and turned it on. She said she loved watching miracles occur.

Many methods may be used to help clients brainstorm new options. The metaphorical case I told was one method for generating new options, for doing something different. As I finished the case, Gerald interrupted me to say,

> John, say no more. I'm one ahead of you. Several weeks ago we purchased a camcorder for recording home videos. Vickie has been telling us that we ought to film something funny around our house so that we can send the tape to *America's Funniest Home Videos* show. She says they pay money for the ones they show on the air and she's into making money.
>
> Here's my plan. I'm going to sit down with my family this Sunday and announce that on Monday we can begin filming our videotape for *America's Funniest Home Videos.* I'll tell Vickie that she can do that thing she does on the kitchen floor on Monday and I'll videotape it. We'll send it in and make money. I'll tell her not to wait until Tuesday or Wednesday or later because the sooner we send in the tape, the sooner we might get it on the air.

Together Gerald and I planned how we would know if change were occurring. We decided to measure his progress using a scaling technique. Each day he would rate the family level using the following scale: 1 = great and 10 = horrible (temper tantrum). Gerald's scale was the reverse of how they are typically constructed, but he thought that 1 was the best.

Gerald and I ended our session with Gerald eager to undertake this new task. The first thing he mentioned he would do was purchase an additional videotape. He and I agreed to have him contact me at the end of the two weeks to assess the movement toward his goal. Two weeks later, Gerald sent me the following short report along with a message that he would not be able to meet with me again, but that he believed the goal had been achieved.

> I promised to give you feedback on my mornings with my ten-year-old daughter, Vickie. Based on a scale where 1 = great and 10 = horrible, the results are:
>   Week #1—3 mornings of 7.0 and 2 mornings of 2.0.
>   Week #2—3 mornings of 5.0 and 2 mornings of 2.0.
> I am greatly encouraged and as yet no need to videotape!!

Gerald also reported that there had been no temper tantrums during the two weeks—a 100% success rate for the family. While there were no temper tantrums, the scale indicates some very good mornings and some that were not; the mean score was 4.4 for the 10 days.

As stated earlier, Gerald and I were not able to continue working together. His follow-up report is the last information available. In reflecting on my work, I realized the family's pattern had been a circular one: (a) Vickie doing a temper tantrum, (b) her parents' anger with her "childish" behavior, (c) Vickie feeling left out of the family, and (d) Vickie doing a temper tantrum to get parents' attention. I am left to speculate about why the intervention worked as effectively as it did. I suspect the introduction of the camcorder served to stop temporarily Vickie's temper tantrums. I also suspect that Vickie stopped long enough to provide the family some relief. During their breathing spell from tantrums, the parents were freed to see the same positive qualities in their daughter that others saw. The parents began treating Vickie more as a part of the family. Vickie had less reason to do tantrums when she felt more accepted.

Brief counselors attempt to interrupt non-useful patterns and help clients establish useful ones. In this case, the interruption alone allows the family system time to establish new workable patterns. It was not necessary to teach the family new patterns. However, if pattern interruption had not been sufficient, other counseling approaches would have been considered. For example, a family therapy approach would suggest that the counselor work with the whole family rather than just the father. A behavioral approach would suggest finding the reinforcing elements that keep the tantrums going. Neither of these or the many other ways of approaching this case would have been wrong, but I suspect they would have been somewhat longer. Brief counselors are quite willing to shift gears and use longer-term approaches if short-term ones are not effective in helping clients reach their desired states and alleviate their discomfort. Brief counselors simply have a preference for the briefest process that works.

CHAPTER 17

Case 2:
More Poohish

CLIENT: *I want a way of changing that makes sense of the way I think about myself and the world.*

This case illustrates the multiple use of brief counseling techniques. Here I began with a more problem-oriented approach but rapidly deployed a solution-focused approach to help dissolve several sticky problems. I emphasized both the client's attempted solutions and exceptions to the problem times (i.e., when the problems did not occur). My emphasis throughout was on what had worked, what was currently working, and what would work. The resource-focused approach inspired hope in the client, an antidote for her feeling down. In addition, the case also illustrates how a brief counseling approach utilizes the client's language for talking about what is and what is to be. The eventual goal of "more Poohish" is definitely the client's language. It instinctively made sense to her.

A month after I had conducted a 30-minute demonstration with Tina at a brief counseling workshop, she sent me a follow-up letter. We had used a four-step approach (Watzlawick et al., 1974) with attention to attempted solutions (Fisch et al., 1982) and elements from de Shazer's (1985) work on exceptions to the problem. I had Tina summarize the problem; we did not linger at this stage. We moved quickly to her attempted solutions and exceptions. As will be noted in her letter, she later used several attempted solutions and exceptions in reaching her goal.

As Tina and I moved into goal-setting, she initially stated her goal as wanting to be "less Eeyorish." I had not remembered well the Winnie the Pooh stories so she had to explain to me that Eeyore was always looking on the dark side of life and finding fault. To place her goal in a framework of what she did want, I asked, "If you were being less Eeyorish, what would you be?" She answered, "I would be more Poohish."

Since Tina's goal of "more Poohish" seemed rather vague in view of my criteria for goals (see Chapter 7), I asked Tina how she would know if she were more Poohish. She answered that she would just definitely know. I believed her. The goal set, Tina and I began to generate ways for her to become more Poohish. Tina's letter reporting her results was one "Dear John" letter I enjoyed receiving.

Dear John,

I was your volunteer client and wanted to write to give you an update. You have my permission to use any of the following in your teaching or writing. Using your brief counseling format, this is what I recall about our session:

1. *Problem*: Due to budget constraints, I am afraid of losing my job as a Child Development Specialist at an elementary school. The fear has translated into a general feeling of apathy and desperation at work. I find it difficult to enjoy my work while wondering if I'll be job-hunting soon.

2. *Attempted solutions and exceptions*: I take good care of myself, exercising daily, doing the outdoor activities I enjoy, resting, eating well, etc. I have written and telephoned my legislators and the members of the School Board to make known my concerns about proposed cutbacks. I do feel good and function effectively much of the time, but I had noticed a decrease in my sense of humor, energy, and centeredness.

3. *Goal*: I cannot really control whether or not I keep my job but I can control how I feel and act at work. This is where I choose to focus. Initially I stated that I wanted to be more joyous, centered and peaceful at work, and to be present with each person with whom I come in contact. A metaphor for this presented itself to me in the form of Pooh and Eeyore from *The World of Pooh*. It seemed that I was much more Eeyorish than Poohish at work. My goal was to be at least 80% Pooh and 20% or less Eeyore.

4. *Tasks*: I was amazed at the ideas that began to flow when I focused my attention on being more Poohish. Some tasks I thought might be helpful were:

- Blowing bubbles (I already do this in traffic jams)
- Wearing my clown nose more often
- Read daily from Anne Wilson Schaef's *Meditations for Women Who Do Too Much*. I decided I had a better chance of doing this if I placed the book on top of my date book.
- Meditate daily. Decided to write this into my schedule, and pull the shade, possibly putting a sign on it saying "Important Conference—Do Not Disturb!"
- Work on resumé instead of listening to the gloom and doom in the teachers' lunch room. John, you suggested a file with RESUMÉ written in black letters on the outside.

A month has passed, and I wanted to let you know what has happened since. First of all, I felt more personal power almost instantly. Perhaps it was the fact that I separated what I could and could not control and made some choices to support myself that caused the change. I also felt playful during the session and that unleashed all kinds of creativity and self-support. I found myself saying things I hadn't thought of. I knew what I needed to do but hadn't thought of it until I verbalized it. Your support and gentle direction helped free me from the rigid victim status I had been experiencing and helped me remember what I already knew. It is to your credit that I cannot recall much of what you did or said, but I remember the ideas that I came up with and the sense of being back in charge of my life. I do recall feeling very validated, gently prodded into action and respected. I was amazed at feeling close to tears when addressing my friends in the audience and experienced a deep sense of gratitude for my job and friends. It was a very powerful experience which left me wrung out but exhilarated.

Since early April many wonderful things have happened which could account for my renewed sense of well-being. My broken ankle has healed and I'm walking like a real person, the sun is out, the flowers have returned, fellow-counselors have called and written to offer support, encouragement, and their thanks for my saying what they needed to say. I have not followed all the tasks I assigned myself and wrestled with some guilt over that until I realized that I don't necessarily need to do all of them, especially since I have more than met my goal of being more Poohish and present at work. I do read the *Meditations* each day. My clown nose and bubbles are at my desk and have been used frequently. I meditated once and was amazed at my creativity afterward. This is one area I want to make a better decision about—perhaps I will make it a habit, perhaps it will be something I do occasionally. The resumé is still in my file cabinet (I even paid my taxes early—I'm not a procrastinator by nature), and I'm in the process of deciding whether or not to pursue this. I know that if and when I need to revise the resumé, I will do it in about an hour so I'm not going to hassle it now.

So there you have it! I keep your handouts from the conference at my desk for quick reference and find I am much more effective in my counseling as a result.

Sincerely,

Tina

A solution-focused approach emphasizes what works or has worked in clients' lives. This single session with Tina is typical of a solution-focused approach. As we worked together, I was impressed by Tina's strengths (e.g., she was taking care of herself physically). We found that her attempted solutions were partially successful (e.g., she was being proactive about proposed cutbacks), and they were not hampering her or posing a problem. As is common for many clients, Tina was not initially aware of how much she had already done. She was not starting from scratch. My role at this stage was to facilitate her hearing the active steps she had already taken, thus letting her experience moderate success. Recognition of success seemed to generate hope.

Tina's goal met the criteria listed in Chapter 7. Her goal of "at least 80% Pooh and 20% or less Eeyore" almost sounds like it was written by a Dreamer who states messages in the positive. Tina proved to be a skilled Realist in that she set a small, short-term, concrete goal that was under her control. She had quickly realized that she could not directly control whether she retained her job but that she could have more control over how she chose to "feel and act at work." The focus on what she could control resulted in her spontaneous use of the Pooh and Eeyore metaphor. Avoiding perfection, she set her goal as being "at least 80% Pooh and 20% or less Eeyore." Finally, Tina did her job as a Critic when we assessed the possible impact of her changes.

Tina's own words describe the release from constraints clients often experience when the focus is solution-oriented. Tina wrote, "I was amazed at the ideas that began to flow when I focused my attention on being more Poohish." Some ideas were playful ("Blowing bubbles—I already do this in traffic jams" and "Wearing my clown nose more often"), while others were more serious ("read daily from . . . *Meditations for Women Who Do Too Much*," "meditate daily," and "work on resumé").

Tina's comment about feeling "more personal power almost instantly" is a phenomenon I have repeatedly witnessed when clients and I focus on solutions. A second phenomenon has been the states of "playful," "creative," and "self-support." A third phenomenon has been clients' sense of being "wrung out but exhilarated." This third comes from having worked very hard while also having experienced significant breakthroughs.

Tina rightly acknowledged that many things happen in life to account for changes and that brief counseling is but one of many things that happened that might have accounted for her being more Poohish. For example, in Tina's view of the changes, Mother Nature deserves some credit for having Spring arrive with its sun and flowers.

Clients often have many resources in their repertoires that they have failed to use. Too much focus on problems can easily result in feeling stuck precisely at those times when clients want to feel less mired in problems or, in Tina's words, "less Eeyorish." One answer is to assist clients and also ourselves to move quickly to identify resourceful patterns or, again in Tina's words, to become "more Poohish." As counselors we need to find our own equivalent for "more Poohish" so that we use our own language of change when we work with clients in that excitement-generating model of counseling known as brief.

CHAPTER 18

Case 3: Walking through Hell

CLIENT: *I'd been in longer-term therapy. I was wary of anything too short.*

As stated previously in this book, brief counseling is not a method for assisting all clients. As with any counseling approach, brief counseling has a range of effectiveness within which it works well and outside of which its usefulness is quite limited. In brief counseling, as with other types of counseling, the client's motivation is often a key factor. Is the client willing to make some changes? As Fisch et al. (1982) might ask, Is the client a window shopper? a complainant? or a customer? In the case presented in this chapter, the client, Kathy, was under considerable pressure to make a decision about what she was to do; she proved to be a most eager customer.

This single counseling session occurred during a time I was on the road doing brief counseling workshops. Kathy had attended an introductory lecture about brief counseling. Following the lecture she had asked if she could meet with me for a single session to discuss a concern. My conditions for the session were that it be tape recorded, that we work with a solution-focused brief counseling approach, and that I have her permission to include a write-up of the case in a book if the session clarified the brief counseling process. Kathy agreed with these conditions. She also later willingly reviewed the transcript and edited it for clarity and confidentiality. As she stated in a letter to me,

> Editing a chapter for a book in which I know the character personally is quite a task! My goals in this editing task were to delete the

unnecessary "garbage"—there was a lot I assume due to the nature of dialogue. My conversations with my cat are sometimes clearer on my part! I deleted repetitive phrases, nonsense, asides, thinking-out-loud, stupidity, and the words "yah" & "uh huh."

I often use the opening part of a first session to assess the clients' strengths. I find this sets an upbeat mood for the session, just as surely as focusing on problems sets a downbeat mood. The focus on clients' strengths and resources helps them identify what has worked in their lives. As a result of rehearsing their assets, clients often feel empowered. Ivey (1994) has written about conducting a positive assets search. Focusing on strengths and resources very early in a counseling process, even as the first activity, prevents clients from "wallowing" through a recitation of what is not working and being discouraged by the negative emphasis on their shortcomings. For those clients who insist on telling us about problems first, we can follow their lead as a way of establishing rapport. In addition, and this occurred in the session with Kathy, counselors and clients can use the identified assets in later work toward new solutions to problems.

Kathy is in her mid thirties. She is a graduate student in a counseling psychology program working on her doctorate. During the introductory lecture on brief counseling, I had discussed ways to demystify counseling (see Chapter 5). Aspects of brief counseling were reviewed by Kathy and me prior to turning on the tape recorder. As Kathy and I were seated to begin the session, I took an active role by stating to Kathy what she might have actually said to herself about her situation. I took my clues from her short conversation with me following the introductory lecture. I find that on occasion we as counselors can come rather close to how our clients might have said it. When we are fairly accurate, clients realize that we have some degree of empathy for their situations. On the other hand, when we're off, clients are quick to correct us and therefore assume a more expert role in the session. Regardless of the outcome, both the client and counselor are launched into the counseling process. As is clear from our opening dialogue, Kathy was fast on the uptake and we moved rapidly into the session.

Assessing Strengths and Resources

JOHN: I'm going to see if I can do a mind-reading act. Two possibilities. The first would be that one of the thoughts that has crossed your mind is, "My god, why is this happening to me *now*?"

KATHY: Yes, happening *now*, plus happening *again*. I would choose those words. Exactly right. [I love to hear clients say, "Exactly right."

It means they are being heard or, more accurately, that my words are making sense to them.]

JOHN: And the second one was, "The only positive thing I can see at this point is that at least it didn't happen when I was taking my licensing exam." [I focus on a potentially positive aspect of the situation.]

KATHY: That's true but I never had the licensing exam on my list; that one didn't come to my mind. But the first possibility is right on.

JOHN: Fifty percent. That's not a bad average!

KATHY: You're doing real good. I'll explain the situation. It will be helpful, won't it?

JOHN: Yeah. [Kathy wants to tell me the past. While my preference is often to begin with where a client wants to go (i.e., future goals), I try to be flexible and begin where clients feel comfortable. However, with Kathy I also begin negotiating for talking about her strengths and resources prior to her recitation of her problem's history.]

KATHY: I've thought about one of the questions you asked in your lecture on identifying goals. I've been thinking about it a lot and that has been helpful in this process. I just wanted to point that out. [My neglect to follow up on this is a missed opportunity from a brief counseling perspective. Pre-session changes can be very powerful, and my regret is that I missed the opportunity to focus on the changes she had already made in relationship to the issues we will be discussing. Kathy said she was going to explain her situation, but didn't. Since she didn't describe the present situation, I use the opportunity to focus on her strengths.]

JOHN: Now, another place that I sometimes start before listening to the story is to first identify what you understand as your strengths as a person. [I have a pen and paper available for clients to jot down key words and phrases that will help them later remember the things they are learning in the session. I hand Kathy a pen and paper at this point. Her in-session writing entitled *Kathy's In-session Notes* is found opposite.]
Put down "management skills" on your list.
[Since "management skills" appear to be a strength, I suggest she put them on her list. I constantly cue clients to record the things they are learning about themselves in counseling so that they can remember and use this knowledge later outside the session.]

Kathy's In-Session Notes

- Survivor
- face fear, vulnerability
- the only way out is through
- heaven is in the center of hell
- sense of humor—laugh at self
- flexible
- YAVIS (Young, Attractive, Verbal, Intelligent, Successful) client
- ★ management skills

- know about self, experienced
- voluntary vs. involuntary crisis
- drawing
- what could be worse?
  myself vs. nomads
- hell is not having a lesson to learn
- "I" statements
- ★ grace under fire—how to walk through hell in a graceful manner
- controlled self—managing self
- ★ head/heart issues

KATHY: To answer that question let me ask you a question. Are you talking about my strengths in general or in relation to the situation?

JOHN: I am talking about your strengths in general as a person. You have lived so many years and have acquired so many . . . [In print the phrase "so many years" comes across sounding like I'm saying the client is very old. That is not my intent and not how the client hears it.]

KATHY: (Interrupting) No, I'm a survivor, and that is a strength. Sometimes I wish I weren't a survivor but it's a strength. I think that's important because when there's a problem, I know I will get through it—for better or for worse. The process is what I don't like.

JOHN: So sometimes you use the expression "seeing the light at the end of the tunnel," for you know there is always a light.

KATHY: Yes. I have been in some very challenging situations in the past few years, and they have given me a lot of strength. When you talk about "what are my strengths," I have had to come face to face with fear. I have come face to face with . . . (She paused here for some time)

JOHN: So you can face fear. [I modify her statement slightly to cast it as a strength.]

KATHY: Yes. I would add to that vulnerability. My vulnerability and my own weaknesses are about the same. My favorite expression instead of "the light at the end of the tunnel" is "the only way out is through." [Kathy modifies my tunnel metaphor to fit her life.]

JOHN: Okay. Is that useful? [I am unclear if what she had just said was perceived by her as a strength. Rather than assuming I know, I check it out.]

KATHY: That's a quote from Trungpa who was a Buddhist. It is a phrase that I read in an article that he wrote. I said it to myself as a mantra. The last time I was in an extremely difficult situation when I had a choice—like now—I read that, and it helped me to understand that in order to overcome the situation I had to enter into it. I have to go inside the problem. I can't skirt around it. My tendency might be to avoid a problem, to not address the problem. [Kathy provides an example of a method she has used in the past to deal with difficult situations. In brief counseling we listen carefully to prior strengths and resources. In the Mental Research Institute model this would be step 2— identifying the client's previous solutions. See Chapter 5.]

JOHN: So saying that and believing that is a strength or a way of helping you cope. [My statement is a very deliberate reiteration of her strength.]

KATHY: The reason I'm here is that I want to go through. [Kathy does not linger long on her strengths; she dives right into the problem part of her story. Her statement can also be seen as a strong motivation to change.]

JOHN: Okay.

KATHY: I'd rather say "Fine, honey, do whatever you need to do, and I will support you." And that's bullshit! The truth is I feel like I have a lot to say about the matter but I want to do it in a dignified way. I will just write things out. [I point to the paper and prompt her to write out the strengths she has been continuing to mention. I am unsure what the content is all about at this point so I wait to have it clarified.]

KATHY: Okay. The other phrase that comes to mind is, "Heaven is in the center of Hell." I think that's Dante's phrase—more or less—you know, like this is easy? Hah! [Kathy pounds on the table with her fist to indicate that her question of being easy is a joke. On the contrary, she finds it very hard.]

JOHN: Put it down. [My directive to have her write down the phrase.]

KATHY: Why do I have to keep reviewing these lessons, as in life lessons?—is another question. That goes back to what you said.

JOHN: I have no clue as to why you keep reviewing these lessons. Note that even on my blackboard there is a phrase from Stephen Covey's book: Organize around priorities. (We both laugh.) In a way I think phrases are sometimes a putting together in capsule form a lot of the learning that we know.

KATHY: Yes, no kidding.

JOHN: The experiences we've had. It is a shorthand for how to access those things at times. [I support the idea that phrases important to Kathy may be a shorthand way of providing her guidance in living.]

KATHY: One of the things that I have been thinking about is things that I also do not like about myself which are not survival skills.

JOHN: I'm going to hold off on those for just a little bit. [Kathy begins to tell weaknesses and I redirect her to stay with the strengths and resources. I'm fully aware that clients will tell me weaknesses soon enough so I am deliberately keeping us away from them for a while longer. It is a way of keeping us on in brief counseling framework. See Chapter 12.]

KATHY: Okay, but that's what keeps creeping into my mind. [In the past, Kathy had been in longer-term counseling; her model of counseling was to focus on problems. My redirecting was a way of teaching her how brief counseling operated. I find that most clients need some orientation to the brief counseling emphasis on the positive.] My strengths . . . the ones I am grabbing onto right now for this difficulty. [Kathy appears lost at this point. To provide more direction, I mention examples of strengths other clients have identified.]

JOHN: Why don't we take one of your strengths, such as your sense of humor.

KATHY: Okay.

JOHN: Ability to laugh at situations and yourself.

KATHY: Yes. (nods in agreement) I also think I am open to criticism. I would say I'm flexible. And sometimes that helps.

JOHN: There is a phrase in the counseling profession that came to me the other night when I was thinking about meeting with you. You would probably be described in the literature as a YAVIS client. [I use a positive label as a way of acknowledging Kathy's strengths.]

KATHY: A what?

JOHN: YAVIS. Five capital letters: YAVIS stands for young, attractive, verbal, intelligent, and successful.

KATHY: There! Once I took a fun personality quiz . . .

JOHN: And?

KATHY: And one of the questions was, "How do you see yourself?" And what I liked best about that entire exercise was that other people agreed with my description of myself. They perceived me in the same way that I perceived myself. This YAVIS was also . . . what was the "S"?

JOHN: Successful.

KATHY: Oh, successful. That's very interesting.

JOHN: Now I would just let you know that with YAVIS clients, the counselor often does minimal work and the client does most by herself because often it is a matter of a little prompting. [Again I seed the idea that Kathy has lots of abilities and that she can do most of the work. This also seeds the ideas that counseling may be accomplished quickly (see Chapter 3) and the idea that Kathy is being treated as an expert on her own life (see Chapter 4).]

KATHY: Yes. That's right. Someone told me once that I am a person who is looking for confirmation of my own solutions. I ask myself, "Do you think this is the right way to handle it?" In fact, I have already got the answer. I really don't want other opinions particularly.

JOHN: Is that the same as the strength in terms of trusting your intuition? [I return to how this applies to the strength of trusting her own intuition.]

KATHY I don't trust my intuition. Isn't that interesting? I trust my intuition about most things except men. You know, that's the truth. And I didn't ever think of that before. I think that happened rather late in my life that I began to realize I was this really lousy assessor of relationships. But that's my own burden to bear. [To this point in the session, we have focused on strengths and not on the issues for which she has sought counseling. It was tempting to respond to her phrase, "really lousy assessor of relationships." With my next question, I derailed slightly.]

JOHN: How large is the sample you're going on?

KATHY: Oh, two—maybe five! I know exactly why I am in the situation I'm in.

JOHN: So you made a generalization based on two—possibly up to five?

KATHY: Yah! We're not talking about a large sample here, John!

JOHN: What you are talking about is your life based on that sample? [I confront mildly.]

KATHY: That's right. [Kathy backs away from the sample metaphor and returns to strengths.]

Clarifying the Problem

JOHN: Okay. Now, I guess as you tell me about the situation and so on, let's bear in mind, "How do I bring this me—these strength aspects of myself—to bear on this issue?" In other words, what do I know about myself? What's there that I know I do and that I have experienced that somehow is going to start to help me to deal with these issues? [I connect the focus on her strengths to the forthcoming discussion of problems—I reframe problems by calling them issues.]

KATHY: I am dealing with "the only way out is through"—as we speak. I immediately took action based on my past, and I said to myself, "You can't skirt around this; you can't avoid this. I have to come to some peace with this." I've called some other people for advice but no one is home—and so it is you and me, John. [Kathy asserts that counselors are not indispensable in her life because friends are her first resource. I consider this a very positive way of looking at life. Clients' family and friends should be their first line of support.]

JOHN: Okay.

KATHY: Ah—the situation—this is about vulnerability, I suppose, and fear. I am trying to be open, and I am trying to be flexible; but all of that is in my head, and my heart is not wanting to be open or flexible or unbiased. My husband has been invited to join a scientific study group in South America.

JOHN: Yeah.

KATHY: It is an educational, scientific, and historical trip. [Considerable identifying detail was omitted here to preserve confidentiality.] My husband Kirk found out about this opportunity two years ago and became interested in it at a time when he was very vulnerable and was looking for an escape.

JOHN: Are those his words or your words?

KATHY: Mine. But he would now acknowledge that, I believe.

JOHN: Okay.

KATHY: It came up again last year at about this time when—at a very bad time in our marriage because neither of us was focused— we were both reacting to life instead of being proactive and finding a solution that was healthy for both of us. We were both lost. So, at that time, I told Kirk the study group tour would have a very negative effect on our relationship. I felt that he was running away from an emotional situation that he couldn't cope with, and I was not happy.

So, eventually he elected not to join the group. I thought the whole issue had gone away. He got a call two nights ago from the leader of the trip explaining that it had been postponed to this winter for X-Y-Z reasons. The group would be sponsored; they had raised several million dollars. Writers and reporters and other professionals would join the team. The trip leader was passionate about conducting the exploration—it has been a dream of his. My husband would be gone up to a year, and at the minimum, half a year. So those are the facts.

JOHN: Facts. The meaning is?

KATHY: The meaning is (long pause) my survival. My question is "Why is this happening again?" You know, why is this coming up again?

JOHN: What is your best guess? [This question focuses back on the client's knowledge and is a soft form of "you tell me."]

KATHY: What Kirk said to me was, "Maybe this trip keeps coming up because I'm really supposed to go"—in other words, his Karma controlling destiny; it is out of our control—maybe he is being tested. This business about timing—perhaps Kirk is trying to resolve certain issues within himself which will be addressed on a trip like this. But he wasn't seeking it out. He has not spent every day of the past year calling this man up on the phone and saying "Is the trip on or off—can I go or can't I?"

JOHN: And so, "why now?"

KATHY: Exactly. One time a visiting lecturer came to a class when I was in college, and she said you have to be passionate about what you're doing in order to make it really work for you. And I really support that. So, I asked Kirk, "Do you feel passionate about this trip?" Because I can tell you things that he does feel passionate about such as athletics. He feels passionate about travel in general. In this case, he seems passionate about taking yet another risk. But that's my opinion. Now I'm dealing with my emotional issues. I am trying to not be biased. And yet I'm struggling.

JOHN: Well, I don't know you—I am not sure "biased" is the word I would use but we all have our agendas—we all have things that we care about and so I don't know that those can somehow be put aside in terms of decisions. [I reframe her use of "biased" as "agenda," a less emotionally loaded word. At the same time, I acknowledged that decisions involve many factors, including emotions.]

KATHY: Well, I don't want to be angry. This is a big goal of mine. I don't want to be angry. I don't want to be a victim. [Often the initial statement of a goal is negatively stated in terms of what the client doesn't want. I will be attempting to have her goal meet certain criteria; see Chapter 7.]

I feel like a mother who wants her child to experience life even though you don't want them to go. You're worried about them. You want to tell them, "no," but you know that you can't. That's the dilemma I feel but it's more from a partially selfish reaction and partially (whispers) a very sad reaction. I feel angry. I feel sad. I feel vulnerable. Why? From a practical point of view, I am in a good job. I just don't have time to cope with major changes now.

JOHN: Uh huh.

KATHY: Kirk manages everything in our household. I don't worry about putting gas in the car. I don't worry about shoveling the snow. I don't worry about cutting the grass. We have a big house. We have a lot of stuff, two cars. Kirk has been very supportive of me as a manager by taking responsibility for our domestic life. I've come to rely on him, and his going away will add a big burden to my life. It's doable; I'll find a way. I can hire someone to help me with difficult tasks; I can hire someone to cut the grass—if I have to.

JOHN: It pulls away a lot of support.

KATHY: It takes away from the support system. And perhaps I haven't been reminding him enough about how much I appreciate that. That's a possibility. But I do rely on him for taking some physical burdens away. So that's the physical part. I feel a burden. I feel heavy. I feel like oh, my God, now I have to do 10,000 other things. It's not as if I am living in a one-bedroom apartment with my cat.

JOHN: Please, let me check something. [Rather than let Kathy continue, I interrupted to clarify and to redirect. See Chapter 13 on interrupting.]

KATHY: Yes.

JOHN: You're talking in terms of Kirk as—what? He does groceries, shovels walks, and so on. What about the relationship? [I am more directing here in moving Kathy to the point rather than allowing her to continue her laundry list of complaints.]

KATHY: Okay. That's a little harder.

JOHN: Yah.

KATHY: Ah. I think (pauses) being married to Kirk is very difficult. Take that as a factual statement—not an emotional response. We have not had an easy marriage, in part because it started off in a crisis situation within two months of getting married, and so we spent the first year and a half of our marriage trying to cope—to survive—to get above the problem and have some peace. So—how can I say this?—because of these circumstances, I learned very early in the marriage that I could not always depend on Kirk emotionally for support, which to me is a very important part of marriage.

JOHN: Let me just check. Can you clarify what this means? [I request more specificity.]

KATHY Yes. Kirk was under psychiatric care and medication for a while. And he was very unstable, and he needed a very strong support system, and I believe that I supplied that. But we all run out of steam eventually.

JOHN: And that could be perceived in some ways as an involuntary crisis.

KATHY: Right. It was definitely involuntary.

JOHN: What you are talking about now is a voluntary crisis. [Here I pull together conceptually my understanding of her crises. The framework for voluntary versus involuntary crisis is my interpretation.]

KATHY: Yes. That's a good point. Putting aside the logistical problems that I have to face, the emotional problems that I have to face are the following. First, I am going to be very lonely. Although I lived alone for many years prior to getting married, it was by choice. But this business of loneliness keeps coming back in my marriage to Kirk. The first year we were together, he was on the road all the time. He was gone three, four, five weeks at a time, and I had to adjust to living in a remote community. I had a single life when he was gone, with more female companions, but when he was in town, I was part of a couple—my social contacts changed. I was a married person—I did everything with Kirk. And then when Kirk got sick—it was like being alone because I couldn't share my worries and concerns. I had to make all the important decisions myself without his assistance. I was finding places to live, locating furniture, handling legal things, talking to doctors—you know—I was in charge. So I didn't have an equal partner. I accepted that role. But I was lonely. And so this business of being alone, physically alone for a year, oh, this is more than I can take while I'm struggling in school. I think that's where the depth of my sorrow comes from. This feeling that I really don't want to be lonely anymore. You know, I didn't come to this city expecting to live here alone. We rented a big house so that we would have plenty of space, and we could entertain. I don't want to deal with that. I'm resisting that.

JOHN: Since you've been in this city have you not been lonely? [I am checking to see if loneliness is an either-or condition of being with or not being with Kirk.]

KATHY: I have been lonely in the sense that I don't have close friendships and that other graduate students are so busy and preoccupied that there is very little time to establish close friendships.

JOHN: What about with Kirk?

KATHY: The situation with Kirk has improved here. He is calmer. He doesn't have the burden of working for an organization, which he hated. He's done a lot of volunteer work and is active in the community. He visits family and friends whom he has not seen regularly for years. He has a very nice life by most definitions. I am grateful for the fact that he is a companion to my cat whom I love dearly, and she doesn't have to be alone all day. That's important to me.

JOHN: Is he a companion to you? [Again, directness on my part.]

KATHY: Is he a companion to me? Yes and no. Yes, he is physically—we share things together, we talk about things. He has a very vivacious personality. He is an interesting person. But he is not a source of emotional support or comfort.

JOHN: Is that the current loneliness and hurt? [I returned the focus to Kathy and her emotions by acknowledging the loneliness and hurt. In brief counseling, emotions are considered an integral part of who a person is but emotions are not dwelt on independent of the context; see Chapter 11.]

KATHY   In terms of my making a decision?

JOHN: Yes.

KATHY: Yes. I feel that I don't have a vote unless I say very definitively, "You absolutely can't do this. This is not going to work."

JOHN: And then?

KATHY: Then—I don't know—maybe he'll mope around, and I don't want to deal with that. I don't want to feel guilty. I really can't do that, John. [Again, possible goals are stated in the negative.] From his perspective, I can understand why this is a good time for him to do this. I am in graduate school. I am extremely preoccupied. I am busy all the time. I study every night; I study on the weekends. I take time out of my schedule to do things with Kirk because I know if I don't, he has told me that things are going to get really crazy—if he is too ignored, he is going to go off the deep end. He has told me that. So I listened. I said to myself, "I'm going to have to redo things." And I have tried. I've worked very hard to spend more time to be there, to be involved. And so from his perspective, I'm in graduate school and I'll hardly notice that he is gone. This is a great opportunity for him.

JOHN: Is this how he phrases it? [Not having her partner present, I check out the accuracy of her report.]

KATHY: This is what I think he is thinking.

JOHN: What has he said? Actually said.

KATHY: He has said, "This is a good time for me to go." He has said that he is not working, again by choice, so he's not so committed to anything that he can't leave. My regret is that by living in this city—he, alone and with me, has created the beginnings of a community for himself. He's very active in the church. He does volunteer work. He participates in Hospice. So I admire and respect the fact that he has made an attempt to get involved in the community. And because of his getting involved in the community, I have also gotten involved with him, which has been good for me. So I feel sad also that in our attempts to be closer as a couple, if he goes away (whistles as in moving fast) that's going to be cut off. I know that if Kirk is gone for a year, he is going to change. He is not going to be the same person as a result of this rather unusual experience. I am also going to change because I will have finished graduate school or be in the last third by the time he gets back, and I will have had to create my own community as I did before. I will have to go back to being like a single person. I will have to learn how to set up a system—not only a physical system to maintain my life, but also a support system to maintain myself emotionally. I have done this before; I know how. I didn't want to have to do it because Kirk was able to fulfill a lot of those roles.

[In the last several minutes, Kathy certainly offered many opportunities for derailing from a brief counseling framework and choosing a more psychodynamic one. Among other themes, Kathy has talked about loneliness, a relationship that doesn't offer to satisfy her emotionally, and the burden of responsibility. These themes could certainly be expanded into long-term counseling and might appropriately be done so, except for one major factor—Kathy has stated she just wants a single session. From a brief counseling perspective, one way of respecting our clients is to not convince them that they must work on all the problem that push our theoretical buttons.]

JOHN: So we're saying if he goes . . .

KATHY: I feel afraid.

JOHN: And so if he goes, that's the end of the marriage? [Again, I have said what I have thought she was suggesting but hadn't yet said by making overt the covert. I'm trusting my listening and yet taking a risk that it may not fit.]

KATHY: That's what I think, and that's the bottom line; but that's not where Kirk is at all. He has told me that if this is going to be totally destructive to my work, then this is not something he should do, but my dilemma is I am unable to say (her voice raises considerably louder) "I'm going to fall apart if you do this!"—because on the one hand, I don't think that it's true.

JOHN: That will be his line anyway. [She appears to be using Kirk's script and I check it out.]

KATHY: I think that's what he might be thinking. You know what I am saying?

JOHN: What would be his strategy? If you did something . . .

KATHY: If I said, "No! Absolutely no!" If I thought that this trip was really detrimental to his health, I would say "No." And I would have a clear conscience, but I can't say, "No! What are we doing this for? This is so stupid." I want to say, "Why do you have to have another adventure?" You know, that's really the bottom line of what my thinking is.

JOHN: Uh huh.

KATHY: But that's very unfair of me. Maybe this is the greatest opportunity in the world for him. I don't know.

JOHN: What's the meaning of this for him?

KATHY: I don't know.

JOHN: Does he know?

KATHY: That's why I asked him. I said, "Do you feel passionate about this?" I don't even remember what his answer was.

JOHN: Well, passion is one dimension.

KATHY: I'm guessing he's doing it because he'll be more important.

JOHN: I don't know him . . . it could be. People like attention.

KATHY: Sure.

JOHN: Here are people seeking him out and saying "We really want you."

KATHY: Right.

JOHN: A powerful need on people's part. They may not feel "passionate" about that but sometimes it is just, "Hey, I'm wanted!"

KATHY: And maybe he doesn't feel as important in the role that he is in now.

JOHN: Is it possible to check out with him as opposed to guessing?

KATHY: Right, but again . . . [Definitely a "yes, but" response.]

JOHN: And maybe he doesn't think in those terms.

KATHY: Yah. If I ask those kinds of questions, which are perfectly healthy, legitimate questions, I might get very defensive answers. I'm stuck with this guy. I was very afraid of marrying Kirk. I thought about it for a long time and there was one main concern. I believed in my heart that he was a nomad—pure nomad, that he was an adventurer, a perpetual wanderer.

JOHN: Uh huh.

KATHY: He needed to diversify and touch the edge of life—meaning push himself to the max on a regular basis in order to feel life.

So he would always be attracted to those kinds of situations, which, while I find them very interesting as an observer, I can't be in all the time. I get undone and so my feeling was I probably shouldn't marry this person. I was back and forth. And so here three or four years later. . . .

JOHN: Yah. Kind of like your worst fear come true?

KATHY: Exactly. And that's the fear part. That was No. 1—facing fear. This makes me cry. You know, I feel like weeping. If Kirk were to go away for eleven months, the person that I am going to become is not a person I am going to like. I'll get angry, I'll just say—"Kathy, there are some things in this life that you don't get. You know, you just didn't get it." I'll go through this phase where I'll hate men. I'll never want to be in another relationship again. I will get so used to being alone that Kirk will no longer be in my mind. I can't even talk to him, John.

JOHN: Uh huh.

KATHY: I cannot pick up the phone and say, "I have a problem." I can't talk to him. I have been through this before, John, on a shorter-term basis.

JOHN: Uh huh.

KATHY: Six weeks, two months. I know it's going to happen. It's too painful.

JOHN: And so what are your options? [This is the first effort to focus on solutions to her present situation. Her response to my question is presented theatrically in a blasé manner.]

KATHY: You know, I am just going to remove myself from this painful situation, become very stoic. People will ask me where my husband is? I'll answer, "Ah, he's on a trip." I don't like this about myself but I can see it coming.

JOHN: So what's the question? [The question is a variation on, "So how is all of this a problem?"]

KATHY: The question is . . . .

JOHN: From what I've heard so far it's like you are fairly convinced he has made a decision about what he's going to do. You could pull out all the stops, and he probably wouldn't go, but then that doesn't sound like that's going to be a real satisfactory solution. On the other hand, you could not pull out all the stops—he goes off, you change . . .

KATHY: He changes.

JOHN: He changes. Your worst fear—when you debated whether you should get married, being married to a nomad—comes true. Is that accurate?

KATHY: Yes.

JOHN: I'd be very surprised if in going through this, you haven't said several times something like the following: It sounds like a bad thing to happen is to be angry, but it's one of those emotions when we get in certain situations—sadness, loneliness.

KATHY: Sure, angry.

JOHN: You walked, as you said, you walked through those before. [I refer back to the reference to her former experiences and her phrase, "the only way out is through."]

KATHY: Yes.

JOHN: This is going to be a longer walk. [She has had the experience before, perhaps one major difference is the greater length of time.]

KATHY: Well, I wish to find something really joyful.

JOHN: I think, according to this (I point to her list of strengths) you have to go through hell first. (pause as both of us are laughing)

KATHY: (nods "yes")

JOHN: That's your framework here. Dante's hell had nine levels . . . [Using her metaphor, I assess how far through hell she is so far. This assumes that Kathy is already into the experience and has made movement toward her implied goal, which at this point seems to be—Get through hell, successfully.]

Where are you at this point in this experience? How much farther do you have to go? [I use a qualitative—non-numerical—scaling technique, as described in Chapter 10, to assess how much of the journey Kathy has accomplished so far.]

KATHY: Yah. (softly) I didn't know life was going to be so hard. I wish they'd told me this. I want to kind of skip it. [Reading this as a suicide reference is not consistent with the other information Kathy supplies. In her review and editing of the transcript, Kathy saw this as an example of her flippant humor which she hadn't edited out.]

JOHN: Yah. You had a father that wrote you doggerel verse. [Kathy had mentioned her father earlier in a reference that she found too revealing of her identity and so was deleted. My reference to his doggerel verse is my deliberate attempt to inject humor at this point because Kathy was beginning a "poor me" response. Kathy laughed and began to look more at options. Deliberate use of humor is one way to lighten the burden during counseling and helps focus on strengths; see Chapter 9.] He probably wasn't saying, "Kathy, I would like to raise you realizing that life is hell and perhaps there is a heaven at the other end."

KATHY: Yah. It has been a lot tougher perhaps in the last three or four years—really tough.

JOHN: Well, it sounds like you have already . . . you are not just at the first level of hell. [I use the levels of hell as a scaling device and point out that she isn't at the first level.]

KATHY: Oh no. I've been there.

JOHN: Yah.

KATHY: Yah. There you go. (Kathy's voice grew more steady as she acknowledged accomplishments.)

JOHN: Do you like to visualize things? Do you like drawings and pictures? [I explore alternative ways of representing her experience.]

KATHY: I have a journal.

JOHN: Because one possibility—like Dante—is to make a record of this. [In making this suggestion I couched it in soft terms like "one possibility."] Thinking about what level you're on now and what you've been through.

KATHY: Maybe I should draw a picture of myself at home. That's a thought.

JOHN: It's kind of like, "Well, what's next? What could be worse?"

KATHY: There could be worse things. (pause)

JOHN: And as you finish walking through hell . . . [The word "finish" in my statement was one of encouragement and support that she would get through this experience.]

KATHY: (laughs) You're great.

JOHN: What's the heaven at the other end?

KATHY: (pause) Well, I think to a certain extent I am responsible for creating it myself. [This is a clear statement that she is responsible for what she is seeking. My next response headed us toward goal-setting.]

JOHN: What would you create? (Kathy begins to cry gently and there are several seconds of silence.) I've got a whole supply of Kleenex here.

KATHY: Coming to this city . . . I don't know if you can call this city *heaven*. . . solved a lot of problems in my life and in my marriage, and it brought me peace of mind. I suppose that's where the anger is. There's a part of me thinks, "You know, Kirk, you couldn't have anything better. Life doesn't get any better than this—in a place where you don't have huge expenses, and you don't have to work full-time, and you can play golf and run.

JOHN: What would you create? [I repeat my question because she hasn't answered it.]

KATHY: In terms of creating heaven? You know, this heaven apparently has a missing quality—something got shoved out. That's what I visualize.

JOHN: Like the nomad Kirk looked around and said, "This isn't quite enough for me."

KATHY: He wasn't even trying—that's part of the reason that I think I am in shock. There is a part of me that is like saying, "Oh, brother," but you know the funny thing is, this little voice inside of me says, "Well, dummy, probably you didn't have to deal with this initially, so you probably will have to deal with this eventually."

JOHN: Kathy versus the Nomad. [I wish I hadn't used "versus" and instead had used a more cooperative term such as "and."]

Searching for Meaning

KATHY: Yah, it is. You know what I really want to know, John? I really want to know what the lesson is—what am I supposed to be learning from all this? I don't want to learn how to be stronger. I think I'm already a pretty strong person. [Another goal emerges—understanding what this all means.]

JOHN: Uh huh.

KATHY: I don't want to learn how to maintain a home and go to school. I know how. Honestly, I know I can do all of these things.

JOHN: Uh huh.

KATHY: (very softly) What's the lesson? Someone could say, "There ain't no lesson this time. You are just supposed to . . . ."

JOHN: That could be. Maybe this level of hell has no lesson. (Both laugh.) And that's what hell is.

KATHY: Oh, I can just see it.

JOHN: Hell does not have any lesson to learn.

KATHY: There you go.

JOHN: Well, I think what we are getting at here is that, as human beings, we like to have meaning and create meaning. It's like "what's the purpose of this?" or "why is this happening?" or "why now?" et cetera, et cetera. And part of it may simply be that there is no good reason! There is somehow no rational explanation.

KATHY: Yes.

JOHN: Kirk's not passionate about this but, on the other hand, he certainly is drawn to it, interested—enough to go away for eleven months.

KATHY: Yes.

JOHN: It must hold some fascination but it may not be understandable.

KATHY: Maybe that's one of the things in my life—I always have to understand everything and it's just not the best. Maybe that's why life's so difficult for me. I like to understand why things are happening.

JOHN: Well, you do that for yourself.

KATHY: To give myself some security perhaps.

JOHN: Yes—but I guess it's another question when we try to understand another person. We're sitting here and you're using words and talking about experiences, and I'm trying to listen and trying to understand but it's like—I don't know if I have a clue. Occasionally, I say some things, and you jot them down as though somehow these words . . . .

KATHY: They mean something to me.

JOHN: But I don't know that I can really understand that.

KATHY: I know what you're saying. (pause) Look—no lesson and no understanding. That's the lesson.

JOHN: That's one possibility. [Having just offered one possible explanation, I quickly acknowledge that it is but one and there are others that may be just as meaningful for her. My phrase is an echo of my earlier, "That could be."]

KATHY: Oh, the things that go through one's head when you're mad! I can just see someone saying, "You should look at this as an opportunity." And, there is a part of me that does. I have noted that. And that's another thing I don't like. [Kathy begins to generate alternatives by herself. Seeing her present situation as an opportunity is an alternative to a situation having no discernible meaning.]

JOHN: When our dreams get stomped on, we get angry, we are resentful. [An acknowledgment of Kathy's feelings in context.]

KATHY: Um hm. The only other thing I am conflicted about is—When do you tell another person, "No"? When do you say, "This isn't doable"? Not that that's what I want to do. I really have to keep repeating that because deep in my heart I wouldn't want to make somebody do something any more than I would want them to make me do something I did or did not want to do.

Recently, I thought about every couple that I knew—and

asked myself, "How would they handle this situation?" because I thought that might help me. I guess I am searching for a role model. Kirk told me that tonight he wants my report. We're going to talk about it. Well, if he has made up his mind, I don't know why we are talking about it. But I do feel I have an obligation to myself to say that—I don't know how to say to him, "I want you to do what you want to do but it will be difficult for me."

JOHN: Well, a parent would say, "No, you can't," or "Yes, you can." [This is a reference to her earlier possibility of responding as a parent.]

KATHY: Yes.

JOHN: But you're not married to a child. [Confrontation using a truism.]

KATHY: No.

JOHN: And it's not a parent-child type of relationship, although . . .

KATHY: Right now, I would like it to be.

JOHN: Yes. You've shared a lot of thoughts and feelings even as we have been talking. I don't know to what extent you have shared those with Kirk. [Rather than simply focus on Kathy, I introduce the interaction between Kathy and her husband.]

KATHY: Well, I am going to, but I needed some guidance.

JOHN: There's a technique in the counseling literature about "I" statements. Have you run across that? Are you familiar . . .

KATHY: In other words, don't use the accusatory.

JOHN: But it's in terms of stating how I see the situation. It's where I stand—I am not playing wimp; on the other hand, I am not playing the heavy, but I am sharing, "This is how I see it, these are my thoughts, these are my feelings about what's happening." It puts the other person in a position of being able to better hear what you've got to say. At the same time, it also allows you much more freedom of expression. [I gave information about how to talk to Kirk using "I" statements. I have some expertise on relationships in general but not necessarily expertise on Kathy and Kirk's relationship.]

I have heard a range of emotions today.

KATHY: You did?

Goal-Setting

JOHN: There has been a change of mind to loneliness to sadness to worry about the marriage—where are we going? and so on, and

"It's not like I am trying to make him feel guilty, but this is kind of who I am, this is my part in the relationship." But I guess one of the things that impresses me is that you went through prior experiences and also keep coming back a survivor. You do it regardless of what happens. I can't quite quote correctly but it is from Hemingway. It's a "grace under fire" type of thing. Even if you're walking through hell, how can you do it in a way that . . .

[I returned to how she is a survivor and added the "grace under fire" metaphor.]

KATHY: Exactly. Exactly.

JOHN: You do it in the best way possible.

KATHY: That's right. That's exactly right. That's my goal. That's exactly my goal. [Bingo! We arrived at a goal that she enthusiastically endorses. While not explicit in terms of criteria I use for goals, Kathy seems to know what it means for her. Here I am willing to trust her to know that the goal fits her.]

JOHN: Just as an aside. It just happens that hell, fire, and all those types of things work as imagery for you.

KATHY: That really is my goal. Truly, that to me is a symbol of having grown up a little bit because my personality is more delegating and more telling people what to do, it just comes naturally to me. What is unnatural to me is to stand back and let it happen in its own natural course—rather than controlling it.

JOHN: Uh huh. Or the control part could be applied to yourself in the sense that the grace under fire is like the matter of managing— like managing myself.

KATHY: Uh huh. (long pause) For me that's very comfortable, and I think it's appropriate. Kirk is a very guilty person. I have found with him that if you say anything that he could inter- pret as a reason to feel guilty, he'll do it. That's his first reac- tion—of all the feelings that we have on this earth, guilt is No. 1 in his mind based on his youth. One of the most diffi- cult parts of my marriage is when I sometimes say things that have no malintent—no intention of making him feel guilty— and he chooses to feel guilty. Somebody with a crystal ball might look in there and watch me saying these "I" statements and say, "She's not saying 'you,' and she's not trying. She's just saying this is how I feel." In prior counseling, I was taught to do "I feel" statements.

JOHN: In that case, how about an alternative strategy. You initially said something about it's kind of a head or a heart issue. [When Kathy raises objections to the "I" statements as a way of talking with Kirk, I have no desire to press forward with them because I am more interested in finding a method that will really fit for her. In brief counseling we use clients' world views as much as possible rather than imposing our own.]

KATHY: Yes, that's true.

JOHN: When we talk about grace under fire, it strikes me this is one of the things that's happening in situations where it's really a blank. It's using the best of both, and so rather than—I am going to go in and use "I" statements which is not . . . [A delightful example of muddiness on my part. I still haven't figured out what I was saying here but Kathy seems to have understood.]

KATHY: Right. It might be interpreted . . .

JOHN: Yah. Just go in and be "you," with all the knowledge and skills that you've had over the years of dealing with relationships and people. [This is a prescription to do what she does best already.]

KATHY: One of my women friends once told me, "Kathy, remember that management seminar we attended? I want you to take everything you learned in that management seminar and use it in your relationship, because you actually have the skills to handle this but you haven't made the connection because it's personal." And that is exactly what you're saying. Because when I think if I had an employee with a problem—the way I would approach the solution would not be the way I would approach it in a marriage because I don't necessarily make the connection that they can work. [As it turns out, my prescription is identical to one that has been recommended before by her friend. Kathy begins to design a solution to her present situation by drawing on knowledge of useful patterns from her past; see Chapter 6.]

JOHN: Uh huh.

KATHY: I think Kirk would understand a head-heart issue. I could say, "My head responds to this, and my heart responds to this."

JOHN: That sounds more natural for you than "I" messages. [A basic maxim in brief counseling is: If something isn't working, do something different. The "head-heart" messages are a better fit for Kathy than "I" messages, so I support those. Use what is natural and easy for the client.]

KATHY: Uh huh. I'll think about this all day. I am going to my meeting this evening—as the German. [At this point Kathy slips into a theatrical style of playing a stereotyped German as appeared in WW II movies. She spontaneously acts out how she is going to present her thoughts to Kirk. Her humorous approach opens up new options and is in keeping with the theme of Chapter 9 on acknowledging fun.] I am the German. You are committee member. Shut up. You want to hear my speech? You shut up and listen to me. You are right. And watch every place you . . . . [Kathy continues as "the German" for a short time. She ends her dramatic speech and comments on it.]
Oh, it's terrible to be angry, you know.

JOHN: That role that you were just in. Who was that?
[Up to that point I had few clues as to what I had just heard.]

KATHY: It's a friend of mine. She's a very good actress. Always talks like that—the German.

JOHN: As you know, I am into short-term counseling. (Both laugh.) [I believe our time is up and so I begin to bring the session to a close in a direct fashion.]

KATHY: Well, that's what I need.

JOHN: And, on the other hand, I would be willing, if you want to touch base, to correspond.

KATHY: Okay, that's very helpful.

JOHN: But why don't I let you be the one who determines if or when it would be appropriate. [I believe in constant choice-making by clients.]

KATHY: Probably I will want to listen to the tape of this session but not right now.

JOHN: Yah.

Commitment to Action

KATHY: This is what I'm going to do. I am going to visualize this whole thing like a committee meeting. Really. This will help me a great deal, and I will just say, "Kathy, this is like the organization you worked for. You had to run the committee meetings, and you just don't go in there unprepared."

JOHN: Would you mind if I made a copy of your notes that you have taken?

KATHY: Absolutely not. But I need them for my meeting tonight.
              Thank you very much.
JOHN: Nice to see you. Keep me posted.

Follow-up Interview

A follow-up interview was conducted six months following our single-session counseling. Kathy talked about our session and its impact on her life. Kathy stated that her problem had been excruciatingly painful and that she had needed it to be resolved quickly, "I was looking for a quick solution." She had several times been in longer-term counseling, never shorter than two months. Kathy had been totally unaware that counseling could be as brief as a single session.

Coping Strategies. For Kathy, the single-session counseling had worked. She summarized it as follows:

> The session was extremely valuable because it helped me to look at the worst that could happen, that is, the dissolution of my marriage, given the nature of our marriage, my husband's background, and knowing how we are as independent individuals. I wasn't ready to deal with that at that time in my life, and the brief counseling helped me to see that. I could say to myself, "So your worst fear exists. Now what?"
>
> I didn't feel I needed to discuss my problem anymore after I left our session. It was a lamentable situation. I didn't like the situation I was in but that's the way it was. You didn't try to change that for me and I felt that was important. You just accepted it. I think the guidance you provided was this: sometimes you can have a very difficult situation and you can deal with it. Coping skills seemed to have disappeared in my situation and you seemed to be reminding me that I had certain survival skills that could be utilized in this circumstance.

Strengths and Resources. I asked Kathy about the resources and strengths we identified in the session. She said before the counseling session that, "I was so overwhelmed emotionally at the time that I couldn't recall any coping skills. I felt I was breaking down. This situation was more than I could manage at the time." We agreed that she had identified most of the resources herself, but she found my focus on her sense of humor as helpful in her tense situation. She added, "I didn't know how to deal with my situation using humor: perhaps in the future I will. For me, humor is a strength."

Role of Feelings. Kathy was used to psychodynamic models of helping in which feelings are often treated as deeply buried. She continued to express herself in this way even as she talked about brief counseling: "The brief counseling limited the amount of digging into a deep pit of emotions that I couldn't deal with at the time. At the same time, we touched on some of my worst fears." When I asked her how we did this without getting her into a "deep pit of emotions," she reflected,

> What I got out of brief counseling was a coping strategy to get me through the next month or two. The brief counseling functioned very well. What I wanted was to get through this with some peace of mind and some sense of respect for my husband's needs. At the time I really believed my needs were greater. I needed some sense of acknowledgment that I had a tough decision. The counseling helped confirm and verify that this was tough, it was a hard decision. The question was, So what are we going to do about it?

Goals and Action Plans. The brief counseling provided Kathy with an action plan for her immediate situation. Following our session she talked with her husband using her management skills, as we had discussed. She continued, "I expressed my needs and tried to say in a healthy way that I couldn't make the decision for him; however, I told him where I was with this situation." Kathy said the use of management skills allowed her to get clarity as to why the trip was so important to her husband; in the process she clarified the situation for herself.

While the use of the miracle question was not used during the session, the outcome of Kathy's talk with her husband resulted in a minor miracle for her. In her words, this was stated as,

> It was very interesting in terms of clarity that within several days I knew I was as fair as I could be. There was a transfer of emotion. It was like I went up to the top of a mountain and I was sitting there like a Buddha. The weight of the problem shifted into my husband's territory. I just saw it happen. It was very bizarre. He suddenly became very emotional, very traumatized. All of a sudden I thought, "If I have to deal with this, I'll deal with it. I'm not going to make this my problem anymore. It's not going to burden me anymore.

Metaphors used by clients can be very powerful and, if possible, utilized (Combs & Freedman, 1990). During our session, Kathy and I had used her image of walking through hell to describe her current situation. She continued to talk about the dramatic changes that had occurred following the session.

> I came out the other side of hell. But what was amazing was that it was like I had just dumped it on another person. It was very bizarre. In this transition, my husband had been very strong, very insistent, very clear about his goals, and very much wanting me to understand. He was very together and I was the one who was not together—and then it went the other way. It switched. He was confused. At that point, I was okay. All this happened within two days of talking to you. I can still remember it so clearly. It just wasn't my problem anymore.

Client Learning. I questioned Kathy about what she had learned from the session. She said, "I learned I'm very comfortable with ambiguity such as where I'll live a year from now or how much I'll earn. What I also learned in this circumstance was that I need to be very clear about what the other person's goals are as well as my own." When I asked if she was doing more of that, she said she was trying to but that it was not easy.

As we explored what she had learned about herself, Kathy shared that early in the situation with her husband she had blurted out to him, "Oh, my greatest fear has come true, I've married a nomad." He had been extremely offended and from that point on Kathy, realizing she had really upset him, hadn't shared her opinions about the situation with him. I compared her behaviors to the extremes of aggressiveness and non-assertiveness. She replied, "That is the essence of our relationship. I go too far and then I go way back. Retreat. Retreat. Retreat. Then I try to be nice to placate the person."

Focus. One way of keeping counseling brief is keeping clients focused (Budman & Gurman, 1988). Kathy in our follow-up interview had this to say on the topic of focus.

> I went off on tangents a lot. That told me I had a huge agenda. There was a long road ahead and at the end of the road was a big decision. Going off from the road there were these little paths with rocks on them. I got to the first crossing and I thought I'll run down one of the little paths.
>
> As I edited the transcript, I saw that I was all over the place. The reason this was a crisis for me was that I had 75 issues that were not resolved in my mind—dealing with feelings of anger, of selfishness, showing consideration, questioning how I got myself into this mess,

angry at all the time. I didn't address issues I wish I had addressed. I saw these tangents as a way of trying to cope with a lot. The crisis was just bringing all this out. I often have a tendency to go off on tangents but not to that degree.

The advantage of brief counseling was that, even though there were all these tangents I wanted to go off onto, I couldn't. There were times in previous counseling when I would go off on tangents for four weeks. On the other hand, you never said to me, "You're off the subject," but you pulled me back gently.

Epilogue

We can never be sure of the outcomes of our brief interventions in clients' lives. The dialogues we open up with clients are open-ended and create new freedoms and new opportunities. Under these conditions of indeterminacy, predictions of our impact become meaningless. Lipchik (1993) stated it well when she summed up a case.

> This has been the story of my perception of the interaction between a particular client and me. I call it a story—my story—because it is a description of only my view of our interactions. I have no evidence that the changes the client reported occurred because of my intent and/or technique. (p. 45)

Sometimes our contacts are so short that we find it hard to know if we have connected and made a difference that really makes a difference. In not only brief counseling but any form of helping, we cannot say that we caused something to occur. At best we can look for evidence that the dialogues we have with clients have opened up new, potentially fruitful options.

As a way of illustrating the indeterminacy of our actions, I offer the following story about a very brief interaction. I am not aware of how our short dialogue affected the other person. I can only report that our dialogue profoundly affected me by reaffirming that human beings have vast reservoirs of strengths that can be accessed and utilized, often in a very short period of time.

Hidden Patterns of Hope

Several years ago a man with moist eyes and a warm smile approached me during a break at one of my brief counseling workshops. He asked if he could talk with me for a short period of time. I knew we had only about five minutes before the group would be gathering again. Acknowledging this very short time, he told me how his wife was a compulsive spender. He had mortgaged their house to pay her debts.

As he shared his story I heard much pain and also great strength. I asked him two questions. The first was, "What is your goal?" He said that his goal was not to change his wife; he saw that as beyond his abilities since she did not see that she had a problem. Given his circumstances, his goal was to be a bit more relaxed. My second question in the very short time we had left was, "How close are you to your goal?" His response was, "I'm almost there." He proceeded to tell me how he had come to terms with the situation. He had faced an extremely painful situation and the immediate future would continue to be painful, but he knew he could do what he needed to do. I commented that from my perspective it took a lot of courage and persistence to accomplish what he had been able to do so far and to face the near future with such strength. The man smiled a smile that conveyed thanks—an acknowledgment that he had been heard. His smile appeared to me a smile of strength.

To this day I do not know the man's name but I remember his moist eyes and warm smile, his tenacity in the face of financial ruin, and his quiet strength. What impact my listening to his story had on him remains a mystery to me. What affect my questions had in affirming him is unknown. In all types of counseling and in any human interaction it is very difficult to discover the impact of our affirming another person as fully as possible.

I am aware that when I look for people's strengths and resources, they often share them with me. When I look for what works, people share with me what works. The image of the man with the moist eyes and warm smile haunts my memory and reminds me that if I had focused on his problems our five minutes might have been very different, so very different.

In the introduction I stressed that (1) brief counseling is not *the* answer to helping people make changes in their lives, and (2) brief counseling is just another collection of tools for our repertoires. I end with the hope that counselors use the tools described in this book only as tools and not as answers. As professionals granted the privilege to assist others, we must continue to care more about the people we work with than the tools we employ. Pedersen (1988) reminds us that we must constantly be aware of our strengths and limitations, be knowledgeable about the world of our clients, and possess a wide range of skills with which to assist. Meeting these challenges is an awesome responsibility. Our fascination with new tools such as brief counseling must not blind us to the fact that in our efforts to help people we also possess the capacity to hurt them. While we can never be certain about our influence on our clients, counseling demands our utmost awareness, knowledge, and skills; brief counseling is no exception.

In the introduction I also invited your involvement; counseling is not a passive activity. We and our clients are confronted with countless choices as we work together. Being granted permission in our society to assist people in making changes in their lives is a responsibility not easily shouldered. As we face the challenges of choices and changes, I offer cheers in recognition of the help you have already provided others. In addition, I offer cheers of encouragement as you continue your journey on the road to being the best counselor you can be. It is my belief that brief counseling will be a valuable tool to assist you on your journey.

References

Amatea, E. S. (1989). *Brief strategic intervention for school behavior problems*. San Francisco: Jossey-Bass.

American Counseling Association. (1996). *American code of ethics and standards of practice*. Alexandria, VA: Author.

American Psychiatric Association. (1994). *Diagnostic and statistical manual of mental disorders* (4th ed., rev.). Washington, DC: Author.

Andreas, C., & Andreas, S. (1987). *Change your mind—and keep the change: Advanced NLP submodalities interventions*. Moab, UT: Real People Press.

Bandler, R. (1985). *Using your brain—for a change*. Moab, UT: Real People Press.

Bandler, R. (1993). *Time for a change*. Cupertino, CA: Meta Publications.

Bandler, R., & Grinder, J. (1979). *Frogs into princes*. Moab, UT: Real People Press.

Bandler, R., & Grinder, J. (1982). *Reframing: Neuro-Linguistic Programming and the transformation of meaning*. Moab, UT: Real People Press.

Benjamin, A. (1974). *The helping interview* (2nd ed.). Boston: Houghton Mifflin.

Berg, I. K., & de Shazer, S. (1993). Making numbers talk: Language in therapy. In S. Friedman (Ed.), *The new language of change: Constructive collaboration in psychotherapy* (pp. 5-24). New York: Guilford Press.

Berg, I. K., & Miller, S. D. (1992). *Working with the problem drinker: A solution-focused approach*. New York: W. W. Norton.

Bergman, J. (1985). *Fishing for barracuda: Pragmatics of brief systemic therapy*. New York: W. W. Norton.

Biehl, B. (1995). *Stop setting goals if you would rather solve them*. Nashville, TN: Moorings.

Bloom, B. L. (1981). Focused single session therapy: Initial development and evaluation. In S. L. Budman (Ed.), *Forms of brief therapy* (pp. 167-218). New York: Guilford Press.

Budman, S. H., & Gurman, A. S. (1988). *Theory and practice of brief therapy*. New York: Guilford Press.

Budman, S. H., Hoyt, M. F., & Friedman, S. (Eds.) (1992). *The first session in brief therapy*. New York: Guilford Press.

Burgess, G. (1968). *Goops and how to be them: A manual of manners for polite infants*. New York: Dover. (Original work published 1900)

Campbell, D. P. (1974). *If you don't know where you're going, you'll probably end up somewhere else*. Niles, IL: Argus Communications.

Clark, K. (1969). *Civilisation: A personal view*. New York: Harper & Row.

Combs, G., & Freedman, J. (1990). *Symbol, story, and ceremony: Using metaphor in individual and family therapy*. New York: W. W. Norton.

Corey, G. (1991). *Theory and practice of counseling and psychotherapy* (4th ed.). Pacific Grove, CA: Brooks/Cole.

Cormier, W. H., & Cormier, L. S. (1991). *Interviewing strategies for helpers: Fundamental skills and cognitive behavioral interventions* (3rd ed.). Pacific Grove, CA: Brooks/Cole.

Corrigan, J. D., Dell, D. M., Lewis, K. N., & Schmidt, L. D. (1980). Counseling as a social influence process: A Review. *Journal of Counseling Psychology, 27*, 395-441.

Cruz, J., & Littrell, J. M. (in press). Brief counseling with Hispanic-American college students. *Journal of Multicultural Counseling and Development*.

Csikszentmihalyi, M. (1990). *Flow: The psychology of optimal experience*. New York: Harper & Row.

Csikszentmihalyi, M. (1993). *The evolving self: A psychology for the third millennium*. New York: HarperCollins.

Csikszentmihalyi, M. (1997). *Finding flow: The psychology of engagement with everyday life*. New York: BasicBooks.

deCharms, R. (1968). *Personal causation: The internal affective determinants of behavior*. New York: Academic Press.

de Shazer, S. (1985). *Keys to solution in brief therapy*. New York: W. W. Norton.

de Shazer, S. (1988). *Clues: Investigating solutions in brief therapy*. New York: W. W. Norton.

de Shazer, S. (1991). *Putting difference to work*. New York: W. W. Norton.

de Shazer, S. (1993). Creative misunderstanding: There is no escape from language. In S. Gilligan & R. Price (Eds.), *Therapeutic conversations* (pp. 81-94). New York: W. W. Norton.

de Shazer, S. (1994). *Words were originally magic*. New York: W. W. Norton.

Dilts, R. B., with Bonissone, G. (1993). *Skills for the future: Managing creativity and innovation*. Cupertino, CA: Meta Publications.

Dilts, R. B., Epstein, T., & Dilts, R. W. (1991). *Tools for dreamers: Strategies for creativity and the structure of innovation.* Cupertino, CA: Meta Publications.

Egan, G. (1990). *The skilled helper: A systematic approach to effective helping* (4th ed.). Pacific Grove, CA: Brooks/Cole.

Fisch, R., Weakland, J. H., & Segal, L. (1982). *The tactics of change: Doing therapy briefly.* San Francisco: Jossey-Bass.

Fletcher, J. L. (1993). *Patterns of high performance: Discovering the ways people work best.* San Francisco: Berrett-Koehler.

Frank, J. D. (1973). *Persuasion and healing* (2nd ed.). Baltimore: The John S. Hopkins University Press.

Frankl, V. E. (1959). *Man's search for meaning: An introduction to Logotherapy.* New York: Pocket Books. (Original work published 1946)

Furman, B., & Ahola, T. (1992). *Solution talk: Hosting therapeutic conversations.* New York: W. W. Norton.

Gardner, H. (1983). *Frames of mind.* New York: Basic Books.

Glasser, W. (1986). *Control theory in the classroom.* New York: Harper & Row.

Gordon, D. (1978). *Therapeutic metaphors: Helping others through the looking glass.* Cupertino, CA: Meta Publications.

Haley, J. (1984). *Ordeal therapy: Unusual ways to change behavior.* San Francisco: Jossey-Bass.

Han Fei Zi. (1985). Waiting for More Rabbits to Bump into the Tree. In Wei Jinzhi (Ed. and Trans.), *100 allegorical tales from traditional China,* (p. 61). Joint Publishing Company: Hong Kong. (Selected and translated from Zhongguo Gudai Yuyan, revised edition, 1978).

Holland, J. L. (1985). *Making vocational choices: A theory of vocational personalities and work environments* (2nd ed.). Englewood Cliffs, NJ: Prentice Hall.

Hoyt, M. F. (1994). Single-session solutions. In M. F. Hoyt (Ed.), *Constructive therapies, Volume 1* (pp. 11-40). New York: Guilford Press.

Imber-Black, E., & Roberts, J. (1992). *Rituals for our times: Celebrating, healing, and changing our lives and our relationships.* New York: HarperCollins.

Ivey, A. E. (1994). *Intentional interviewing and counseling: Facilitating client development in a multicultural society* (3rd ed.). Pacific Grove, CA: Brooks/Cole.

Ivey, A. E., Ivey, M. B., & Simek-Morgan, L. (1993). *Counseling and psychotherapy: A multicultural perspective* (3rd ed.). Boston: Allyn & Bacon.

Janis, I. L. (1983). *Short-term counseling: Guidelines based on recent research.* New Haven, CT: Yale University.

Kabat-Zinn, J. (1994). *Wherever you go there you are: Mindfulness meditation in everyday life.* New York: Hyperion.

Kelly, G. (1955). *The psychology of personal constructs. Vols. I and II.* New York: W. W. Norton.

Korzybski, A. (1933). *Science and sanity*. Lakeville, CT: The International Non-Aristotelian Library.

Lipchik, E. (1993). "Both/and" solutions. In Steven Friedman (Ed.). *The new language of change: Constructive collaboration in psychotherapy* (pp. 25-49). New York: Guilford Press.

Littrell, J. M. (1996). *Counselors as catalysts in transforming schools: Educational leadership in action*. Research grant from the Department of Professional Studies, Iowa State University, Ames.

Littrell, J. M., & Angera, J. (in press). A solution-focused approach in couple and family therapy. In J. West & C. Bubenzer (Eds.), *Social construction in couple and family counseling*. Washington, DC: American Counseling Association.

Littrell, J. M., Malia, J. A., Nichols, R., Olson, J., Nesselhuf, D., & Crandell, P. (1992). Brief counseling: Helping counselors adopt an innovative counseling approach. *The School Counselor, 39*(3), 171-175.

Littrell, J. M., Malia, J. A., & Vanderwood, M. (1995). Single-session brief counseling in a high school. *Journal of Counseling and Development, 73*(4), 451-458.

Littrell, J. M., Zinck, K., Nesselhuf, D., & Yorke, C. (1997). Integrating brief counseling and adolescents' needs. *Canadian Journal of Counselling, 32*(2), 99-110.

McGinnis, A. L. (1990). *The power of optimism*. San Francisco: Harper & Row.

McMaster, M., & Grinder, J. (1980). *Precision: A new approach to communication*. Beverly Hills, CA: Precision Models.

Mills, K. R. (1992). *The effect of information redundancy and format upon comprehensibility of consent information to chronic alcoholics*. Unpublished doctoral dissertation, Iowa State University, Ames.

Molnar, A. & Lindquist, B. (1989). *Changing problem behavior in schools*. San Francisco: Jossey-Bass.

Nadler, G., Hibino, S., with Farrell, J. (1995). *Creative solution finding: The triumph of full-spectrum creativity over conventional thinking*. Rocklin, CA: Prima Publishing.

NLP Comprehensive Training Team. Andreas, S., & Faulkner, C. (Eds.). (1994). *NLP: The new technology of achievement*. New York: William Morrow.

O'Hanlon, B. & Wilk, J. (1987). *Shifting contexts: The generation of effective psychotherapy*. New York: Guilford Press.

O'Hanlon, W. H., & Hexum, A. L. (1990). *An uncommon casebook: The complete clinical work of Milton H. Erickson, M.D.* New York: W. W. Norton.

O'Hanlon, W. H., & Weiner-Davis, M. (1989). *In search of solutions: A new direction for psychotherapy*. New York: W. W. Norton.

Ornish, D. (1993). *Eat more, weigh less*. New York: HarperCollins.

Pedersen, P. (1988). *A handbook for developing multicultural awareness*. Alexandria, VA: American Association for Counseling and Development.

Perls, F. S. (1969a). *Gestalt therapy verbatim*. Moab, UT: Real People Press.

Perls, F. S. (1969b). *In and out the garbage pail*. Moab, UT: Real People Press.

Peter, L. J. (1977). *Peter's quotations: Ideas for our time.* New York: William Morrow.

Phillips, M. L. (1993). From the editor. *Anchor Point: The Magazine for Neuro-Linguistic Communication,* 7(1), 1.

Prochaska, J. O. (1996, December). *Staging: A therapeutic revolution with entire populations.* Workshop presented at the meeting of The Brief Therapy Conference, San Francisco.

Prochaska, J. O., Norcross, J. C., & DiClemente, C. C. (1994). *Changing for good: The revolutionary program that explains the six stages of change and teaches you how to free yourself from bad habits.* New York: William Morrow.

Reynolds, D. K. (1984). *Playing ball on running water.* New York: Quill.

Reynolds, D. K. (1995). *A handbook for constructive living.* New York: William Morrow.

Rogers, C. R. (1961). *On becoming a person.* Boston: Houghton Mifflin.

Sanford, K. D., & Littrell, J. M. (1997). *Efficacy of social support task interventions in single-session counseling.* Manuscript submitted for publication.

Satir, V. (1972). *Peoplemaking.* Palo Alto, CA: Science and Behavior Books.

Schwartz, P. (1991). *The art of the long view.* New York: Doubleday Currency.

Selekman, M. D. (1993). *Pathways to change: Brief therapy solutions with difficult adolescents.* New York: Guilford Press.

Seligman, M. (1975). *Helplessness: On depression, development, and death.* San Francisco: Freeman.

Seligman, M. E. P. (1994). *What you can change and what you can't: The complete guide to successful self-improvement.* New York: Alfred A. Knopf.

Simpson, C. (1996). *Jenny's Locket.* Nazareth, PA: Pearl Press.

Sinetar, Marsha. (1987). *Do what you love, the money will follow.* New York: Dell.

State of Iowa Department of Education. (1990). *Rules of special education.* Des Moines, IA: Iowa State Office Building.

Sternberg, R. J. (1996). *Successful intelligence.* New York: Simon & Schuster.

Strong, S. R., & Claiborn, C. D. (1982). *Change through interaction.* New York: John Wiley & Sons.

Talmon, M. (1990). *Single-session therapy: Maximizing the effect of the first (& often only) therapeutic encounter.* San Francisco: Jossey-Bass.

Talmon, M. (1993). *Single session solutions: A guide to practical, effective, and affordable therapy.* Reading, MA: Addison-Wesley.

Thomas, Jr., R. M. (1995, July 16). John Weakland, an originator of family therapy, is dead at 76. *The New York Times,* p. 32L.

Thompson, R., & Littrell, J. M. (in press). Brief counseling with learning disabled students. *The School Counselor.*

Vangstad, C., & Littrell, J. M. (1997). *Bomb squads to defuse acting out children.* Unpublished manuscript, Iowa State University, Ames.

Walter, J., & Peller, J. (1992). *Becoming solution-focused in brief therapy.* New York: Brunner/Mazel.

Watzlawick, P., Weakland, J. H., & Fisch, R. (1974). *Change: Principles of problem formulation and problem resolution.* New York: W. W. Norton.

Weakland, J. H., Fisch, R., Watzlawick, P., & Bodin, A. M. (1974). Brief therapy: Focused problem resolution. *Family Process, 13,* 141-168.

Wurman, R. S. (1989). *Information anxiety.* New York: Bantam Books.

Wurman, R. S., with Leifer, L. (1992). *Follow the yellow brick road: Learning to give, take, and use instructions.* New York: Bantam Books.

Zinck, K., & Littrell, J. M. (1998). War and peace. In L. Golden (Ed.), *Case studies in child and adolescent counseling* (2nd ed., pp. 164–173). Upper Saddle River, NJ: Merrill/Prentice Hall.

Recommended Readings

Amatea, E. S. (1989). *Brief strategic intervention for school behavior problems*. San Francisco: Jossey-Bass.

Andreas, C., & Andreas, S. (1987). *Change your mind—and keep the change: Advanced NLP submodalities interventions*. Moab, UT: Real People Press.

Bandler, R. (1985). *Using your brain—for a change*. Moab, UT: Real People Press.

Bandler, R. (1993). *Time for a change*. Cupertino, CA: Meta Publications.

Berg, I. K., & Miller, S. D. (1992). *Working with the problem drinker: A solution-focused approach*. New York: W. W. Norton.

Bloom, B. L. (1992). *Planned short-term psychotherapy: A clinical handbook*. Boston: Allyn & Bacon.

Budman, S. H., & Gurman, A. S. (1988). *Theory and practice of brief therapy*. New York: Guilford Press.

Budman, S. H., Hoyt, M. F., & Friedman, S. (Eds.) (1992). *The first session in brief therapy*. New York: Guilford Press.

Cade, B., & O'Hanlon, W. H. (1993). *A brief guide to brief therapy*. New York: W. W. Norton.

de Shazer, S. (1985). *Keys to solution in brief therapy*. New York: W. W. Norton.

de Shazer, S. (1988). *Clues: Investigating solutions in brief therapy*. New York: W. W. Norton.

de Shazer, S. (1991). *Putting difference to work*. New York: W. W. Norton.

de Shazer, S. (1994). *Words were originally magic*. New York: W. W. Norton.

Dilts, R., Grinder, J., Bandler, R., Bandler, L. C., & DeLozier, J. (1980). *Neuro-linguistic programming: Vol. 1. The study of the structure of subjective experience*. Cupertino, CA: Meta.

Duncan, B. L., Solovey, A. D., & Rusk, G. S. (1992). *Changing the rules: A client-directed approach to therapy*. New York: Guilford Press.

Fisch, R., Weakland, J. H., & Segal, L. (1982). *The tactics of change: Doing therapy briefly*. San Francisco: Jossey-Bass.

Fletcher, J. L. (1993). *Patterns of high performance: Discovering the ways people work best*. San Francisco: Berrett-Koehler.

Friedman, S. (Ed.) (1993). *The new language of change: Constructive collaboration in psychotherapy*. New York: Guilford Press.

Furman, B., & Ahola, T. (1992). *Solution talk: Hosting therapeutic conversations*. New York: W. W. Norton.

Gilligan, S., & Price, R. (Eds.). (1993). *Therapeutic conversations*. New York: W. W. Norton.

Hoyt, M. F. (Ed.) (1994). *Constructive therapies, Volume 1*. New York: Guilford Press.

Hoyt, M. F. (Ed). (1996). *Constructive therapies, Volume 2*. New York: Guilford Press.

Molnar, A. & Lindquist, B. (1989). *Changing problem behavior in schools*. San Francisco: Jossey-Bass.

NLP Comprehensive Training Team. (1994). *NLP: The new technology of achievement*. New York: William Morrow.

O'Hanlon, W. H., & Weiner-Davis, M. (1989). *In search of solutions: A new direction for psychotherapy*. New York: W. W. Norton.

Selekman, M. D. (1993). *Pathways to change: Brief therapy solutions with difficult adolescents*. New York: Guilford Press.

Talmon, M. (1990). *Single-session therapy: Maximizing the effect of the first (& often only) therapeutic encounter*. San Francisco: Jossey-Bass.

Talmon, M. (1993). *Single session solutions: A guide to practical, effective, and affordable therapy*. Reading, MA: Addison-Wesley.

Walter, J., & Peller, J. (1992). *Becoming solution-focused in brief therapy*. New York: Brunner/Mazel.

Watzlawick, P., Weakland, J. H., & Fisch, R. (1974). *Change: Principles of problem formulation and problem resolution*. New York: W. W. Norton.

Weiner-Davis, M. (1995). *Fire your shrink*. New York: Simon & Schuster.

Weiner-Davis, M. (1992). *Divorce busting: A revolutionary rapid program for staying together*. New York: Simon & Schuster.

Zeig, J. K., & Gilligan, S. G. (Ed.). (1990). *Brief therapy: Myths, methods, and metaphors*. New York: Brunner/Mazel.

Index

thoughts, changing, 138, 139–140
  see also beliefs
time:
  causal connections in relation to, 27,
    38
  change and, 13
  effective counseling and, 171,
    172–79
  -limited counseling, 3–4, 79 (*see also*
    brief counseling)
Times They Are A-Changin', The, 4
Tin Woodsman (*Wizard of Oz*), 39, 48
Topdog/Underdog, 120, 149
Tough Love approach, 70–71
Transactional Analysis, xiv, 120, 149
triggers for derailment, 147, 148, 149,
    150, 151, 211
Truman State University, 181
Trungpa, 202
trust, 43–46, 72, 90, 137
Trust Walk, 53

understanding, 216, 217
University of Michigan, 140

Vanderwood, M., 54
Vangstad, Claudia, 172, 181–82
victim status, 195, 207
visual:
  aids, 54
  motion (interrupting client), 155
vulnerability, 202, 205

"Waiting for More Rabbits to Bump
    into the Tree," 95, 105
Walter, Glen, 109, 114, 115, 122
Walter, J., 15, 68, 126
Walter, Rosie, 109, 114, 115, 122
war stories, 153–54
Watzlawick, Paul, 13, 14, 22, 31, 53, 73,
    102n, 172, 173, 175, 177, 178,
    180, 188, 193
Weakland, John H., 10, 13, 14, 172, 173
weight (excess), 32–33
Weiner-Davis, M., 44
*What You Can Change and What You
    Can't*, 60
When Harry Met Sally, 117
Whitaker, Carl, 94
Wilk, J., 64, 125
Winnie the Pooh, 194, 196
Winthrop college, 115
Wizard of Oz, 39, 47
Wizard of Oz, 47, 48, 162
Working with the Problem Drinker, 18, 59
World of Pooh, The, 194
Wurman, R.S., 53, 81

YAVIS, 201, 204
Yorke, C., 8
Young, Lorrie, 112

Zinck, K., 5, 8